ON THE BORDERS OF THE ACADEMY

Also published by The Graduate School Press of Syracuse University

The Mentoring Continuum
From Graduate School through Tenure

Collaborative Futures
Critical Reflections on Publicly Active Graduate Education

Building Community
Stories and Strategies for Future Learning Community Faculty and Professionals

Pedagogy, not Policing
Positive Approaches to Academic Integrity at the University

Interrupting Heteronormativity
Lesbian, Gay, Bisexual and Transgender Pedagogy and Responsible Teaching at Syracuse University

Building Pedagogical Curb Cuts
Incorporating Disability in the University Classroom and Curriculum

Using Writing to Teach

ON THE BORDERS OF THE ACADEMY

Challenges and Strategies for First-Generation Graduate Students and Faculty

Edited by
Alecea Ritter Standlee

Library of Congress Cataloging-in-Publication Data

Names: Standlee, Alecea Ritter, 1979- editor.
Title: On the borders of the academy : challenges and strategies for first-generation graduate students and faculty / edited by Alecea Ritter Standlee.
Description: New York : Graduate School Press of Syracuse University, [2018] | Includes bibliographical references and index.
Identifiers: LCCN 2018016396 | ISBN 9780977784783
Subjects: LCSH: First generation college students--United States. | Graduate students--United States. | College teachers--United States. | People with social disabilities--Education (Higher)--United States. | Education, Higher--Social aspects--United States. | College teaching--Social aspects--United States.
Classification: LCC LC4069.6 .O6 2018 | DDC 378.1/98--dc23 LC record available at https://lccn.loc.gov/2018016396

This volume is published with support from the
Syracuse University Graduate Student Organization

For more information about this publication, please contact:

The Graduate School Press
304 Lyman Hall
Syracuse University
Syracuse, NY 13244

http://graduateschool.syr.edu/programs/graduate-school-press

Manufactured in the United States of America

CONTENTS

Table

CONTRIBUTORS

Marcus Bell completed his Ph.D. at Syracuse University in 2017, and is now an assistant professor of sociology at Onondaga Community College. In his work, Marcus utilizes a combination of qualitative and historical/comparative methods to examine the intersection of race, citizenship, and social policy in the United States. He is especially interested in the macro-level construction of racial ideology over time, as well as the micro-level internalization and representation of racialized experience. He also examines the relationship between various racial groups and the state, with a particular focus on the policing of American citizenship. In 2014 Marcus was named a junior fellow of the Yale Urban Ethnography Project, and in 2016 he was awarded the Sociology Dissertation Fellowship from Syracuse University. Marcus has published book chapters on racial inequality in education, extrajudicial police violence, and mass incarceration. He is currently working on several articles that highlight the construction of white racial identity in predominantly black schools.

Selene Cammer-Bechtold is a fourth-year doctoral student who focuses on education, rural sociology, and the intersection of those two fields. After taking an undergraduate degree in social studies education and history, she decided to switch to sociology after various sojourns in the service industry, finance, and higher education. Her tentative dissertation project focuses on the experiences of teachers from urban and suburban backgrounds after finding positions in rural districts. Other research interests include education reform, notably Common Core implementation in

New York State, and the experiences of students from disadvantaged and first-generation backgrounds.

Saran Donahoo is an associate professor and interim chair in the Department of Educational Administration and Higher Education and the director of the College Student Personnel Program at Southern Illinois University in Carbondale. She earned both her doctorate and her A.M. at the University of Illinois at Urbana-Champaign. She completed her B.A. in secondary education at the University of Arizona. Her published works include three co-edited books and articles in *Teachers College Record*, *Equity and Excellence in Education*, *Christian Higher Education*, *Urban Education*, and *Education and Urban Society*, as well as an array of book chapters. Additionally, she has served as the associate editor for media reviews for the *Journal of Student Affairs Research and Practice*. Her honors including receiving the Joyce Cain Award for Distinguished Research on African Descendants from the Comparative and International Education Society (CIES) and the AERA Division J Outstanding Publication Award.

Rosanne Ecker, a former practicing clinical psychologist, served as Associate Director for Graduate Career Services at Syracuse University, where she met individually with students to help them develop job-search strategies and materials for both the academic and the non-academic job search. Rosanne also developed career programs for doctoral students, working collaboratively with the Syracuse University Graduate School and Graduate Student Organization.

Malar Hirudayaraj, Ph.D., is Assistant Professor of Human Resource Development in the Department of Service Systems at Rochester Institute of Technology in Rochester, New York. Her research interests are focused on issues of social justice and diversity in graduate employment, particularly the impact of the educational biography of graduates on their employability in professional positions.

Aaron Hoy is a Ph.D. candidate in the Department of Sociology at Syracuse University's Maxwell School of Citizenship and Public Affairs. His research and teaching interests include families, sexualities, and sex/gender. His dissertation research uses in-depth interviews with currently married and divorced gays and lesbians to explore the meanings of same-sex marriage. To date, his research has been published or is forthcoming in a range of sociology and interdisciplinary journals, including the *Journal* *of Divorce and Remarriage* and *Population Review*. He received his M.A. in sociology from Syracuse University in 2014 and his B.A. in sociology from Ohio University in 2010.

David Marquard is an assistant professor at the University of North Carolina, Pembroke. He is also the founding director of The Literacy Commons, an organization that provides literacy outreach in North Carolina.

Kathleen Mullins is a full-time faculty member in the English and Communication Department at Front Range Community College in Westminster, Colorado. She holds master's degrees in English Studies and Student Affairs Administration in Higher Education. She continues to explore issues of social class and working-class identity in her work with developmental reading and writing students as they navigate higher education for the first time.

JanRose Ottaway Martin grew up in the foothills of the Cascade Mountains in Western Washington. Her passion for work with poverty-driven studies comes from her own history of rural poverty combined with the year she spent in Denmark witnessing more supportive and humanistic approaches to the issue. JanRose completed a bachelor's in sociology at Western Washington University. After spending two years in the Peace Corps in Guinea, West Africa, she came back to the states and got her master's in social work. JanRose worked for several years at an outpatient mental health facility in downtown Seattle, where her work focused on co-occurring disorders and homelessness. She now works at the county level managing outpatient behavioral health programs. Her research interests include low-income students in higher education, the intersection of co-occurring disorders and poverty (including diagnosis and new treatment models), and innovative community-driven public health interventions in Africa.

Meghan J. Pifer is an assistant professor of higher education at Widener University. Her research explores colleges and universities as organizational contexts, as well as the salience of identity and individual characteristics, and interpersonal networks and relationships, within those contexts in shaping individual and organizational outcomes.

Elvia Ramirez is an associate professor of ethnic studies at California

State University, Sacramento. She received her Ph.D. in sociology from the University of California, Riverside. Her research interests include Chicano/as and Latino/as in higher education, graduate education, social inequality, and Mexican immigration. Some of her recent publications include "Unequal Socialization: Interrogating the Chicano/Latino(a) Doctoral Education Experience," in the *Journal of Diversity in Higher Education* (2017), and "Qué estoy haciendo aquí? (What Am I Doing Here?): Chicanos/Latinos(as) Navigating Challenges and Inequalities during Their First Year of Graduate School," in *Equity and Excellence in Education* (2014).

Karley A. Riffe is a doctoral candidate at the University of Georgia's Institute of Higher Education. Her research explores the interrelationships between higher-education institutions, those who work within them, and the external environment as these relationships affect institutional mission fulfillment.

Vincent Serravallo is a first-generation college graduate and academic from working-class origins. His parents and their parents, none of whom went beyond grade school, were brickyard workers, garment workers, and construction laborers in New York's Hudson Valley dating back to the early 1900s. Brought up with a high regard for education, he received his bachelor's degree in sociology from the State University of New York at Oswego. After graduating, he worked at a large insurance company to earn money for graduate school. Based on the union campaign he experienced at that job, he wrote a master's thesis at the University of Kansas that analyzed employers' aggressive anti-union campaigns. In a later study, he found that university administrators used union-avoidance methods nearly identical to those of private businesses when faced with union drives by faculty. For his doctorate in sociology at the City University of New York Graduate Center, he combined ideas of Karl Marx and George Herbert Mead to study the influence of less-alienated labor on intergenerational mobility in a working-class community. His present research concerns academic labor in an era of changing higher education. He currently lives in Rochester, New York, and is an associate professor of sociology at Rochester Institute of Technology, where he teaches social and cultural theory, sociology of work, social inequality, and foundations of sociology.

Sarah Smith is the pseudonym of a millennial white woman who spent her childhood growing up in a suburban trailer park in the Midwest. A first-generation college student from a low-income background, she attended a large state university in the Midwest and received her bachelor's degree in biology in 2008. Unable to find full-time work during the Great Recession, she took a number of part-time jobs until a lab where she had worked as an undergrad offered her an entry-level research position. After three years in the lab, she went on to graduate school at the same state university for a master's degree in public policy and graduated in 2016. She took a year off from school to be a caregiver for her family before starting the next stage of her career.

Alecea Ritter Standlee is a first-generation Ph.D. and college professor. Raised in poor rural communities by low-wage service workers in the Pacific Northwest, Alecea found her niche in higher education. After completing her undergraduate degree at the University of Idaho, she worked for multinational computer company, Dell Inc., but quickly realized her passion was in education. She would go on to earn a Ph.D. in sociology from Syracuse University, as well as an M.A. in women's studies at the University of Cincinnati. Her dissertation, "The Real Virtual World: Techno-Mediated Relationships in the Lives of College-Age Adults," conducted under the supervision of postmodern theorist Prof. Jackie Orr and feminist scholar Prof. Marjory DeVault, explored how communication technologies are used to establish, negotiate, and maintain interpersonal relationships. This experience solidified her commitment to principles of inclusion, social justice, and active scholarship. As a qualitative researcher, Alecea believes that giving voice to underrepresented research participants will yield robust and valuable data about the social world. Today, as a professor at Gettysburg College, she specializes in teaching and research in the areas of social theory, gender, sociology of technology, and social inequality, with a particular emphasis on the impact of first-generation status on the college experience. Her current scholarship examines the social and cultural implications of communication technologies on the role of socio-economic status, gender, and geographic location in the formation of interpersonal relationships and complex social networks.

Taren Swindle is an assistant professor in family and preventive medicine within the College of Medicine at the University of Arkansas for Medical Sciences. Her research program focuses on strategies for obesity prevention and nutrition promotion for young children in low-income families. Specifically, Dr. Swindle's work seeks to leverage the link between the early childcare environment and the home to promote healthy eating and behaviors for children. She received her Ph.D. in educational psychology and research from the University of Memphis in 2013.

Michelle M. Tokarczyk was born in the Bronx, New York City, and lived there until she was nine years old, when her family moved to the more suburban Queens. She attended Herbert Lehman College—back in the Bronx—and received her doctorate in English from SUNY Stony Brook. She has been active in the Working-Class Studies Association and is known for her critical work as well as her poetry. Tokarczyk is a professor of English at a private liberal arts college in the eastern United States.

Mauricio Torres is a doctoral candidate in sociology at Syracuse University's Maxwell School of Citizenship and Public Affairs. His areas of expertise include race and ethnicity, law and punishment, education, and affect. In addition to the chapter featured here, he is the coauthor of "Trayvon Revisited: Race, Fear, and Affect in the Death of Trayvon Martin," along with Mary Cannito-Coville and Dalia Rodriguez. His dissertation, titled "Leaning In: Diversity Work and Campus Culture at a Quaker Boarding School," interrogates the complexities of diversity work in the context of Quaker education and its limits as an anti-racist project.

Jim Vander Putten received his Ph.D. in higher and postsecondary education from the University of Michigan, and is an associate professor of higher education at the University of Arkansas at Little Rock. He coordinates the higher education doctoral concentration in Faculty Leadership and the higher education M.A. concentration in Health Professions Teaching and Learning. He serves as vice president for the Arkansas State Conference of the American Association of University Professors, and his research interests include the influences of social-class origins on faculty work life, education research quality, and threats to academic freedom in an age of anti-intellectualism.

ACKNOWLEDGMENTS

This volume owes is origin to the work of Syracuse University Graduate School Programs and Career Services staff and students. These programs, and the committed staff who operate them, have worked with Syracuse University graduate students for years and have come to identify the challenges faced by the students and faculty for whom higher education was entirely new territory. Mentors and leaders, some of them first generation themselves, have worked to provide a map of unfamiliar and sometimes hostile terrain to graduate students and faculty members alike. Publication was enabled by financial support from Syracuse University's Graduate Student Organization. Additional thanks must be extended to Dr. Glenn Wright and Thomas Jefferson West III, who have contributed their time and editorial support to this project. A special thanks to Jason Ritter who contributed the wonderful cover image as well as many hours of emotional support to his spouse—the book editor, Alecea Ritter Standlee. Finally, profound thanks to the volume's contributors, who have waited patiently (let us not say how long!) for its release.

INTRODUCTION

Alecea Ritter Standlee

The 21st century, though not long underway, has already become an era of paradigmatic shifts in the culture and experience of higher education, especially in the Western world. Higher education in the United States, for example, is in the midst of great transformation. Even as higher education becomes ever more essential for lifelong success, the cost of college is increasing. Financial support for public institutions has declined, and student financial aid burdens graduates with more debt than ever before. These shifts are fundamentally linked to the history of increasing accessibility and decreasing exclusivity of higher education in the latter half of the 20th century. As a result of shifting social expectations and the rise of egalitarian philosophies of education, institutions of higher learning have worked to provide a more diverse and less stratified experience for students and faculty, making higher education more accessible to more students. At the heart of this transformation is the first-generation student. In order to understand this transformation, it is essential to discuss what first-generation and working-class status means, as well as some of the specific challenges students with this status face in today's academy.

Before we consider the challenges and controversies that surround first-generation students and faculty in higher education, we must first address a matter of definition. On the surface, first-generation academic status is easily defined: it applies to graduate students and faculty whose parents did not graduate from, or perhaps even attend, college. Yet this group is deeply diverse and profoundly complex. Traditional intersectional frameworks that link together social class (which may function as a proxy for first-generation status), racial identity, and gender identity are a useful starting point for defining first-generation students. However, seeking to better understand the experience of the first-generation student requires a much more complex approach. While in some cases class status can provide insight into first-generation status, specifically for poor and working-class individuals, no simple correlation between these terms can be assumed. An educated parent may be financially successful or destitute, and their education may have taken place at an elite university or a struggling community college. Similarly, a less educated parent may be financially successful, thus allowing a very different educational experience for a child than a financially desperate parent could provide. Furthermore, racial identity, especially if coupled with immigrant status, may be profoundly impactful for first-generation academics. Due to the diversity of intersectional identities among this group, it is difficult to articulate a universal experience, though the authors in this volume effectively express shared experiences among many, if not all, first-generation scholars.

To further compound this complexity, many authors in this volume have elected to utilize a culturally specific class identity that in some cases functions as proxy for their first-generation identity. The identity of "working class," like "first generation," carries with it a host of meanings, some of which include undertones of racial identity—often whiteness—within the highly contested political environment that we currently inhabit. During the contentious 2016 election year, the discursive identity of "white working class," which has a long and complex racial history, was again a central tool to maintain racial and class hierarchies. In the aftermath of the election, due in part to partisan media and through the efforts of a revitalized white supremacist movement, the term "working class" became a proxy for a particular brand of racialized narrative. This narrative focused on maintaining racial barriers between working-class whites and non-whites, policed carefully by both poor whites—who faced the decline of their own white privilege, while struggling to deal with class marginalization—and wealthy political elites who benefit from an internally divided working class. Despite the co-option of the label "working class" as a political tool to support racial hierarchies, many working-class people of all races struggle against this narrative as they enter both the work force and higher education.

In addition, working-class status, as a marginalized identity, may extend to individuals who would normally be excluded from the category "first generation," in the sense that one or both parents may have completed some form of higher education, but were not able to parlay that into movement up the socio-economic ladder. These "mixed-status" students may experience a cultural environment and childhood socialization similar to more traditional first-generation students, despite some parental familiarity with college. In order to address some of these complexities, we must cultivate a tolerance for ambiguity. Therefore, in this volume, the terms first generation and working class, rather than being constrained by strict definitional guidelines, are allowed to serve as self-defined identity categories. Like racial, religious, or sexual identity categories, first-generation and working-class status are narratively constructed and often contested by the very individuals who define themselves as such. In addition, evolving social and political contexts add to the shifting nature of these conceptual frameworks. At times, this means that contradictions and slippery abstractions may emerge in the volume. Yet if we value the voices of first-generation and working-class scholars themselves, as well as the knowledge gained through research, such discursive slippage must be embraced. Discursive flexibility is essential to knowledge generation in this evolving field, as the diverse contributors (and, in many cases, their research participants) attest.

Definitions notwithstanding, much recent research has been done on the experiences and challenges faced by first-generation and working-class undergraduate students, in both public and private institutions of higher learning. What has emerged is evidence of an educational system that is struggling with the demands and the limitations imposed by a changing political environment and by shifts in the demographic makeup and cultural identities within the student population. From the perspective of the first-generation student, the challenges and demands of entering the higher educational environment are immense. Some of these challenges are the result of external forces that target higher education with attacks that are disproportionally visited upon the historically marginalized, including poor and working-class first-generation students. The recently passed 2017 tax bill, which pays for tax cuts for high earners and corporations in part by targeting higher education, along with the massive budget cuts to state-supported public colleges and universities we have seen in recent years, undermines accessibility to college for first-generation and low-income students. This trend has begun to reverse some of the educational gains made in the late 20th century. As educational access and upward mobility become more difficult for the poor and working class, anti-intellectualism and distrust of science and information grow—as does, not coincidentally, income inequality and the power of social and political elites. Today, working-class and first-generation students, even as they struggle to adapt and internalize the social norms of their new educational environments, continue to face difficulties shaped by regressive forces that seek to undermine higher education as a means to maintain social hierarchies and concentrate power into the hands of a few.

Research in this area has made profound contributions to general knowledge about the experience of first-generation students, especially undergraduates. Committed institutions have developed programs to better support the needs of this group, and lobbyists and activists have worked to push back the rising tide of anti-intellectualism that endangers access to quality higher learning for all students, including those in the first generation. At the same time, graduate students and faculty members from first-generation and/or working-class backgrounds face profound disconnections and challenges as they enter the academic job market. The experiences of graduate students and faculty members have been less comprehensively researched than those of undergraduate students, and the goal of this volume is to contribute to the emerging field of study in this area. Unlike undergraduates, who, while they may struggle to adapt and succeed, generally view higher education as a temporary—albeit profoundly transformational—life stage, many graduate students and most faculty members view higher education as their life's work. In order to understand their experiences, it is necessary to look at the interactions between both the individual and his or her class status, the institutional expectations and norms of individual colleges and universities, and the broader social environment of higher education. In order to understand the experience of the first-generation and working-class graduate students and faculty members represented in this volume, it is useful to begin with a discussion of the broader cultural environment in which higher education, and those committed to it, are situated.

Situating Higher Education, Past and Present

Historically, the United States has been a leader in educational innovation. This is, no doubt, in part because of the complex relationship between public education and civil society. That an educated public is necessary to allow for effective and informed participation in the democratic process is not a concept that originated in the United States, but nonetheless has informed federal and state support for education since the creation of the earliest public schools. Yet even as public primary and secondary education were embraced by educational activists and reformers in the 19th and 20th centuries, higher education remained, in many ways, the province of the rarified social classes.

Access to higher education has been denied again and again to marginalized groups within American society. Women and people of color have been viewed as unfit to enter the hallowed halls of knowledge, and have faced opposition, both explicit and implicit, in accessing higher education. Yet educational institutions arose to meet the needs of those otherwise left out in the cold. Women's colleges and Historically Black Colleges/Universities played an essential role in allowing access to higher education. Higher education has functioned as a gateway to middle- and upper-class lifestyles, imparting intellectual gifts as well as financial and social capital on a select few. Despite these emerging spaces of inclusivity, educational attainment for marginalized racial groups remained well below that of their white counterparts for much of the 20th century, while women remained underrepresented in many fields. A major reason for the persistence of these inequalities is evident in their intersection with class status.

For the poor and working class, educational attainment remained low throughout the early 20th century, though whites and men did slightly better than other groups. Thus, in the middle of the 20th century, demands for fundamental transformations in higher education emerged. Access to educational resources led to the ability to more directly engage in civil society, and the demand that the benefits of higher education be extended beyond the middle and upper classes to the poor and working class began a new transformation in higher education. The demands on educational institutions, communities, and governments were reflections of an era of civil and cultural engagement, when change was embraced and social upheaval was normalized. Higher education responded with varying degrees of enthusiasm, but doors previously closed to the poor and working class opened, and higher education became a space in which students who benefited from intergenerational transmissions of educational privilege sat side by side with first-generation students, who were, fundamentally, strangers in a strange land.

This change in access led to a fundamental shift in the cultural view of higher education. No longer a space of exclusivity, higher education has become increasingly important for long-term financial and career success. Yet, as is often the case when a space of privilege is made available to the marginalized, it becomes subject to delegitimization. For example, when women enter a previously masculine-dominated work space, the status and financial rewards of that industry tend to decline. This reflects a cultural misogyny that associates femininity with being "lesser." Higher education is increasingly inhabited by women, people of color, and the poor and working class in the form of first-generation students. As a result, higher education has been targeted by individuals and groups who, unable to maintain the elitism of the space, have focused on devaluing it.

For most of its history, higher education represented, at its core, the expansion of the human mind and scientific development, the encouragement of intellectual curiosity, and the cultivation of a flexible mind. Effectively, the goal was to foster a broad set of knowledge and skills that allowed for long-term career success, deep and profound engagement in civil discourse, and personal happiness. In response to the demands for access to and equality in higher education, political actors, beginning with Ronald Reagan and today including a significant majority of conservative political figures, began to characterize higher education, not as a means to develop a comprehensive understanding of the universe, a space to develop a profound life philosophy or to make scientific discoveries that contribute to the sum total of human knowledge, but rather as a means to get a job. Furthermore, attempts to undermine educational quality, especially in public higher education, have taken the form of pressure on institutions to present speakers with no scientific or educational merit on equal terms with luminaries in their field. The effect of these transformations has been to deny the historic benefits of higher education to women, people of color, and perhaps most completely to the poor and working-class students who fought so hard for access to these benefits, even as it stabilizes and even expands the concentration of power among elites. In the current social environment, explicit attacks on higher education have had profound consequences. A 2017 study of social attitudes found that over half of all registered Republicans consider higher education harmful to the country, and support for educational budget cuts as well as increased taxation on institutions and students has grown. States across the United States have cut budgets to higher education, forced the hiring of business leaders as university presidents, and undermined educational freedoms in the form of political attacks and the removal of tenure protections. Meanwhile, current federal government leaders have proposed increased taxes on colleges and universities, implemented cuts to and limitations on student lending and, as this volume goes to press, are working toward widespread cuts to public education as a whole. Such successful attempts to increase barriers to education have become increasingly successful, resulting in a concentration of power among the wealthiest and most politically powerful citizens. This allows for the increasing control of elites over financial, political, and discursive realms, rendering higher education and the media, which have historically functioned as sites for democratic discourse and the transmission of knowledge, as embattled resisters or even co-opted tools of the powerful.

At the same time, we have seen the normalization of cultural discourse that calls into question the value of higher education, creating a narrative that focuses increasingly on credentialing and applied labor, specifically for the working class. While upper-class families continue to consider high-quality education a necessary part of their world, poor and working-class families are increasingly encouraged to view education as either a credentialing barrier to a regular income or an unnecessary indulgence. This discourse also constructs higher education, specifically the liberal arts tradition, as not simply elitist, but destructive to working-class identities and culture. Higher levels of education have long been linked with socially progressive attitudes and a decline in discriminatory behavior, and political actors who work to maintain social stratification have seized upon this reality as a means to undermine the value of education by defining it as propaganda. The consequences of these events cannot be overstated, as first-generation and working-class families have increasingly internalized the notion that education is a useless hoop to jump through at best, and undesirable or even harmful to people at worst, rather than as a means to a more stable, healthier, and happier life. As education becomes less accessible due to limitations on financial support, and less desirable due to discursive constructions that make it seem worthless or destructive to working-class and poor families, first-generation students who do enter higher education face significant barriers to their success.

In this ideological struggle about the meaning and nature of higher education, the first-generation and working-class student has become the site of conflicting narratives. On one side, social and political actors normalize the idea that the first-generation and working-class student is most in need of, and demanding of, a career-focused trajectory that values credentials and efficiency over knowledge generation and acquisition. The other side of the philosophical divide argues that what first-generation, working-class students need and want most are the foundational educational resources that foster intellectual curiosity and critical thinking, both of which have been at the root of higher education since antiquity. Faced with this narrative conflict, and struggling with a hostile political environment, institutions have responded in a variety of ways. Some have adopted a vocational, career-focused model, moving away from the ideal of a comprehensive education—as evidenced by the decline in support for general education curricula and the rise of educational models that focus on rapid degree completion rather than quality of instruction. Others—most commonly elite institutions—have in effect demanded class assimilation from new students, implicitly communicating expectations that student conform to upper-class norms of behavior and adopt upper-class cultural identities in order to succeed. Such institutions can become cultural monoliths profoundly alienating to first-generation and working-class students.

Institutions whose social norms and identity are rooted in a history of upper-class, elite culture can find their traditions and expectations under attack, both from groups that question their elitism and from groups that challenge the value of their educational goals. One response may be to resist changes in culture and defend age-old institutional traditions. This can impose demands for conformity that are challenging for all individuals within the institution, but profoundly so for first-generation students, faculty, and staff. For example, collegiality and departmental "fit" often require that faculty and grad students demonstrate class conformity through their knowledge of art, music, and international travel, as well as their skill in adopting upper-class customs in social situations like formal dinners and cocktail parties. Upper-class expectations about conflict management styles, self-promotion, social networking, family and work structures, and physical appearance and dress, can shape perceptions of fit and belonging for first-generation faculty and graduate students. All of these factors can play a role in how successful graduate students and faculty are in securing grants, finding appropriate mentorship, and advancing within the profession.

Thoughtful institutions will attempt to create genuine flexibility in accommodating a changing student and faculty population, and continue to provide quality comprehensive education in the true liberal arts sense. Institutions that work to include diverse race, class, sexual, and cultural identities within their faculty and staff, as well as within their curriculum, provide a more positive and welcoming environment. Some institutions require courses that address diverse class and racial experiences, while others maintain theme housing or student support groups for first-generation, nontraditional, and other marginalized populations. Focusing on inclusion and support not only helps first-generation students succeed, but also fosters a more diverse, adaptable, and emotionally intelligent student body and faculty culture.

Whatever their strategies, colleges and universities across the country have faced profound changes, many of which are linked with the rise in first-generation, working-class, and other previously excluded groups. Even as institutions of higher learning struggle with both the real differences in their increasingly diverse student bodies (both graduate and undergraduate) and faculty, and the pressures imposed by external actors seeking to preserve cultural exclusivity, students and faculty members also struggle with new cultural and social expectations, many of which are currently in flux. Faced with conflicting demands to support free speech and condemn hate speech, to embrace diversity but also welcome conservative outlooks, faculty and students may experience a kind of intellectual paralysis. At the same time that they struggle to support and integrate first-generation students, institutions are faced with political and financial coercion to reinforce and even recreate barriers to upward mobility. Furthermore, faculty and students find it difficult to navigate a first-generation and working-class identity increasingly controlled and defined by a small group of anti-intellectual and anti-equality figures. To date, relatively few scholars have written on the difficulties faced by first-generation and working-class graduate students and faculty in academia. This volume seeks to provide an outlet for innovative research and personal narratives in this area. Here we find mentors and peers sharing the strategies that have allowed them to survive, and sometimes thrive, in academic settings across the country.

Understanding the Experience of Working-Class Faculty

As many of the researchers and essayists in this volume discuss, first-generation and working-class academics often find themselves in a liminal space, negotiating transitions and conflicts between the upper-middle-class norms of their peers and work environments and the norms embedded in their working-class histories. While the scholars represented in this volume approach the experiences and needs of working-class and first-generation academics from a variety of perspectives, taken together they provide a rich discussion of the issues surrounding higher education in general and class-based challenges in particular.

The first section focuses on first-generation career academics—those who have spent, or are poised to spend, their working lives in higher education. Engaging such issues as work environment, marginality, social capital, and educational background, these contributors provide a profile of the contemporary first-generation faculty member, conveying a deeper understanding of the unique challenges faced by first-generation professors and academic professionals as they work and teach within the academy. In this discussion, we see several key elements central to understanding the experience of working-class and first-generation faculty members in higher education. They articulate the fundamental truth that higher education is shaped by its history as a middle- and upper-class environment. The social and cultural norms of higher education are, at a very basic level, a reflection of the cultural norms of upper-middle-class Americans.

In Chapter 1, Vincent Serravallo explores the fundamental challenges of moving into and across the cultural and class boundaries of higher education. As a working-class academic—that is, an individual from a working-class home who has now entered the rarified heights of academe—he effectively describes the very real cultural differences and challenges faced by such class transgressors. Jim Vander Putten also engages with the challenges of class transgression as he addresses the transformational role educational experiences in the lives of college faculty from working-class and first-generation backgrounds.

Michelle Tokarczyk brings together the issues of first-generation and class status by addressing the complex interactions among her own lived experience, the institutional norms of a liberal arts college, and the tensions that exist between institutions and faculty members as a result of class difference. Meghan Pifer and Karley Riffe's chapter investigates the perceptions of academic work within the academy as they are articulated and understood by working-class and first-generation academics, as derived through a content analysis of their self-reflective writing. Among the most profound of their findings is the degree to which working-class academics struggle with the kind of inter-class border crossings that Serravallo so ably delineates. Together, these chapters provide a powerful picture of the cultural environment of academic workers and highlight some of the ways in which social class plays a profound role in success and survival.

As Serravallo and Pifer and Riffe discuss in detail, the social norms of higher education are often fundamentally different from the norms of working-class Americans. This can have profound effects on working-class and first-generation academics' mobility within an institution. Failure to effectively conform to social norms may lead to the kind of interpersonal conflict between colleagues that can damage departments for decades. Furthermore, any attempt to introduce working-class norms into an institutional culture can be viewed negatively not only by colleagues, but by students and administrators. Working-class academics run the risk of being viewed as "difficult" or "gauche," which can have long-term career impacts.

Yet "passing" as upper-middle class, which involves conforming, is not without its risks. At times, establishing the trust needed to build social capital within one's new class environment can mean the abandonment of old bonds and the unlearning of skills previously considered essential. In effectively passing as a member of the elite, working-class academics are encouraged to entirely differentiate themselves from other members of their birth class. Furthermore, as Tokarczyk notes, working-class and/or first-generation academics may also experience "imposter syndrome." The persistent sense of not belonging has both personal and professional consequences. This section provides a comprehensive and thought-provoking assessment of the challenges faced by the working-class/first-generation faculty members within the academy. For those interested in entering this environment and who will engage in class transgression to do so, the experience can be both challenging and rewarding. Graduate school is the entry point and "makes or breaks" their professionalization as academics.

Graduate Students and Academic Professionalization

The second section of this volume is devoted to the experience of academic professionalization and graduate school socialization. These contributors focus on addressing lived experiences of graduate students as a labor force, as students, and as individuals engaged in the difficult work of reshaping their understanding of the world. The scholars represented in this section have worked to identify and articulate an academic culture in which the demands and the limitations imposed by changing educational environments are disproportionally visited upon the historically marginalized, including poor and working-class first-generation graduate students. Within an increasingly competitive and challenging environment, first-generation students, who lack the social capital of many of their peers, face unique challenges. As working-class and first-generation graduate students engage with the process of academic socialization and professionalization, they experience not only new expectations and new modes of social and intellectual engagement, but also experiences that conflict with their own sense of identity and values.

Kathleen Mullins explores the experiences of working-class graduate students, challenging conventional narratives rooted in individualistic explanations of these academic success stories, while also identifying important "resilience factors" such as access to strong K–12 educational programs, emotional support, and lived experiences that foster responsibility and self-discipline. She challenges the notion of a universally positive experience in these supposed success stories, arguing that graduate school confronts first-generation students with high expectations for acculturation to the norms of academia. As a result, cultural differences that are accepted in undergraduate students become increasingly difficult to manage for students at the graduate level.

David Marquard elaborates on this theme, examining the narratives of working-class graduate students who experience their engagement with the culture of academia as a frustrating experience of "outsider status." Highlighting issues such as anger and shame, he addresses the emotional and narrative consequences of this marginalization, as working-class graduate students struggle to fit into their new environment. Mullins and Marquard both address experiences of loss rooted in family and class identity, and the sense of marginality experienced by working-class graduate students inside the classroom and within academia in general.

Faculty and academic professionals often expect graduate students to be comfortable with the social and cultural discourse of higher education, and with the middle- and upper-class environment in which it has historically been situated. Elvia Ramirez expands upon this issue, discussing the ways in which not only class and first-generation status, but also race and ethnicity, play a profound role in academic professionalization. Addressing the personal experiences of Latino/as and the institutional norms and expectations that surround them, Ramirez effectively illustrates the sense of marginality experienced by working-class students in general and by working-class students of color in particular. She notes how cultural practices normalized within higher education can create an environment of hostility for first-generation Latino/as that is rooted in both race and class differences.

The writing team of Aaron Hoy, Marcus Bell, Selene Cammer-Bechtold, and Mauricio Torres further this discussion by analyzing the specific structures that make the academy a foreign and even hostile place for working-class and first-generation students, and for students of color. The neoliberalization of higher education has fundamentally reshaped higher education in ways that have profound impacts on both daily practices and career trajectories. As first-generation academics, the authors of this chapter acknowledge the ways in which their experience of the academy is shaped by the increasing focus on professionalization and consumerism, with a corresponding decrease in attention to the creation of knowledge. Yet they also ably articulate the ways in which acknowledging such forces in no way keeps them from being subject to them.

JanRose Ottaway Martin provides a comprehensive discussion of the "leaky pipeline," the educational phenomenon that occurs when certain populations, most notably women, people of color, and working-class students decline in educational participation at increasing rates that correspond with higher levels of education. Malar Hirudayaraj wraps up the section by addressing the consequences of the "leaky pipeline" as she addresses the ways in which the challenges and institutional structures discussed in this section can result in working-class and first-generation students being forced to opt out of higher education altogether. Ottaway Martin and Hirudayaraj both address the consequences of shifting cultural expectations and access around educational attainment, while also acknowledging that many improvements must occur to provide all students with the real benefits of higher education, especially at the graduate level.

Surviving and Thriving in Academia

Finally, in deference to the power of narrative voice and the profound ways in which the silencing of a population or group can be an act of violence—a means to take away individual voice and with it, the right to self-definition—the final section of the book is devoted to the narrative voice of the marginalized. This section provides personal essays from first-generation students and academics themselves, granting insight into the struggles and strengths of living and working in an unfamiliar landscape. These chapters give the reader insight into the lived experience of first-generation academics, while providing practical advice for survival and success.

Sarah Smith and Saran Donahoo tell us powerful and compelling stories that take us on journeys real and imagined. Smith discusses her journey from extreme poverty to a career in higher education, and Donahoo uses the allegory of Dorothy and Oz to emphasize the profound importance of social capital in the form of mentors, peers, and institutional support mechanisms. Finally, Rosanne Ecker and Taren Swindle discuss some of the practical ways in which academic institutions and first-generation and working-class students themselves can mobilize support and resources. Ecker describes a range of programming initiatives to support first-generation graduate students, while Swindle offers a practical guide to networking and acculturation for the same population. This section of the book provides a more immediate sense of what it is like to live and work as a permanent resident in a strange space during a time of transformation.

Moving Forward

Taken as a whole, this volume asks and perhaps even answers some profound questions about higher education, from the perspective of a population that is simultaneously both "insider" and "outsider." The struggle of higher education in the 21st century is rooted in such questions. How, for example, do we make higher education a space simultaneously welcoming to the needs of the historically marginalized and resistant to the forces of neoliberalization and delegitimization that are levied against it by powerful actors? How does one embrace the institutional values and expectations of knowledge work, while still maintaining the connections and values that come with a working-class identity? How do we resist the array of social forces that are working to undermine educational access—discursively, politically, and culturally? As working-class and first-generation students and faculty members enter the hallowed halls of higher education—not as travelers moving through, but as settlers who will be leaders—we must think deeply about our own road to success, and how our identities and experiences can reshape and, in some cases even preserve, the core values of our new home. As women, people of color, and those from the working class enter higher education, we face profound challenges, yet bring with us possibilities for profound transformation.

The authors in this volume discuss strategies and tools for confronting the challenges of higher education, and also highlight some of the battles we face from both inside and outside the walls of the academy. There is no question that in welcoming the marginalized, higher education has opened its doors to transformation, even as it faces resistance from forces that seek to recreate hierarchies and protect concentrations of power. Working-class and first-generation academics must be leaders in shaping that transformation, both to open the path for those who follow and to reject the forces that would use our identities to undermine higher education, denying the real benefits of knowledge to the breadth of the population. The challenges higher education is currently facing are mirrored within the United States more broadly. Powerful political forces promote the delegitimization of scientific knowledge and a general sense of anti-intellectualism as a means to police class borders and reinforce boundaries of power. Ultimately, this volume seeks to provide first-generation graduate students, faculty members, and their allies and mentors insight into the changing face of higher education and the unique challenges faced both by newcomers to the academy and by the "outsiders within."

PART ONE

Mapping the Terrain

Understanding Academic Labor

1

Changer in Paradise

Escaping Marginality and Shaping Academic Labor

Vincent Serravallo

Consider Norman Frost. This is not his real name, but he was the first in his family to get a college degree, and in the late 1960s he became an economics professor. However, when asked to discuss his experience of moving up into academia, he tells us he is not fully living out what most would agree should be a happy success story. Instead, he describes an inner turmoil involved with his trajectory: "Being a working-class academic is sometimes very lonely. It's difficult to relate to most colleagues, but it is also difficult to relate to working-class folks, who tend not to trust you since you got to be a 'Doctor'" (Ryan and Sackrey 1984, 257).

Frost's experience is not unique. In actuality it is typical of a pattern of experience shared by many first-generation academics from working-class backgrounds. No fewer than five volumes—published between 1984 and 2006 and based on full and composite narratives of 138 academics—illustrate this pattern.[1] They overwhelmingly describe tremendous anguish and ambiguity involved in their achievements. Their testimony describes in stirring detail the major challenge for those like us who are pioneering their path to the university: the difficulty of crossing the borderline of social class and class culture. As first-generation academics, you will be joining a professional occupation composed mostly of people whose lifestyles and temperaments are not only very different than ours, but hold sway as the standard we must meet. That is the borderline separating what the subjects see as two separate worlds.

However, several of these narratives comprising the literature by and about first-generation academics contain clear counter-views. While acknowledging the difficulties of crossing the borderline, many subjects also expressed a will to confront and overcome this predicament. For example, let us consider Nancy LaPaglia, a humanities professor from a working-class family: "Although I recognize that dissimilar domains exist, I want to be everyplace. I am not actually alienated from either sphere—the working class or academe. I am not simply rebelling against one position or another. I am opposing fixity and trying to have the best of both worlds" (Dews and Law 1995, 185–86). Thus, while the upward mobility of first-generation academics from working-class origins is fraught with unease, not all aspirants accept it as insuperable, and many attempt to outfit their new academic world with what they see as the commendable features of their old world.

I will address the realities of both Frost's and LaPaglia's experiences, but I will focus on the latter, the attempt "to have the best of both worlds." Put another way, I will suggest ways to achieve a working life in the academy that is more in your control. Let me first discuss in more detail the two representative statements.

Marginality, Habitus, and Hope

The first statement, by Frost, is a crucial forewarning. It depicts the inner malaise resulting from a life between and betwixt two worlds, the working class and the academy. There is overwhelming consistency in the narratives of those contributors to the literature who succeeded in attaining a tenure-track academic position: they see themselves as long occupying an unhappy location somewhere on the borderline of the old world of their origins and the new world of their professional destination, of having a foot in each world but being strangers in both.[2] They poignantly describe an anomic predicament characterized by such now-familiar glum metaphors as being "caught in the middle," "in limbo," or "far away from home." They feel they are impostors, unable to achieve complete class assimilation and uncertain about even wanting to.

Robert Park (1928) was among the first sociologists to reflect on this condition.[3] He identified the "marginal man" as a personality type associated with racial and ethnic group members whose international migrations simultaneously placed them in the terrains of home culture and host culture, but who felt at home in neither. Characteristic traits of marginality included "spiritual instability, intensified self-consciousness, restlessness and malaise" (893). Contemporary students of social class continue to examine the symptoms of Park's marginal man, but reconceptualize them within the theoretical framework of Pierre Bourdieu (1977). Bourdieu refers to particular dispositions, tastes, and lifestyles as *habitus*, a powerful subculture that emerges from the material conditions of social class. Those attempting to move into a new position face a new habitus while the old habitus continues to exert its hold. Bourdieu refers to this as a "cleft habitus" (Lee and Kramer 2013).

The familiar imagined territories of old world (origins) and new world (academe) actually represent two different and opposing social relationships: the working class and the professional-managerial class, each with its distinct dispositions, roles, and power.[4] Credentials and good work might bring the aspirant from lowly origins to the doorway of a professional position, but due to the workings of social class and class culture, he or she is not prepared to embody the new dispositions, perform the new roles, and exercise the new power as is expected of all members of the new world. The professional-managerial class habitus that dominates the academy is difficult to master for many of those not born into it, and this is by far the most common obstacle identified in the literature.[5]

Park and Bourdieu, however, did not perceive marginality or cleft habitus as deterministic and fixed. Park recognized the creativity and change that migrations of racial and ethnic groups offered their host countries, and Bourdieu held that habitus may change or reshape the conditions from which it arose. The second statement above, by LaPaglia, evidences this. She believes she is "not actually alienated from either sphere—the working class or academe." Recent research on college undergraduates from working-class origins suggests that her claim is not unique (e.g., Lee and Kramer 2013). While the marginality problem that first-generation academics have discussed over the past 30 years is powerful, it is not necessarily insurmountable. Many of these academics have tried to escape the marginality trap and make a contented life in the new world. I will use my experience as a first-generation tenured professor from working-class origins to develop these "escape plans" primarily for the benefit of those just starting their full-time (or temporary full-time) academic appointments, but much of what I outline will benefit graduate students as well. Before I formally present my suggested strategies, though, let me begin with a small personal example.

Challenging Gauche with Class

Soon after I received tenure, my chair asked me to organize the department holiday season collection for our secretary. I had happily contributed each year since being hired, and never failed to note the significant transition this represented in my life: the once very poor graduate student was now lending financial support to an assistant! However, a colleague with an Ivy League background said something to me that reminded me of the class-cultural differences that my above-the-national-median salary did not overcome. The pool of cash reached triple digits, and I opted to do what had been customary for my extended family and friends: give her the cash—the "long green with the short future," as my backroom-gambling hometown neighbor put it. This did not sit well with my Ivy League colleague, whose parents are college graduates, one a professor. "That's so gauche," the professor smugly protested with wrinkled nose.

This professor is a good person with a sharp and creative mind, but I took this as a stinging affront on my class character—a clear statement that I was too low-mannered for the ways of the professoriate. So, I asserted my areas of expertise (sociology of work and social inequality), appeals to social justice, and my working-class customs to firmly yet civilly make several points: that our secretary did not have the luxury of a professor's flexible work schedule to drive to the mall in the event a gift had to be returned; that while our faculty politely interacts with the office staff, we do not form relations close enough to know their tastes in gifts; that office staff, who do not have incomes as high as those of faculty, most likely find cash much more practical than some gadget. And I informed my colleague with much pride (and via anecdotes) that cash-giving was a normal practice for many people with working-class origins—one that might recall the joys of children getting handed a few singles spontaneously by an uncle simply because he had not seen them in a few weeks. I turned the situation around and made it clear that elements of middle-class culture would not set the standards of my workplace. Later, I informed my colleague that our secretary happily told me that cash was perfectly fine.

Since then, there have been other such incidents too numerous or too subtle to recall in detail, but my ability to escape marginality and reshape my "paradise" (as Ryan and Sackrey would have it) grows as the months and years go by. Let me use my experience to suggest how you too can accomplish this. I will start at the general level of academic work, offering some foundational insights for maneuvering within the world of academia, and will then move to the more specific, day-to-day aspects of an academic position.

Our Roots, Your Roots

You might be the first in your family to become an academic, but you are not *the first* first-generation academic. Fortunately, you have predecessors, and they have confronted the challenges and felt the trepidations you might now experience. You also have your personal background of achievements in your particular academic endeavors. Draw on your own experiences and those of your predecessors.

Learn from Our Predecessors

My first suggestion is that you read, as early as possible, the books that have focused directly on first-generation academics' experiences, beginning with the earliest of the lot, *Strangers in Paradise*, by Ryan and Sackrey (1984). *This Fine Place So Far from Home* (Dews and Law 1995), *Caught in the Middle* (Grimes and Morris 1997), *Reflections from the Wrong Side of the Tracks* (Muzzatti and Samarco 2006), and *Working-Class Women in the Academy* (Tokarczyk and Fay 1993) also provide abundant lessons from first-generation academics whose common background nonetheless admits variation by sex, sexuality, race, age, and geography.

The narratives provided in these texts are thoughtful accounts that will help you better articulate your unique predicament and create the academic future you want. All of my information about first-generation academics in this essay is based on this literature and my own experiences.

Read and discuss the books in reading groups composed of your first-generation colleagues, including graduate students. You are likely to form bonds with academics who share your origins. As Julie Cannon puts it, they are likely to "*know* what life on the other side of the tracks is really like" (Muzzatti and Samarco 2006, 108; emphasis in original), and since life on that side varies, you will gain further insight into your own experience by knowing theirs.

Moreover, because the texts explicitly discuss such issues as social class, social mobility, gender, bureaucracy, subculture, intersectionality, and organizational power, they will enhance the coursework of graduate students—especially those in the social sciences—and may inspire ideas for a course paper, poem, song, film, master's thesis, or dissertation. Junior faculty members might be inspired to conceive and design research projects.

We Are Not Impostors

To enter academia is to enter various realms: your particular discipline, our wider occupation of college professor, and your particular academic workplace—plus their respective subcultures. Trepidation in entering all three areas has marked the experiences of those from working-class origins. They often claim to feel like impostors, pretenders, fakes, or spoilers, and they fear they will someday be found out as such. Many believe they lack the abilities involved in the everyday expectations of their academic job, and feel ignorant of or unsuccessful at performing the lifestyles, dispositions, and overall presentation of self associated with academicians as a class. As one subject in Grimes and Morris's study put it: "As a professional sociologist, I have always felt like an outsider to the profession. This lack of fitting in stems from two sources. First, I have always felt academically less well prepared than most sociologists…. The second source of alienation comes from life in a strange [class] culture" (1997, 143).

You can avoid this predicament by honestly acknowledging your abilities. By this I certainly do not mean to suggest that you engage in an inspirational campaign of self-affirmation; I do not suggest that you will be smart if you repeatedly tell yourself you are smart, or that you must believe that being born into the working class was a blessing for your future.[6] Instead, you must remember that you passed high selection standards to be admitted into graduate school in the first place. As the chair of the Sociology Department at the University of Kansas pointedly told me when I expressed self-doubt, "You wouldn't *be* here if you weren't capable." As a new faculty member, you must acknowledge that your accomplishments and experiences got you the offer of a tenure-track job, which dozens or hundreds of other applicants did not get. You must also consider that your candidacy was sponsored by letters and perhaps phone calls from renowned authorities who believed in your abilities.

To confirm your competencies, revisit some of your past work, such as a class paper, master's thesis, dissertation, computer code, creative works, or peer-reviewed publications. You could also review the awards or public acknowledgments you have received for service to the community, the discipline, your university, or someone's research. At times you might cringe over something you wrote or did, but it is more likely that you will take pleasure in your proven competencies.

Windows on Academe

Becoming an academic involves much more than attaining expertise in an area of concentration. It demands socialization into an occupational subculture. Regardless of discipline and the particular school in which they work, academics constitute an occupational subculture. They share a specialized language, carry out familiar rituals, and agree on certain norms, beliefs, and values (Rothman 1998, 44–61). This is true for most occupations. As a seamstress in the "shops," for example, my mother was a "sleeve setter" who had to "fill the bobbin" for every new "bundle" she got, and might have to work on "repairs" found by the "trimmer." In the academy, the "tenure-track" professor who got the "new line" due to her "strong CV" will often have to teach fewer "new preps," and have a "lighter load" while on "probation." When I pumped gas in the days of "full service," we all believed that customers in old clunkers tipped more than those in luxury cars; most academic departments are guided by an opposing belief that applicants from prestigious universities are the best job candidates. Masons value the good workmanship of their brick walls, and professors value the scholarly work of searching for knowledge. Just as firefighters create and share norms about how to save lives, and home health-care aids share norms about how to care for the infirm, professors share norms for how to teach, do research, and deliberate department and university business.

Every academic department in its particular school will manifest a unique combination of features of the wider occupational subculture. This is the workplace subculture, and I will discuss this further on. But when considering the professoriate as a whole, there are important organizations and organs that are very helpful for socializing the newcomer to the dominant language, values, and norms of academe.

AAUP and The Chronicle

One organization you should become familiar with is the American Association of University Professors (AAUP). Established in 1915, the AAUP is the national association promoting the interests of the academic profession. As described on its website (http://www.aaup.org),

> The mission of the AAUP is to advance academic freedom and shared governance; to define fundamental professional values and standards for higher education; to promote the economic security of faculty, academic professionals, graduate students, post-doctoral fellows, and all those engaged in teaching and research in higher education; to help the higher education community organize to make our goals a reality; and to ensure higher education's contribution to the common good.

This organization will inform you of the elementary shared beliefs and language of the academy and provide position statements on existing and emerging issues. It was instrumental in promoting the modern idea of tenure, and its statements on academic freedom and governance are highly regarded by faculty members, administrators, and policy makers. "Collegiality" is a concept currently affecting many academic workplaces, and the AAUP has written a position statement on it. This is of special concern for first-generation academics, due to the common claim that working-class life does not prepare one for, and is at odds with, the gentle art of debate between colleagues.

One of the most important publications on academe is *The Chronicle of Higher Education.* Published weekly during the academic year, and daily in its online version, *The Chronicle* provides news, information, opinions, and discussion forums on nearly every aspect of academia. It is read and discussed by administrators and faculty members alike. If you cannot afford a subscription, your department or the dean's office most likely subscribes, and it is probably in your school's library. A related source is *Inside Higher Ed,* a free online newsletter and blog.

Needless to say, you should not automatically accept the AAUP's views, nor should you substitute the AAUP for other advocacy bodies, such as unions. You would be best informed if you complemented *The Chronicle* with other publications on higher education that provide more depth and alternative views.[7] But familiarity with the AAUP and *The Chronicle* will help you to become informed about the major issues and debates in the profession, so you can speak intelligently about them, and will help you absorb the basic beliefs and language that mark the occupational subculture. Escaping the impostor self-image and making your place in academia will follow from the confidence and authority you can develop from these resources. There is always the possibility, moreover, that once more at home in academe, first-generation academics from working-class origins could be part of a movement to reshape the academic subculture.

The Innards of the University

Hundreds of students enter a college or university and leave about four years later with a degree. The work that goes into scheduling their classes, teaching their classes, determining their grades, deciding their financial aid, feeding and housing them—and that is just a short list of their needs for completing their degree—is overwhelming. This feat is accomplished because the school is a complex organization comprised of many parts, rules, and overarching values. The structures (offices, departments, councils, governing bodies) are guided by rules (policies and procedures), all of which are shaped by wider values (such as articulated in a mission statement), and this set of relationships makes the "machine run" regardless of a school's unique qualities, such as student population, Carnegie classification, endowment size, or the personality of its president. Learning the structures, rules, and values of your particular school and academic department is essential for an easy transition into your studies or your job, and for giving your input on how it works. In this section I will focus on the social structure of the college; I will discuss work at the department level further below.

Your Place in the Social Structure

Rather than seeing yourself as entering an intimidating academic monolith, consider that you now occupy a position, such as assistant professor, within a complex but ordered group. Read the history of your institution, preferably published by a historian, to get an overview of the organization you are in or joining. Then, learn about how the school "works." Examine your school's organizational chart to learn the major units. Institutions of higher education are typically divided into two main spheres: finance and academics. The former includes such departments as budget, human resources, and financial aid. The academic division, where most of our time is spent, includes the office of the president and other senior academic administrators, including provosts and deans. There are several units making up the academic division, such as student affairs, academic affairs, and some form of an academic or faculty senate. Within these bodies are countless committees charged with carrying out the school's academic business. Find your place in the organization and identify the major committees of the various units and their duties. You might be informed of these structures during an orientation for new hires.

Among the important structures are the governance bodies. The basic elements of academic labor—teaching and research—are shaped and strongly guided by policies and procedures created by large and small governance bodies constituted by academics. A common refrain of academics is the need to "just do my work and not get involved with university politics." This attitude is based on the myth of academic individualism. The academic cannot work in isolation from his or her colleagues and governance bodies. Doing one's own research project, for example, is often shaped by policies on human subjects, internal and external grants, release time, and many others; these policies are formed by governance bodies. If faculty members do not participate in such groups, they will face policies given to them by administrators. By the time you can serve on governance bodies that formulate such rules, you will not only feel more at home in academia, you may be in a position to remodel that home.

A faculty senate (sometimes called an academic senate or faculty council) is the typical governance group representing the faculty, and it is essential that you familiarize yourself with its bylaws, including those concerning membership. The minutes of senate meetings are often made public, and it would be worthwhile to review them to get a sense of the pressing issues of the day and the debates about them.

All of the divisions, committees, and governing groups shape the school's operations, but the school's board of trustees has the final decision-making powers. Typically, trustees will hail from the business world, and will likely be older, white males with high incomes. Few if any academics will be among them. See who the members are to get a sense of how your school is directed.

A union may be another structure in your academic workplace. About one-third of professors nation-wide are union members. If your school is unionized, learn the union bylaws, study its contract, and know your union representatives. It would also be helpful to learn how the school became unionized, and about the union's history.

Know the Rules and Use the Rules

Your work and the work of the various groups and committees in the school are guided by formal policies and procedures. Read your university's policies and procedures manual or bylaws, as they will provide the official rules on nearly all aspects of your work. This includes not only the rules about tenure and promotion, but about many other important elements, such as the charge and membership of institution-wide standing committees, the various faculty ranks and their duties, grievance procedures, academic conduct, intellectual property, attendance, foreign travel programs, final exams, graduation requirements, grading and grade disputes, salary, retirement, and so on. The purpose of reading the bylaws is not to become your school's policy wonk, since the complexity and detail of the typical policies and procedures manual are overwhelming. Instead, the purpose is to help you speak more authoritatively about the important issues that arise or know where in the policies one would look to get the official word on an issue. Without this knowledge, you may feel aloof and further disinclined to interact with colleagues on important matters. Ryan and Sackrey well understood this:

> One way to cope as a newcomer anywhere is to learn the rules before the bumbs [*sic*] on your head get too large and too many. To some, such a strategy of acceptance and achievement also demands a rising-to-the-occasion of playing at others' rules as well as or better than they do, particularly to keep from feeling overwhelmed, inferior, incompetent, or all three. (1984, 131)

Regarding the benefits of "playing at others' rules as well as or better than they do," it is crucial to know how to use the rules that academics use, or claim to use, to conduct their meetings: *Robert's Rules of Order* (Robert et al. 2000). It is a long, complex book that few have mastered or even read from cover to cover, but its main elements are crucial for making the first-generation academic feel more in control in the academy. Since the typical school will implicitly affirm the dictum that it is an "institution of laws, not men," *Robert's Rules of Order* may serve as a leveling agent—preventing class background or habitus from bearing any advantage—since the rules of conducting business apply equally to all. Potentially harmful strategies that we might find in an informal meeting, such as grandstanding, bullying, and steering the deliberations for personal interests, are not allowed when *Robert's Rules of Order* are followed.

A final point to keep in mind about rules: you will find that in many cases, actual practices (often called traditions) will sometimes vary from the official policies. The formation of and compliance with informal rules in the academic workplace is important, and I will discuss this in a later section.

College Values

All of the units and the rules that guide them are informed by wider values agreed to by your university's leaders. All schools promote the value of an educated person, but schools will vary regarding what aspects of an educated person they will stress. Some might value "career education," while others stand for "liberal learning for the public good." All institutions will have some form of a mission statement, and it is important to read it so as to learn the major values that guide your institution.

The values proposed in the mission statement also shape the long-term planning of a university. A university's official plan for the next five or ten years is usually known as its strategic plan. Read the current strategic plan and see who was involved in creating it. While often self-congratulatory and marked by hyperbole—and generally used to gain funding—the strategic plan does inform the faculty of the school's priorities in such areas as curriculum, enrollment, learning, and research. A plan, for example, that calls for more interdisciplinary programs, more external grants, and more diversity, may shape an academic department's expectations, and thus help determine whether or not you will get support for your research plans or your ideas about designing a new course.

Your Department

The academic department is a workplace that requires direct and long-term relations with departmental colleagues. It will have its formal and informal norms, specialized language, and shared beliefs that help workers know how to do the work. This is the workplace subculture—a localized version of the occupational culture. The point, then, is to conduct the same kind of review of your department's bylaws and committees as you do for your university.

However, no matter how detailed and deliberate, a department's formal policy has some degree of ambiguity and thus is open for interpretation—hence, the role of informal norms created and shared by the people with whom you most closely work. "Candidates for tenure must provide evidence of effective teaching," a formal department policy might state, but departments and tenure committees have gone to war over what constitutes "effective" teaching. As a result, tenure candidates and their assessors share informal expectations, such as attaining generally high ratings on student evaluations, the exact number for which varies by department. Departments are not likely to have formal rules about granting a break time during class, but you will soon be told explicitly or learn indirectly through observation and hallway talk about what is the "rule," if there is one. The same goes for attire, assessment methods, course material, office hours, how to deal with unruly students, grade disputes, and so on.

One of the primary features of the occupational subculture of college professors is professional autonomy. It is expected that we will independently determine our pedagogy, course syllabi, grading policy, and selection of research topics. In fact, a common finding in the research on first-generation academics is that they are most at home, and feel less marginality, when in the classroom or when doing research. Such professional autonomy must never be taken for granted.[8] Nonetheless, there are helpful limits to such autonomy. For example, you will benefit from the informal norms of seasoned colleagues regarding how many pages students should be asked to read or write, and what is the "right" number of tests to give. Thus, if norms in your department are not clear, explicitly ask your department colleagues what is expected for your performance: How much reading is to be expected of students? Is it customary to give breaks at the mid-point of class? Is there an agreement about students' use of laptops and other online devices during class time?

Contested Academic Cultures

Learning the aforementioned enables you to maneuver in your work with more authority (especially since relatively few academics possess all this information), and it provides you greater opportunity to change your workplace subculture; after all, subcultures are constructed and therefore can be changed. For example, my self-esteem rose considerably, and I felt much more at home and in control of my life, when I was elected to be the moderator for the monthly meetings of the approximately 140 faculty members of the College of Liberal Arts, while not yet tenured. Carefully reading and applying *Robert's Rules of Order*, I set the parameters for discussion and often directed or silenced senior colleagues from higher class origins during deliberations.

In another instance, while serving on the university budget committee I used my knowledge of *Robert's Rules of Order* and my academic concentration areas to challenge proposals that I felt disadvantaged students from low-income families. Two or three outspoken committee members wanted to cut costs by eliminating student financial aid to qualified students applying for high-demand majors. It is highly unlikely that these academics came from lower-income backgrounds. "We have a large number of students wanting to enroll in programs that have a great placement record, so we don't need to offer them financial aid," they argued. The other committee members nodded in agreement, and the chair was ready to accept the proposal without a vote. However, I asserted the elementary rules of conducting a meeting and made the chair ask for a motion, provide time for deliberation, and call a vote. As in the instance of my "gauche example" above, I asserted my knowledge of social inequality in higher education's admissions policies to argue that such a proposal would exclude qualified but low-income students and thus rob them of their dreams solely because they were low-income. Alas, my objection to the proposal was outvoted, but I had it formally included as the dissenting view in the committee's published recommendations to the president and the entire university. When the issue came before our faculty senate, the president acknowledged my point as crucial for maintaining the right balance between diversity and budget. My effort did not revolutionize my school, and we do not yet know how the administration will decide on the matter, but it does demonstrate that ideas from first-generation academics that promote the interests of first-generation students can be put on the table as legitimate items for university-wide debate, using the very processes and policies practiced by the university. Had I not been familiar with those processes and policies—and had I not pursued membership on the committee—economic background would not have been identified as an issue.

The growing areas of contention in higher education present opportunities to build on the work of our first-generation predecessors. Examples include the focus on family income as an aspect of diversity, and the extension of the tenure probation period for having or adopting a child. Other trends open to debate include the emphases on instructional technologies, research, global education, interdisciplinarity, collegiality, and job placement. Along with knowing the rules and structures that make the university machine run, make good use of your experience as a first-generation academic from working-class origins to help shape (or curb) the future of these trends.

Cultural Divides at the Individual Level

My preceding suggestions—reading the literature on the experience of first-generation academics, acknowledging your accomplishments, and learning the structures, norms, and values of the profession and the workplace—make but the foundation on which to confront the major challenge: relating to a new social class culture. We must deal on a face-to-face basis with the individual people who occupy positions and are agents of the policies and values guiding our academic workplaces. Most often, these individuals, your colleagues, demonstrate great ease in the academy. They embody proper academic behavior and attitudes as a result of the anticipatory socialization they received at the hands of parents and educators. You must interact with these colleagues seemingly born to the academy. This interaction is often unnerving and sometimes intolerable, but always inescapable. These are the colleagues who formally assess your performance and judge your progress; ultimately, they decide your future. Your "hard" record of achievements in the areas of teaching, research, and service may or may not be sufficient for favorable overall judgments of your performance—but your interpersonal abilities are sure to be an important unofficial criterion. Nor do the anxieties of social interactions always diminish as one's career advances; most of the first-generation academics whose pain of marginality has been reported in the literature have attained tenure, and several have advanced up the academic hierarchy into administrative positions.

No Faking It

My first general suggestion is that you realize the power of habitus, and avoid the tendency to fit into the professional class by mimicking its members and masking your origins. Accept the reality that full assimilation into the academic class is unlikely. To the extent that academic culture is understood to connote middle- or upper-class status, membership in this culture cannot be faked. Many first-generation academics have attempted a two-pronged strategy of masking the stereotypical ways of their old world while mimicking the ways of those in the new. Some, like Donna LeCourt, feel they were good at it:

> With such attempts at mimicry, I successfully rewrote myself and my thinking.... [I]t extended beyond schooling to trying to revise eating habits, conversational patterns, the way I dressed, even how I decorated my apartment.... I also learned how to "mask" working-class markers well—a skill I still employ when I believe the context demands that my appropriately professional and middle-class face appear: the cocktail party at the job interview; the seemingly innocuous dinner where I know to leave sports, television and the heated political debate at home; the reminder that admitting where I received my undergraduate education will immediately diminish

> me the eyes of my interlocutor. My body learned in these years how to move in professional-class ways: how do dress, speak and socialize differently; what to say and what to silence. Although I no longer seek a complete masking, I learned much in those years about what I risked when the mask slipped and how to consciously choose when that slippage might occur. (Muzzatti and Samarco 2006, 93–94)

Self-conscious mimicking and masking, as the above statement represents, is qualitatively different from the "code-switching" required of all of us as we move within and between many different social settings. Taking the role of the other, as George Herbert Mead (1934) explained, is a necessary part of socialization in general. Learning the elements of professional-class culture by close observation is vital in anticipating your colleagues' responses and demonstrating your ability to integrate into your workplace. You may take comfort in realizing that you have been engaged in this sort of thing for many years since entering school (Lehmann 2014). Indeed, some of the recent commentators have made reference to and applied W. E. B. DuBois' (1994 [1903]) notion of double consciousness to their experiences of the class divide (Moses 1995; Cannon 2006).

Deliberate imitating and suppression as described by LeCourt, however, is of a different order that demands a great deal of energy and stress to maintain in the long term. LeCourt herself hints at the need for never-ending attention to managing the risk of being found out. Thus, it is important not to fall prey to insincere and exaggerated efforts of self-presentation. In addition to the constant stress, it denies the source of unique power and talent your origins offer for your work and for academe in general (Granfield 1991). To repeat, full class assimilation is very unlikely, but as I hope to demonstrate, it is also neither necessary nor desirable.

Collegiality

Collegiality is a broad and complex term, but I will use it in the practical sense of interaction norms for faculty members of all ranks in various formal and informal settings. In simple terms, we recognize collegiality as the expectation that we interact with politeness and respectfulness of others' views and ideas. Passions are tempered by appealing to reason; we may refute and disprove with gusto, but the target is the idea, not the person. Currently, there is a trend to formalize collegiality into written policy, as this section of a 2013 internal "collegiality statement" from an academic department in my university exemplifies: "We expect that disagreements will be asserted calmly and respectfully, and will not devolve into personal attacks that would undermine the professional reputation of the individual and the department."

Asserting disagreements "calmly" is perhaps the epitome of academic collegiality, and as ethnographies such as those by Khan (2011), Lareau (2003), and Cookson and Persell (1987) find, it seems to be done with great ease by those with middle- and upper-class upbringings. The common socialization practices of middle- and upper-class parents and the schools their children attend nurtures curiosity, confidence, and reasoning over physical responses: brain over brawn. Kohn and Schooler (1983) identify features of parents' work as the source of these different socialization practices. Highly paid, prestigious occupations tend to require independent judgment and creative problem-solving, and those in them tend to emphasize these values and develop them in their children. Those in occupations requiring close supervision and regimented tasks tend more to socialize obedience to authority; their work offers them less opportunity to demonstrate to their children the ways of logical persuasion to resolve problems and conflict. Collegiality seems to be inching toward acceptance as an explicit factor in tenure and promotion, as the previously quoted departmental collegiality statement goes on to make clear: "In grievous cases, shortcomings of collegiality may be factored into annual faculty reviews and decisions on tenure and promotion." In this case, the academic's career heavily depends on collegiality.

Having witnessed as a small child my father terminated from the area's largest employer for punching a co-worker who referred to him by an ethnic slur; and having witnessed many uncles use the same technique in smaller, unregulated workplaces; and having witnessed as a teenager my neighbor bawl out and mercilessly slap two teenagers bloody for bullying his sons; and having witnessed as a graduate student my upper Manhattan neighbors resolve disagreements with deadly bullets; and having witnessed as a tenured professor deadly force on the street below my bedroom window (having chosen to make my home in a residential area mixed by class and race); and witnessing throughout my life most family members arguing with loud voices and contorted faces—after a lifetime of watching and expecting conflict to be settled with great emotion and violence, the calm demeanor I am expected to assume as an academic has not come naturally. I favor it as much as my colleagues, and I have come to master it no less than most of them. Still, my colleagues might not need to expend the self-conscious effort to first suppress passion, as I must; it is an ease I will not likely ever attain.

If your experience is like mine, observe and practice civil debate regularly. You might already be familiar with a variety of physical and nutritional means to promote calm (like yoga, meditation, tai chi, distance running, and substitution of chamomile tea for five-hour caffeine energy shots), and you are likely aware of the extensive literature on the art of listening and rhetoric. However, practicing civil discussion will produce the best results. If time permits, practice by writing out in advance an exchange you will face. You can practice for collegial interactions by engaging in imaginary debate with talk show callers, TV pundits, and so forth.

However well you master the collegial demeanor, know that you have the freedom to integrate styles of interpersonal relations from your origins. Thus, apply as much of your old-world ways of social interaction as will comply with the calmness code. Asserting the wit and color of working-class and folk communicative styles is one of the most commonly mentioned tactics first-generation academics employ for not only integrating with, but enhancing collegial culture. Incorporate some of the civil terms, expressions, and rhetorical devices you have learned from friends and family. For example, as Ryan and Sackrey's informant Douglas Brent (another pseudonym) explains:

> Part of being rural is to use colorful figures of speech.... Perhaps it is a way uneducated people use their imagination; they play with language in different ways than do the educated. I grew up in this environment, and have picked up many of the figures of speech. You don't describe someone as simply happy; "he or she is as happy as a pig in a new suit." As the example indicates, many of these are earthy. (Ryan and Sackrey 1984, 291)

First-generation academics have also identified career mobility and self-promotion as alien to their upbringing, and some have become disillusioned with academe because of this. Testifying, perhaps, to Kohn and Schooler's point about the value of obedience in working-class families, they believed they were raised to be humble, to just do their work and let others acknowledge their achievements. Overvaluing humility, however, may jeopardize one's chances for achieving a variety of awards, such as merit raises, research partnerships, tenure, and promotion. If you wish to remain true to modesty, you will have to decide for yourself how much self-promotion you will employ for what you believe is essential for your academic career. An honest, not "padded," documented presentation of your accomplishments will satisfy the requirements of your assessors without undermining your integrity. When preparing your materials for an annual evaluation or tenure review, it will be beneficial to include any truthful descriptions that enhance your work. For example, if the editor puts your published article first in a journal, describe it as the "lead-off" article. If you are among others on a publication, describe the amount and importance of your contribution. If you assisted students via long electronic discussions, include a printed copy to demonstrate your commitment to teaching. Do the same for unsolicited favorable emails from students. As any quantitative methodologist will tell you, numbers do not speak for themselves. Thus, high student evaluation ratings or high numbers of students who took the next-higher-level course with you could be explained as examples of effective teaching or significant improvement. You might also apply these honest enhancers when requesting your teaching schedule or committee positions.[9]

Cultural Literacy

By far the most common element of the marginality problem reported by first-generation academics is their ignorance of middle- and upper-class academic culture. For example, as Christine Overall explains: "Growing up in working-class Toronto, I had, unlike my middle-class colleagues, little or no access to foreign travel, classical and contemporary art, dance and theatre, fine cuisine, elegant clothes, middle-class manners, and influential people" (Dews and Law 1995, 215–16). Of course, it can be, and very likely will be demoralizing to attend receptions and dinners during which the topic of conversation moves to the areas Overall mentions. To repeat my earlier claim, you cannot fake the knowledge necessary in these situations. Some first-generation faculty members avoid the agony by not attending such events. Attendance, however, is often required—and may provide a good opportunity to learn. As an academic you will have opportunities to become familiar with many aspects of professional or middle-class culture; take advantage of them.

One increasingly available opportunity for travel is to direct a study abroad program. You might also have opportunities to attend an academic conference abroad. The more time you share the academic workplace with your middle- and upper-class colleagues, the more you are likely to adopt some of their tastes, dispositions, and habits. Thus, when in the company of those with high academic cultural literacy, tactfully probe for clarity and elaboration—that is, ask questions. To be clear, this is not to feign interest or flatter; it is a good way to develop your knowledge. The longer you remain in academe, the more experience you will gain with questioning colleagues whose interests and work is unrelated to yours. If someone is discussing an obscure topic, ask this colleague to relate it to something that pertains to your field. I might know nothing about nineteenth-century French literature, but I could ask the authority on this topic what if any French-language novels or poems address the issues of, for example, the eight-hour movement taking place in the U.S. around that time, or of labor issues in general.

In an actual situation early in my career, renowned Harvard law professor Charles Ogletree spoke at my university, and I was invited to a dinner in his honor with a small group of colleagues. Ogletree taught Barack and Michelle Obama law at Harvard, and has been on several TV news shows and documentaries. During the dinner, my colleagues and he engaged in lengthy name-dropping of famous lawyers and TV news personalities, and I felt excluded and uncomfortable; it seemed like a conversation out of my league. During a lull in the conversation, however, I mentioned my interest in critical labor law and asked Ogletree about his experience in that area. To my delight, he showed sincere interest in and a great deal of knowledge about this topic. I felt at ease during the substantive discussion that ensued. I am certain that much of this was due to Ogletree's approachable personality, but my query initiated the dialogue.

Conclusion

The growing research on first-generation academics from working-class origins shows a variety of experiences with the challenges of entering academe, and a variety of strategies to attain a successful career once in it. It is true that the marginality problem is a dominant, commonly shared feeling for most of us. After all, academe is a social institution maintained by unfamiliar norms and values that pressure one's thoughts and actions to conform. First-generation academics are new to these pressures and understandably feel out of place, strange, and ill at ease. Some respond by attempting to fully assimilate. We recall LeCourt, who said, "I successfully rewrote myself and my thinking." Muzzatti and Samarco also suggest this strategy when they claim that "the survival, perhaps even more so than the success, of professors from the working and underclasses is highly contingent upon our sanitizing of fugitive knowledge, our obfuscation of class position, and our muzzling of class consciousness" (2006, 79). However, the experience of most of the contributors, plus my own, testify to the obstacles of a pathway based on constant self-conscious attempts to mimic and fake the norms and values others easily personify. Moreover, sociologists inform us that while the norms and values of academia are powerful, they are not absolutely powerful. First-generation academics have the capacity to challenge, modify, or replace the social forces shaping them, and much of that capacity, what sociologists call agency, is nurtured in our particular life histories—certainly including our working-class origins. Thus, many reject full assimilation. Some, like Ryan and Sackrey's pseudonymous George Puck, believe they can ignore the culture of the academy and attempt to insulate themselves within its sphere. Puck claims,

> I spend two days a week on campus.... I *never* visit the office of another professor except when I must do so on business.... In my view, I run my own small college within a university two days a week. The rest of the University can go to hell with itself.... And I think that the institution needs me a great deal more than I need it. (182–83, emphasis in original)

However, Puck himself admits that this approach is possible only for a small privileged class of tenured senior academics in certain colleges. It is also a very individualistic work life, at odds with academia's reliance on group collaboration, interdisciplinary research, and the general social nature of knowledge construction.

Between these two extremes of either total assimilation into academic culture or the complete rejection of it is a pathway that offers hope at both the personal and wider social levels. Some first-generation academics make an effort to hold on to certain elements of their "old world" background and apply them in the "new world" of academe. In this way, one attempts not just to escape the torment of marginality, but to reshape our academic world. It is an approach expressed by Laurel Black: "I am seeking a way to keep the language of the working class in academia, not just in my office with my working-class office mate, to nurture its own kind of vitality and rawness and directness..." (Dews and Law 1995, 25). This orientation seeks to retain within academia the knowledge and experience of the working classes. Of course, there is no monolithic working-class knowledge and experience. There is instead a variety shaped by race, ethnicity, region, gender, occupation, and many other factors. Nonetheless, first-generation academics share an outsider standpoint that can be asserted rather than masked or suppressed.

We should use it to educate our non-first-generation colleagues as well as our students. When I was doing fieldwork for my dissertation on how working-class parents socialize their children, for example, a fellow graduate student and good friend from the upper-middle class told me matter-of-factly not to schedule interviews with these families over the summer because that is when people are on vacation. I informed him that my subjects do not "go on vacation" over the summer or any other time. Trips to visit family in nearby counties and states are common, but vacation as the middle class understands it—a private family excursion—is not part of their lives.

We can use it to raise the consciousness of colleagues by having them confront insensitive classist comments, like I did with a professor who asked a student during class and in front of dozens of other students, "Why don't you have the [assigned] textbook? Can't afford it?" White, male, and the son of a medical doctor, he was apparently unaware of the humiliation such a question could evoke, especially in low-income students in an expensive private university like ours.

Depending on our disciplines, we can conceive or enhance our research projects and our classroom lectures by integrating the experiences and ways of life of our family backgrounds. My discipline, sociology, affords me much opportunity of this kind, and most of my formal research examines working-class life. In the lecture hall, I discuss unfair labor practices to exemplify deviance. I show some of the posters and music of the Industrial Workers of the World to exemplify counterculture. And, what better way to teach about intersectionality or the cultural capital of the lower classes than to describe my life growing up in a working-class family? A chemistry professor of working-class origins from my hometown brought into his lectures his family's informal knowledge of chemicals in their traditions of wine- and bread-making; physics and biology professors could surely do the same.

Asserting features of the "old world" knowledge and experiences assists the individual academic in maneuvering through the marginality dilemma, it raises the consciousness of colleagues about class inequality, and it helps build the confidence of first-generation undergraduates and inspire them to carry on. As you progress in your academic career, know that these three main benefits constitute the paradise of academia as much as do commonly celebrated elements such as the professor's high occupational prestige and freedom to explore and debate the truth. That is the paradise your unique first-generation biography has the power to create.

Notes

1. Dews and Law (1995) have 26 first-generation academic contributors, Muzzatti and Samarco (2006) 18, Ryan and Sackrey (1984) 26, and Tokarczyk and Fay (1993) 21. The study by Grimes and Morris (1997) involves 47 subjects. All of the contributors in this literature originate from working-class families, but this might not be the case for all "first-generation academics." Some first-generation professors and graduate students may have parents or guardians who have no college degree or did not attend college, yet achieved jobs or incomes characteristic of the middle class or even the upper class. Small business owners, inheritance beneficiaries, or even big-prize lottery winners are examples. While this presents the possibility of diverse, and more likely "higher" lifestyles and life chances within the category "first-generation academic," the number in such a group is likely very small. Thus, while "academics with working-class origins" might offer a more homogeneous population, I will use the two terms interchangeably.

2. The most commonly referenced problems of assimilating into the new class culture are rooted in deficient cultural literacy, e.g., a lack of knowledge of world travel, food, and high culture; wrong taste in clothes; weak vocabulary; and improper presentation of self. Some also report difficulties in adjusting to calm and polite manners of deliberation during committee meetings.

3. DuBois (1994 [1903]) conceptualized the turmoil of a divided self in his notion of "double consciousness" well before Park. But DuBois' formulation was rooted in the circumstances of forced migration by enslavement, not the free migration to another country or the choice to attempt to advance up the class, occupational, or educational hierarchy.

4. The Ehrenreichs' notion of a "professional-managerial class" serves well to represent academics: they are "salaried mental workers who do not own the means of production and whose major function in the social division of labor may be described broadly as the reproduction of capitalist culture and capitalist class relations" (Ehrenreich and Ehrenreich 1979, 12).

5. There is more to the marginality problem. Ryan and Sackrey believe that academics from the working class also experience the "internalization of class conflict." As they put it, "It became clear for us that to grow up working class, then to take on the full trappings of the life of the college professor, *internalizes the conflicts in the hierarchy of the class system within*

the individual, upwardly mobile person" (1984, 5; emphasis in original). That is, as members of the professional-managerial class in higher education, first-generation professors help reproduce the structure of class inequality that disadvantages students from their own class background. A college degree, perhaps now more than in the past four decades, is a major factor in attaining prestigious and high-income jobs (Wysong, Perrucci, and Wright 2014, 232–33), and college professors provide that advantage by sorting students via letter grades, letters of reference, and other formal means of evaluation. One possible response is for the first-generation academic to participate in various opportunities for social change, but activism is not commonly accepted as progress toward tenure or promotion. In some universities, however, such activism, if resulting in peer-reviewed publications, is accepted as "engagement" scholarship.

6. On the problems that follow from this line of thinking, see Ehrenreich's (2009) autobiographically inspired critique.

7. An example is the online, open-access journal *Workplace: A Journal for Academic Labor.*

8. Recent trends in higher education include the emphasis on accountability (e.g., instructional assessments, goals and outcomes), pressure to employ particular instructional technologies (e.g., online courses, flipped courses), a variety of policies that transfer academic judgment to nonacademic personnel (e.g., professional advisors and commercial online student evaluation systems), and strong expectations for team teaching and study abroad. Karp (2003), Slaughter and Rhodes (2004), and Tuchman (2009) are excellent starting points for research on the simultaneous rise of faculty responsibility and erosion of faculty autonomy. The current interest in collegiality may be explained, in my view, as administration's effort at social control in response to faculty resistance to the erosion of their autonomy.

9. Another aspect of working-class culture that might be part of your background is experience with collective bargaining, and this could be leveraged in certain circumstances in nonunionized schools—for example, with respect to starting salary. If a school has formally offered you a job, and states your salary, you are in a position to consider reasonable negotiation of the salary, along with other expenses, such as moving and office equipment. Of course, this assumes you have first done research on the prevailing wages for both the locality and for your rank and discipline nationally. Your proposal might be rejected, but you can try.

Works Cited

Bourdieu, Pierre. 1977. *Outline of a Theory of Practice.* New York: Cambridge University Press.

Cannon, Julie Ann Harms. 2006. "White, Working Class, and Feminist: Working within the Master's House and Finding Home Again." In *Reflections from the Wrong Side of the Tracks: Class, Identity, and the Working-Class Experience in Academe,* edited by Stephen Muzzatti and Vincent Samarco, 101–16. Lanham, MD: Rowan and Littlefield.

Cookson, Peter, and Caroline Hodges Persell. 1987. *Preparing for Power: America's Elite Boarding Schools.* New York: Basic Books.

Dews, C. L. Barney, and Carolyn Leste Law, eds. 1995. *This Fine Place So Far from Home: Voices of Academics from the Working Class.* Philadelphia: Temple University Press.

DuBois, W. E. B. 1994 [1903]. *The Souls of Black Folk.* New York: Dover Press.

Ehrenreich, Barbara. 2009. *Bright-Sided: How the Relentless Promotion of Positive Thinking Has Undermined America.* New York: Metropolitan Books.

Ehrenreich, Barbara, and John Ehrenreich. 1979. "The Professional-Managerial Class." In *Between Labor and Capital,* edited by Pat Walker., 5–45. Boston: South End Press.

Granfield, Robert. 1991. "Making It by Faking It." *Journal of Contemporary Ethnography* 20 (3): 331–51.

Grimes, Michael D., and Joan M. Morris. 1997. *Caught in the Middle: Contradictions in the Lives of Sociologists from Working-Class Backgrounds.* Westport, CT: Praeger.

Karp, David L. 2003. *Shakespeare, Einstein and the Bottom Line: The Marketing of Higher Education.* Cambridge, MA: Harvard University Press.

Khan, Shamus Rahman. 2011. *Privilege: The Making of an Adolescent Elite at St. Paul's School.* Princeton, NJ: Princeton University Press.

Kohn, Melvin, and Carmi Schooler. 1983. *Work and Personality: An Inquiry into the Impact of Social Stratification.* Norwood, NJ: Ablex.

Lareau, Annette. 2003. *Unequal Childhoods: Class, Race and Family Life.* Berkeley: University of California Press.

Lee, Elizabeth, and Rory Kramer. 2013. "Out with the Old, In with the New? Habitus and Social Mobility at Selective Colleges." *Sociology of Education* 86 (1): 18–35.

Lehmann, Wolfgang. 2014. "Habitus Transformation and Hidden Injuries: Successful Working-Class University Students." *Sociology of Education* 87 (1): 1–15.

Mead, George Herbert. 1934. *Mind, Self and Society: From the Standpoint of a Social Behaviorist.* Chicago: University of Chicago Press.

Moses, Wilson. 1995. "Ambivalent Maybe." In *This Fine Place So Far from Home: Voices of Academics from the Working Class,* edited by C. L. Barney Dews and Carolyn Leste Law, 187–99. Philadelphia: Temple University Press.

Muzzatti, Stephen L., and C. Vincent Samarco, eds. 2006. *Reflections from the Wrong Side of the Tracks: Class, Identity, and the Working-Class Experience in Academe.* Lanham, MD: Rowan and Littlefield.

Park, Robert. 1928. "Human Migration and the Marginal Man." *American Journal of Sociology* 33 (6): 881–93.

Robert, Henry, Sarah Corbin Robert, Henry M. Robert III, William J. Evans, Daniel H. Honemann, and Thomas J. Balch. 2000. *Robert's Rules of Order Newly Revised.* Cambridge, MA: Perseus.

Rothman, Robert. 1998. *Working: Sociological Perspectives.* Upper Saddle River, NJ: Prentice Hall.

Ryan, Jake, and Charles Sackrey, eds. 1984. *Strangers in Paradise: Academics from the Working Class.* Boston: South End Press.

Slaughter, Sheila, and Gary Rhoades. 2004. *Academic Capitalism and the New Economy: Markets, State, and Higher Education.* Baltimore, MD: Johns Hopkins University Press.

Tokarczyk, Michelle M., and Elizabeth A. Fay, eds. 1993. *Working-Class Women in the Academy: Laborers in the Knowledge Factory.* Amherst: University of Massachusetts Press.

Tuchman, Gaye. 2009. *Wannabe U: Inside the Corporate University.* Chicago: University of Chicago Press.

Wysong, Earl, Robert Perrucci, and David Wright. 2014. *The New Class Society: Goodbye American Dream?* Lanham, MD: Rowman and Littlefield.

2

Educational Experiences of Faculty from Working-Class Backgrounds

Jim Vander Putten

The meritocratic ethos in American society supports the idea that all children should have equal opportunities for educational access and eventual occupational advancement. This is not always the case, however, and people tend to maintain their current positions in their present social class: "There are quite strong tendencies for children of those at the bottom of the income distribution to find their children at the bottom, with a parallel tendency for those at the top of the income distribution to find their children at the top" (Bowles, Gintis, and Groves 2005, 1).

Decades of social science research has confirmed the relationships of a wide variety of social, educational, and behavioral outcomes between parents and children (Duncan et al. 2005). In regard to education, Harris, Terrel, and Allen (1999) found that highly educated parents may produce home environments with higher levels of cognitive stimulation. Parents with higher levels of education often organize routines and resources in ways that prepare their children to be successful in school (Michael 1972). Annette Lareau (2011) documented the stark contrasts in parental routines between middle-class and working-class parents, and illustrated the formidable pragmatic challenges and economic constraints faced by the latter in attempting to best prepare their children. Casey Mulligan (1999) found that attainment in school is persistent across generations, and that the strong correlation of educational level with skills and earning potential over an individual's lifespan has significant implications for the continued reproduction of social class.

It is important to consider this intergenerational research in the context of college and university faculty. Lipset and Ladd (1979) found that roughly 60% of the fathers of the (over 60,000) respondents to the 1969 Carnegie Commission on Higher Education Faculty Survey came from professional, managerial, and business backgrounds, while only 25% were from working-class social origins. Examining the faculty demographic profile in the 15 years following the Lipset and Ladd study, Stetar and Finkelstein (1997) reported that the percentage of faculty from professional- and managerial-class families had scarcely changed between 1969 and 1984, although the class demographics of university students changed significantly during that time to include more students from low-income families.

What are the implications of this for faculty from working-class backgrounds? What aspects of their educational experiences were significant in shaping successful academic performance and high educational aspirations for these children, characterized by Kenneth Oldfield (2007) as "humble and hopeful"? Reported here are the results of a qualitative study investigating the educational experiences (pre-K through college) of faculty from poverty- and working-class backgrounds. The study results can provide deeper insights into the specific ways in which these faculty differ from their more advantaged colleagues and can also inform the design of preparation programs for undergraduate and graduate students from poverty- and working-class backgrounds who aspire to faculty careers. Two primary research questions guided this study: 1) What are the educational experiences of faculty from poverty- and working-class backgrounds? 2) How did these experiences influence their educational persistence and aspirations?

Literature Review

The theoretical framework for this study is based on research that addresses three areas: a) sociological theory in general, and in particular theory relevant to a working-class subject position; b) educational experiences of students from working-class backgrounds; and c) college and university faculty from working-class backgrounds.

Sociological Theory and the Working Class

The concept of *social class* means different things to different people.

To some, class refers to categories of people occupying common positions within societies stratified by status (Parsons 1970). To others, classes are defined as conflict groups determined by their positions related to authority or power structures (Dahrendorf 1959). Richard Sobel saw class as a function of the "economic and structural conditions within which social actors contend" (1989, 2). In addition, Max Weber and subsequent theorists have viewed social classes as groups of people with similar opportunities in life that have distinct economic implications (Weber 1922; Giddens 1973). Finally, Marxists define social class in terms of structural positions within the social organization of production (Wright 1979).

In this study, I use Marxist theory in general, and the work of Erik Olin Wright (1978; 1979) in particular, to analyze social class in the context of the working class. It is important to acknowledge that the Marxist concepts used to analyze 19th- and 20th-century industrial capitalism cannot simply be applied to contemporary society. Wright's work is particularly useful in bridging this historical divide. He defines the working class as those people who: (a) occupy the working-class position within the social relations of production, i.e., wage labor which is excluded from control over money capital, physical capital, and labor power; or, (b) are linked directly to the working-class through immediate family or class trajectories; or (c) occupy working-class positions within political or ideological apparatuses, i.e., positions which are excluded from either the creation or execution of state policy and ideology. (1978, 96). Thus Wright accounts for workers who are not directly involved in relations of production, and discusses class interests in political and ideological as well as economic terms.

Marxist scholars have analyzed social class in relation not only to American society in general, but to the American educational system in particular. For example, Bowles and Gintis (1976) argued that the historical purpose of education is to reproduce the class system from one generation to the next, and that the hierarchy in American education exists at every level to accomplish this purpose—from the tracking system in public schools directing some children up and others down, to elite universities reserved primarily for the upper class. A number of scholars have documented various aspects of this hierarchy (Espenshade and Radford 2009; Golden 2006; Khan 2010; McDonough 1997; Schmidt 2007; Steinberg 2002; Stevens 2007), while others have begun to examine the early educational experiences of elites in this process (Kendall 2002; Khan 2010).

Few authors, however, have narrowed the analysis to American higher education, and fewer still to college and university faculty from working-class backgrounds. Jencks and Riesman (1968) devoted a chapter to social stratification in their lengthy analysis of American higher education, and combined economic and occupational class to form the single concept of social class:

> When we speak of the upper-middle class, for example, we will mean families headed by someone with a professional or managerial job, usually making at least twice as much as the average American family. When we speak of the lower-middle class we will mean families headed by clerical or sales workers or small businessmen, usually earning fairly close to the median national income. When we speak of the working-class we will mean families headed by a blue-collar worker, again with income close to the national average. (65–66)

Looking briefly at the literature on working-class academics, Dews and Law (1995) considered possible definitions based on income, parental education level, and occupation. Their contributor Julie Charlip commented pointedly on the limitations of an income-based definition:

> If you earn thirty thousand dollars a year working in an assembly plant, come home from work, open a beer and watch the game, you are working-class; if you earn twenty thousand dollars a year as a school teacher, come home from work to a glass of white wine and PBS, you are middle-class. (1995, 26)

This effectively illustrates the problem of using a single criterion such as parental education level, occupation, or even the cover term "first-generation college" to accurately measure the construct of social class origin or capture the essence of working-class culture (Rubin 1976).

Educational Experiences of Working-Class Students

Viewing the educational experiences of students through the lens of social-class origins has been attempted by several notable contributors to the literature. Sennett and Cobb (1973) identified the long-term costs of membership in the working class, beginning with K–12 education, while Lillian Rubin examined day-to-day working-class life. The title of Rubin's book, *Worlds of Pain: Life in the Working-Class Family* (1976), accurately indicates findings from her chronological exploration of working-class families involving marriage, family formation, relationship intimacy, family issues emerging from the nature of working-class occupations, and individual views on the quality of leisure time. Lareau's (1987; 1993; 2011) focus on the intersection of social class and education yielded important knowledge about parental influences on their children's educational and career aspirations.

MaryBeth Walpole (2003) focused on college students from low-socio-economic-status (low-SES) backgrounds, and compared them to students with different racial and ethnic identities, genders, and sexual orientations. Just as students from these latter groups have been historically under-represented in higher education, so have students from low-SES back-grounds. In fact, until recently much of the research on student diversity in higher education has adopted a monolithic, single-identity approach that fails to acknowledge that "no one is just one thing," in Edward Said's apt phrase. The assumption seems to be that if a student maintains a primary identification with one background characteristic, then other characteristics are essentially irrelevant. As a result, while students from different racial and ethnic groups, genders, and sexual orientations may also be from low-SES backgrounds, the class aspect of their identities tends to be subsumed and largely ignored. A common assertion among scholars whose work focuses on social-class identities and social inequality is that there are two groups of students on campus who are painfully aware of their class origins: students from upper-class backgrounds and students from poverty- and working-class backgrounds. Although a student's race, ethnicity, and gender can often be identified by visual cues, ever since torn blue jeans became a fashion trend, markers of student economic background have become mostly invisible.

Terenzini, Cabrera, and Bernal investigated the college choice proces-ses, in-college experiences, and outcomes of college completion for low-SES students. Regarding college choice, they found that "nearly one-half of the lowest-SES-quartile high school graduates do not enroll the follow-ing fall in any postsecondary institution, a nonenrollment rate nearly five times higher than that of high-SES students (48 versus 11 percent)" (2001, v). In terms of college academic experiences and the levels of involvement in academic-related areas, the highest-SES-quartile students were more actively engaged in their course work than were students from the lowest SES quartile. Finally, looking toward graduate school and possible faculty careers, Terenzini, Cabrera, and Bernal found that

> from 20 to 35 percent of the students who entered postsecondary education in 1989–90 reported that they intended to apply, or had

> applied, to a graduate or professional school. Five years later, however, far fewer reported having entered a postbaccalaureate program (4 to 6 percent of the students in the upper two SES quartiles versus less than 2 percent of the lower two quartiles). (2001, vi)

These findings raised important questions about the opportunities for students from low-SES backgrounds to complete graduate school and enter the professoriate.

Faculty from Working-Class Backgrounds

Stetar and Finkelstein (1997) examined trends in the social origins of faculty using parental education and occupation data from 1969 to 1989. They concluded that, "Although … there has been some modest diversification of faculty with respect to religious origins in recent decades, their socioeconomic roots … are remarkable with respect to how slowly the profile has changed over the past twenty years." (289). Nor has the situation changed appreciably in the decades since. Ironically, increases in overall American affluence are likely to have a negative impact on working-class representation in the professoriate, as a larger proportion of the middle class gains access to the faculty career pipelines enjoyed by the elite. The ongoing marginality experienced by faculty from a working-class background has obvious implications for how institutions define and interpret concepts like "faculty diversity" and "underrepresentation," as will be discussed later in the chapter.

Ryan and Sackrey's pioneering book focused on working-class academics' upward social mobility and its effects on individuals:

> It became clear to us that to grow up working-class and then take on the full trappings of a college professor's life, *causes the conflicts inherent in the hierarchy of the class system to be internalized within the individual, upwardly mobile person.* With this idea in mind, and with a yet undefined structure for our book, we began to wonder if other upwardly mobile academics had experienced similar feelings of estrangement or dissatisfaction and, perhaps most important, had internalized conflict. (1984, 4; emphasis in original)

However, the majority of Ryan and Sackrey's contributors were white males in the social sciences. In response, Tokarczyk and Fay (1993) produced a similar volume whose contributors solely comprised female working-class academics in the humanities. Dews and Law's (1995) edited volume took a more general approach that included men and women in a variety of academic disciplines. Shepard, McMillan, and Tate's (1998) and Rosen's (2013) edited volumes focus on the influence of faculty social-class origins on teaching for a diverse array of English faculty from working-class backgrounds. Adair and Dahlberg's (2003) edited collection of essays focuses specifically on women from poverty-class backgrounds and examines personal experiences with social services systems and educational experiences as students. Kathleen Welsch's (2005) edited volume explores the relationships that female working-class academics in college and university writing programs have with their parents, while Oldfield and Johnson (2008) assembled the first collection of essays by queer scholars from working-class backgrounds.

The empirical social sciences have also contributed research on working-class academics. Judith Barker (1995) expanded on Ryan and Sackrey's (1984) ideas on internalized conflict and investigated social mobility for working-class academics. Her qualitative results identified a series of themes describing working-class academics; they (a) possess fewer financial resources; (b) experience feelings of invisibility due to the myth of classlessness in academe; (c) have few working-class-based professional and social support systems; (d) experience insecurity about their intellectual ability; and (e) often have fears of inadequacy in social and professional situations. Grimes and Morris (1997) focus specifically on sociology faculty from working-class backgrounds.

Methodology

Guided by the literature reviewed above, the definition of "faculty from working-class backgrounds" used in this study consists of three clearly operationalizable criteria:

- both parents possessing a high-school education at best;
- low-income status during childhood through undergraduate college years;
- parent(s) in blue-collar occupation(s), including farmer, maid, coal miner, factory worker, and so forth.

In combination with these more specific criteria, three more subjective or experiential criteria provide a larger perspective on the definition:

- overall background in which the family unit did not participate fully in a middle-class lifestyle;

- faculty members perceive their own distance from a middle-class lifestyle;
- faculty members identify with the concept of the working class.

Data Collection

The sample of participants is diverse and was selected in terms of their discipline, rank, race, gender, tenure status, and the degree to which they met the criteria comprising the working-class definition in use here. Long interviews were conducted with 12 faculty from working-class backgrounds employed at different types of institutions: two each from a community college, a Master's-1 (M1) institution, a Research-1 (R1) institution, a liberal arts college, a medical school, and a Historically Black College/University. This group of interviewees was identified through snowball sampling (i.e., asking participants to recommend other faculty from working-class backgrounds who may be interested in participating in the study) and was comprised of seven women and five men, with four faculty of color.

Data Analysis

As noted by Creswell (2013), qualitative researchers are interested in meaning: how people make sense of their lives, their experiences, and structures of their environment. In keeping with this perspective, content analysis for this study was conducted from the faculty members' points of view, and their own reports of their early educational experiences were used to identify categories that characterize various aspects of these experiences.

This study is based on a subset of data from a 20-question semi-structured interview protocol that was sequenced chronologically, with questions ranging from family background and educational experiences to choice of first faculty position. The goal of the research was to explore the educational experiences of faculty from working-class backgrounds, and to gain insights into these experiences by grounding the analysis of working-class academics in the context of their family histories and subsequent academic careers. The study uses social class as an analytic concept (Dahrendorf 1959) to understand the educational experiences of faculty, rather than using social stratification as a descriptive concept (Strauss 1975) to conduct social-class analysis for the purpose of refining the definition or mapping the boundaries of the working class. In other words, faculty social origins in general, and working-class origins in particular, were used as the frame of analysis for the lived experiences of the research participants. Efforts to evaluate the accuracy of my definition of "working class" within the broader continuum of social-class positions were beyond the scope of the study. Furthermore, it is important to acknowledge that the concomitant background factors of race and gender are closely linked with social class, and exert influences on faculty perceptions of their educational experiences that are often difficult to disentangle.

To ensure consistency in data collection, all interviewees were asked the same questions. Each interview lasted approximately 90 minutes, and was recorded and transcribed. Renata Tesch's (1990) eight-step qualitative process was used to cluster topics and themes from the interview transcripts. In short, an initial coding of the data was completed, followed by a second review for data reduction and to facilitate a shift to a conceptually oriented approach to coding the data (i.e., identifying coding subcategories, making subcategory coding assignments, and clustering the subcategories into primary themes in the codes). As a consistency check, a third review was completed to reassess the accuracy of coding assignments. A second researcher was available to resolve coding differences.

Results

The research design and data analysis used in this study enabled me to chronologically organize the educational experiences of faculty from working-class backgrounds by education level: "Pre-K to Middle School" and "High School to College." Presented below are exemplary quotes in each category, addressing issues such as early conceptions of class consciousness, parental influences on education and work, and awareness of the consequences of social mobility. They illustrate specific ways in which intergenerational transmission of social and educational aspirations occurred for working-class faculty in this study.

Pre-K to Middle School

One professor of philosophy described a conversation with her mother during first grade:

> I had two students in my class at school … [whose families] owned their own homes. And they would come in with pleated skirts, even wore uniforms to mass. I was going to visit them, and my mother was sort of saying, be careful, don't have their aspirations because

> they are wealthier than us, and I think that with house ownership that became in her mind a determining factor.

An assistant professor of philosophy talked about growing up in a Midwest company town:

> My dad never finished his associate's degree.... They [both parents] had white-collar jobs, but we were never up with all my friends whose parents all had bachelor's degrees or higher. One of my best friend's dad has a Ph.D. He was vice president at [an international food production company].... We tried to fit in to that group, I could never.... I could tell that ... my friends' parents always looked down on me because I came from somebody who didn't go to college....

As an assistant professor of developmental education in an HBCU explained,

> we were reared in an environment where neither of my parents were formally educated past eighth grade. That sometimes serves as a deterrent to students who are growing up in that environment, because you think you need someone there to say, "you need to aspire for this or aspire for that." They had that push there for us, but you really can't see the importance of something, I guess, if you haven't really been there.
>
> You know about it but you don't really understand unless you've been there. But my mom and my dad were very insistent upon us getting an education, and after graduating from high school, that wasn't enough.

One of the medical school professors discussed his strong academic abilities, yet attributed the resulting educational and occupational opportunities to chance:

> I was never forced by my parents to achieve and do well in school and then I really never started to do exceptionally well until the sixth grade and seventh grade.... I always liked to please people and one way to do that was to be a good student. And then there came a time of understanding on my part that knowledge was power or knowledge was the ability to shape one's life the way another can't.
>
> I was trying to break away from the stereotype ... limiting me.

> But it was a way that I could empower myself to determine my own destiny for a change. I hold my background to be very important to me.... What happens if the opportunity comes? Opportunities are created. It was luck, but I always thought it was due to my background, and how I got from charity case to Yale....

The other medical school professor in the study provided a quintessential example of parental encouragement to aspire to more than a working-class occupation:

> [My parents] encouraged me a lot to get a good education.... I worked construction with [my father] on summers, and he'd say, "You want to do this all your life? Stay here. You want to do something better, use your brain." Even when I was a little kid, I did well in school. That was rewarded. I was told that's good. That's going to get you out of here. You won't have to work like your father. And really it was early on in my life I decided I wanted to be a doctor. I knew that from the time I was about four or five years old.

Many of the comments in this category focused on the influences of social-class awareness at an early age. One impact of this awareness was to provide motivation for faculty to excel in elementary and secondary school, while another was to reinforce the differences between the "haves" and the "have nots."

High School to College

The exemplary quotes in this category provide insights into the accumulated educational disadvantage associated with working-class social positions that emerge during the college-going process, and the significant costs of significant upward social mobility. An assistant professor of philosophy talked about influences on the college choice process:

> Everybody's talking about how much knowledge you have about colleges. I picked colleges because I knew, OK, everybody else was going there. I [might have] no idea where [a college] was. I got accepted to the University of Michigan but I didn't think we could afford to have me go to Michigan.... They'd accepted me to Grand Valley State University based on my ACT scores. And my mom, she was a big influence—she knew that Grand Valley State was a party school: "I really don't want you to go there. You can go

> somewhere better." But that was the extent of it. So I didn't have that influence.

The professor of philosophy also illustrated the idea that for poverty- and working-class academics, you can never really go home again:

> My mother always said, and I do recall her saying this, to go to college if I had the opportunity. It was a big thing for at least my parents. They were giving up my bringing in an income. My father had more difficulty with me being in college, I remember him sitting me down. And I think also there was really a problem whether he was going to be able to continue talking with me.

One of the medical school professors told a fascinating story about a social mobility fork in the road:

> I was in sixth grade or seventh grade with a job at the A&P [supermarket] and started off as a bagger there. I worked through dairy, and went to the meat department, which is the highest paying. I was the best in the department, and one time the head of the meat department came up to me, and said, "How would you like to go to butcher school? We like you and we want you to become a butcher." And I said, "Thank you.... I am very honored that you think that high[ly] of me, but I have a scholarship to go to Yale, so I think I am going to go to Yale instead." I was soon to become an A&P butcher—which was, you know, it pays the best—or I could go to college.

One faculty member of color is a professor of English at a Research-1 institution, and recalled his feelings of being out of place attending an elite private liberal arts college:

> As soon as I got to Amherst College, I was with people such as I had never been with before. Most of my high school classmates came from families where the previous generations had not attended college ... and a few of us at Amherst were in that position.
>
> I looked around me, I listened to people.... Oh, the familiarity with books and learning. It was really clear from then and thereafter for the next four years and certainly from time to time afterwards in graduate school, I would wonder what would it be to have been from a family where there were say, two previous generations of people who had gone to universities and who had grown up

> with books like this, rather than, you know, a set of encyclopedias.

A psychology faculty member in a community college spoke of the lack of understanding her parents had for more education after high school:

> I was a good student, and it was a source of pride for [my parents] and I got lots of positive strokes. When I got to the college level and was working full-time and going to school part-time, there tended to be a lack of understanding of why I would put myself through that. And it's not like it was a terrible thing, but it was like, "why would you do it?"

These comments illustrate some of the ways in which the pre-college experiences of academics from working-class backgrounds differ from those of their more privileged faculty colleagues. They provide insights into factors, influences, and characteristics that allowed these faculty to experience continued academic success through postsecondary education, graduate education, and into full-time faculty work. In sum:

- from early in life, the participants possessed social-class consciousness and awareness of being "different," "the other," or "less than" their more advantaged classmates;
- as a result of this social-class awareness, participants recognized that their more advantaged classmates were on different educational and life trajectories;
- participants observed the importance of social networks within the middle and upper classes that did not extend to the working class;
- these perceptions culminated in the participants' realization of the importance of excelling academically to increase the range and scope of future life opportunities.

Considering these results in the context of Terenzini, Cabrera, and Bernal's (2001) discouraging findings on the educational experiences of low-income students, it becomes readily apparent that the faculty in this study were among the few who succeeded. This points to a distinct limitation of the present study: all interviewees demonstrated the ability to persist through graduate degree completion, raising an obvious question: What about the students from working-class backgrounds that didn't persist? Where are the "cracks in the pipeline" that result in a 38% rate of high-school freshmen earning a diploma and going on to college immediately after graduation (Committee for Economic Development 2005)?

Discussion and Conclusions

In the context of previous research on the intergenerational transmission of educational aspirations, it becomes evident that the early awareness of social-class identity demonstrated by the subjects in this study provided them with broader perspectives on the world of work and the role of education in accessing working-class and middle-class occupational opportunity structures. Instead of viewing a high-school diploma and resulting full-time job as the norm for their children, parents of the interviewees, with few exceptions, defined success in terms of college graduation and entry into a profession.

One theme that emerged from the "Pre-K to Middle School" results focused on interviewees' early recognition of social-class differences based on social conventions (such as styles of dress, peer perceptions of social-class status, and parents' social circles), parental education levels, and occupations. Interviewees were painfully aware of the differences between them and their more privileged classmates. One exemplary quote poignantly illustrates the undercurrents of emotion that ran through this section of the interviews:

> I think we knew that we were poor.... I remember one time, [it] was Valentine's Day and we didn't have money to buy valentines to take to school [to exchange with classmates], which was a big deal then, and I remember [my stepfather] borrowing money from a co-worker or something so that we could have them.

Lareau (2011) explored this phenomenon in detail, and extended the range of early perceptions of social-class differences to include relative affordability of expenses related to children's organized sports, summer camps, and—most relevant for the purposes of this study—private schools. Lareau found that working-class parents were not reluctant to discuss financial issues with their children, and these discussions were often cast in terms of price: how much something costs, and how much money the family possessed. In contrast, middle-class parents rarely discussed financial issues with their children, and Lareau asserted that this contributed to middle-class children's sense of entitlement. For many of the interviewees, though, the unspoken issue was not financial, but rather related to Sennett and Cobb's (1972) concept of the "hidden injuries of class," and the implied question, "I wonder how much better my life experiences would have been if I had the same privileges and opportunities?" One interviewee alluded to it this way:

> I recall [my parents] talking about relatives.... I remember my father had one sister who managed to finish high school and of course, you know, they had this idea that she thought she was better than they were because she finished high school. Particularly my mother—it affected my mother more and maybe because she didn't even get a diploma from elementary school. There was a lot of discussions about that, all the time. I was always conscious of social class, class divisions, whether it was based on ethnicity.... But it was always ... there was always the economic factor, or the intellectual factor, and so I grew up with a kind of attitude and perception about a person, especially persons who were making decisions for all others. My mother and father were involved in the Protestant work ethic: you put in a good day's work for a good day's pay, and this is what they were very proud of.

These social class differences often persist and become more pronounced as students from working-class backgrounds enter the professoriate. Working-class faculty possess ambivalent feelings about the reference group and social class with which they identify. On one hand, a working-class upbringing exerts significant influence on how one views the world (Sennett and Cobb 1972; Komarovsky 1967). On the other, their entry into a middle-class profession and the effects of their current social-class position provides another influence. The disparity between the social class of one's background and the social class of one's current work environment creates discontent for working-class faculty (Ryan and Sackrey 1984; Tokarczyk and Fay 1993). This significant social-class transition (from blue-collar to professional/managerial) creates feelings of being "out of place." Sennett and Cobb (1972) labeled these feelings as *status incongruity*, defined as "the discontent as a result of upward mobility from the social class of one's origin to a higher social class." This status incongruity has been described as "living on the margin"—not belonging to either of two distinct worlds (London 1992).

A second theme throughout the "Pre-K to Middle School" data was the interviewees' early academic success. Nainby and Pea (2003) have discussed the importance of successful educational experiences, including challenging school environments in which academic achievement was the primary criterion to determine social popularity, access to the highest curriculum tracks, and expanded options for Advanced Placement courses and exams, all of which set the stage for admission to prestigious colleges and universities. Many of the interviewees in this study clearly attributed their success to educational opportunities that made it possible to complete the terminal degree and enter the professoriate.

The *High School to College* results in this study focus primarily on college choice and out-of-class experiences. Hossler, Braxton, and Coopersmith (1989) identified three interrelated steps in the process of choosing a college: the development of predispositions to attend college, the search for potential institutions, and the choice of one institution among competitors. In terms of a predisposition toward higher education, three of the twelve participants in my study reported parental encouragement and high educational expectations, whereas the remaining nine lacked such encouragement or faced active resistance to their educational ambitions, reflecting a common experience for students from working-class backgrounds.

For the interviewees in this study who attended prestigious colleges and universities, students from "other cultures" meant students from middle- and upper-class backgrounds rather than students from other countries. The feelings of marginalization experienced by these interviewees during high school and college can be likened to international culture shock, as is palpable in the case of the previously quoted Amherst College alumnus who described his classmates as "people such as I had never been with before," and marveled at their "familiarity with books and learning."

Looking further along the educational pipeline, Terenzini, Cabrera, and Bernal (2001) found that student interest in attending graduate or professional school differed across socio-economic groups, and that students in the lowest-SES quartile were both less likely to apply or intend to apply to graduate school and less likely to actually attend. In contrast, Leonard Baird (1976) reviewed existing literature and concluded that graduate school attendance was not strongly related to socio-economic background, and Mullen, Goyette, and Soares (2003) noted little influence of social-class background on graduate educational attainment. However, the operationalization of social-class origins in these latter studies was based solely on family income (Baird 1976) or on parental education level (Mullen, Goyette, and Soares 2003), which are insufficient proxies for social-class measures. In contrast, the first three measureable criteria in the more comprehensive definition of social-class origins—namely, faculty from working-class backgrounds—used in this study generated data that was diametrically opposed to those previous research findings. Working-class social origins exerted considerable positive and negative influences on graduate education attainment for the faculty in this study.

There is also evidence that one's social class exerts influence on the type of doctoral institution attended. Dwight Lang (1984; 1987) asserted that higher education sustains a system with distinct status divisions that often make it difficult for individuals from modest backgrounds to enter top private universities. Donald Light (1973) found a relationship between class background and both access to and successful completion of the doctorate at prestigious graduate schools. In addition, his document analysis of faculty pedigrees, using the graduate catalogs of the top 12 graduate schools, revealed that 83% of the faculty at these graduate schools held their highest degrees from the same elite institutions. Similarly, in their analysis of a sociology faculty search process, Smelser and Content (1980) found that 73% of the sociology faculty in the five top-ranked departments received their degrees from either their own department or another among the top five. Robert Townsend arrived at similar results in his analysis of the undergraduate institutions attended by Ph.D. recipients in history. Most notably, he concluded that

> The doors to graduate study in elite private universities are largely closed to students who received their degrees in public colleges and universities outside of a few with top-tier Ph.D. programs.... Receiving an undergraduate degree from an elite school appears to be an important marker of future success in the academic job market. (2005, 1)

Applying these findings to graduate students who persist, graduate, and enter the professoriate, several researchers have established historic patterns of stratification along lines of social-class origin. Lipset and Ladd (1979) reported results from the 1969 and 1975 Carnegie Commission on Higher Education faculty surveys that inquired into faculty social origins. Their results for faculty were at odds with the findings on occupational outcomes of higher education for those in other professions. Whereas the expansion of higher education increased the proportion of working-class students in high-status occupations overall, Lipset and Ladd found that social-class origins continued to influence who became a faculty member and at what types of institutions they were employed. More specifically, they found parallel results between institutional prestige and social class: more prestigious research-oriented universities employed faculty from higher social classes at a disproportionate rate, and faculty offspring were most likely to work at the most prestigious schools; middle-class offspring were more likely to work at less-prestigious, second-tier institutions; conversely, faculty from working-class and farm backgrounds were most likely to be employed at lower-status colleges. The findings on institutional prestige and social class were confirmed by Boatsman and Antony's (1995) study of 1989 Cooperative Institutional Research Program (CIRP) survey data on college and university faculty, which indicated that the association of higher social-class origins with higher prestige for their affiliated institutions continued to apply even after controlling for age cohort, ethnicity, and gender.

These correlations in faculty social origins have distinct implications for faculty from working-class backgrounds, as well as for graduate students who aspire to faculty positions. As the ranks of full-time, tenured or tenure-track college and university faculty become more elite, the criteria weighted most heavily in graduate admissions at top-ranked doctoral programs—college grades, GRE scores, and the prestige of an applicant's undergraduate institution (Posselt 2016)—are likely to be barriers for students from working-class backgrounds. These barriers will prevent access to the best graduate schools and subsequently to faculty positions at the most prestigious institutions, and the cycle of social reproduction of faculty will continue.

The themes that emerged from the data in the present study confirm some of Lareau's (1987; 1993; 2011) results concerning social-class influences on children's early educational experiences, and extend them to faculty from working-class backgrounds. Unfortunately, the subfield of research in the sociology of higher education categorized as "faculty diversity" has focused primarily on race and gender, with scant attention devoted to faculty social class origins. In my previous work, I have noted the methodological shortcomings of this incomplete conceptualization of faculty diversity (Vander Putten 2014). Studies whose research design excludes social origins are unable to differentiate between, say, the children of Michelle Obama and the children of an African American female custodian who works at a university. The findings and knowledge claims emerging from such studies are limited in accuracy and trustworthiness; they fail to establish convincing arguments that faculty experiences documented in the research are solely attributable to race, ethnicity, or gender, since they exclude faculty from poverty-class and working-class backgrounds who have often had many of the same personal and professional experiences (e.g., Barker 1995).

Institutionalized preparation programs for women graduate students (especially in predominantly male academic disciplines) and graduate students of color have been in existence on university campuses for many years, and continue to expand. If the professoriate is to have a reasonable chance of achieving faculty social-class diversity to approach parity with race, ethnicity, and gender diversity, programs like the University of California system-wide First-Gen Faculty campaign, which provides working-class college students who aspire to the professoriate with role models and mentors (Flaherty 2017), will need to be widely adopted in highly ranked research universities across the country. This study can help provide the impetus for such a transformation, as the themes emerging from my analysis strongly argue that social-class origin is a valid component of faculty diversity that should be considered in combination with race and gender.

Works Cited

Adair, Vivian, and Sandra Dahlberg. 2003. *Reclaiming Class: Women, Poverty, and the Promise of Higher Education in America.* Philadelphia: Temple University Press.

Baird, Leonard. 1976. "Who Goes to Graduate School and How They Get There." In *Scholars in the Making*, edited by Joseph Katz and Rodney Hartnett, 19–48. Cambridge, MA: Ballinger.

Barker, Judith. 1995. "White Working-Class Men and Women in Academia." *Race, Gender and Class* 3 (1): 65–77.

Boatsman, K. C., and Jim Antony. 1995. "Faculty Equity: Class Origin, Race and Gender in the American Professoriate." Paper presented at the conference of the American Educational Research Association, San Francisco, CA.

Bowles, Samuel, and Herbert Gintis. 1976. *Schooling in Capitalist America: Educational Reform and the Contradictions of Economic Life.* New York: Basic Books.

Bowles, Samuel, Herbert Gintis, and Melissa Groves. 2005. *Unequal Chances: Family Background and Economic Success.* Princeton, NJ: Princeton University Press.

Charlip, Julie. 1995. "A Real Class Act: Searching for Identity in the 'Classless' Society." In *This Fine Place So Far from Home: Voices of Academics from the Working Class*, edited by C. L. Barney Dews and Carolyn Leste Law, 26–40. Philadelphia: Temple University Press.

Committee for Economic Development. 2005. *Cracks in the Educational Pipeline: A Business Leader's Guide to Higher Education Reform.* Washington, DC: Author.

Creswell, John. 2013. *Research Design: Qualitative and Quantitative Approaches.* 4th ed. Thousand Oaks, CA: Sage.

Dahrendorf, Ralf. 1959. *Class and Class Conflict in Industrial Society.* Palo Alto, CA: Stanford University Press.

Dews, C. L. Barney, and Carolyn Leste Law, eds. 1995. *This Fine Place So Far from Home: Voices of Academics from the Working Class.* Philadelphia: Temple University Press.

Duncan, Greg, Ariel Kalil, Susan Mayer, Robin Tepper, and Monique Payne. 2005. "The Apple Does Not Fall Far from the Tree." In *Unequal Chances: Family Background and Economic Success,* edited by Samuel Bowles, Herbert Gintis, and Melissa Groves, 23–79. Princeton, NJ: Princeton University Press.

Espenshade, Thomas, and Andrea Radford. 2009. *No Longer Separate, Not Yet Equal: Race and Class in Elite College Admission and Campus Life.* Princeton, NJ: Princeton University Press.

Flaherty, Colleen. 2017. "First-Gen Faculty: University of California Plan Forges Connections between Students and Professors Who Were the First in Their Families to Attend a Four-year Institution." *Inside Higher Ed,* June 2. https://www.insidehighered.com/news/2017/06/02/university-california-plan-links-first-generation-students-similar-professors

Giddens, Anthony. 1973. *The Class Structure of the Advanced Societies.* New York: Harper & Row.

Golden, Daniel. 2006. *The Price of Admission: How America's Ruling Class Buys Its Way into Elite Colleges—and Who Gets Left Outside the Gates.* New York: Crown.

Grimes, Michael, and Joan Morris. 1997. *Caught in the Middle: Contradictions in the Lives of Sociologists from Working-Class Backgrounds.* Westport, CT: Praeger.

Harris, Yvette, Denise Terrel, and Gordon Allen. 1999. "The Influence of Education Context and Beliefs on the Teaching Behavior of African American Mothers." *Journal of Black Psychology* 25: 490–503.

Hossler, Don, John Braxton, and Georgia Coopersmith. 1989. "Understanding Student College Choice." In *Higher Education: Handbook of*

Theory and Research, vol. 5, edited by John Smart. New York: Agathon.

Jencks, Christopher, & Riesman, D. 1968. *The Academic Revolution.* Chicago: University of Chicago Press.

Kendall, D. 2002. *The Power of Good Deeds: Privileged Women and the Social Reproduction of the Upper Class.* Lanham, MD: Rowman & Littlefield.

Khan, Shamus. 2010. "Getting In: How Elite Schools Play the College Game." In *Educating Elites: Class Privilege and Educational Advantage,* edited by Adam Howard and Ruben Gaztambide-Fernandez, 97–112. Lanham, MD: Rowman & Littlefield.

Komarovsky, Mirra. 1967. *Blue-Collar Marriage.* New York: Random House.

Lang, Dwight. 1984. "Education, Stratification, and the Academic Hierarchy." *Research in Higher Education* 21:329–52.

Lang, Dwight. 1987. "Equality, Prestige, and Controlled Mobility in the Academic Hierarchy." *American Journal of Education* 95 (3): 441–67.

Lareau, Annette. 1987. "Social Class Differences in Family–School Relationships: The Importance of Cultural Capital." *Sociology of Education* 60: 73–85.

Lareau, Annette. 1993. *Home Advantage: Social Class and Parental Intervention in Elementary Education.* Philadelphia: Palmer.

Lareau, Annette. 2011. *Unequal Childhoods: Class, Race, and Family Life.* 2d ed. Berkeley: University of California Press.

Light, Donald. 1973. *The Impact of the Academic Revolution on Faculty Careers.* Washington, DC: American Association for Higher Education.

Lipset, Seymour, and Everett Ladd. 1979. "The Changing Social Origins of American Academics." In *Qualitative and Quantitative Social Research: Papers in Honor of Paul F. Lazarsfeld,* edited by Robert Merton, James Coleman, and Peter Rossi, 28–43. New York: Free Press.

London, Howard. 1992. "Transformations: Cultural Challenges Faced by First-Generation Students." In *First-Generation Students: Confronting the Cultural Issues,* edited by L. Steven Zwerling and Howard London, 5-11. New Directions for Community Colleges, No. 80. San Francisco: Jossey-Bass.

McDonough, Patricia. 1997. *Choosing Colleges: How Social Class and Schools Structure Opportunity.* Albany: SUNY Press.

Michael, Robert. 1972. *The Effect of Education on Efficiency in Consumption.* New York: Columbia University Press.

Mullen, Ann, Kimberly Goyette, and Joseph Soares. 2003. "Who Goes to Graduate School? Social and Academic Correlates of Educational Continuation after College." *Sociology of Education* 76:143–169. doi: 10.2307/3090274

Mulligan, Casey. 1999. "Galton vs. Human Capital Approaches to Inheritance." *Journal of Political Economy* 107 (6): S184–S224.

Nainby, Keith, and John Pea. 2003. "Immobility in Mobility: Narratives of Social Class, Education, and Paralysis." *Educational Foundations* 17 (3): 19–36.

Oldfield, Kenneth. 2007. "Humble and Hopeful: Welcoming First-Generation Poor and Working-Class Students to College." *About Campus* 11 (6): 2–12. doi: 10.1002/abc.188

Oldfield, Kenneth, and Richard Greggory Johnson III, eds. 2008. *Resilience: Queer Professors from the Working Class*. Albany: SUNY Press.

Parsons, Talcot. 1970. "Equality and Inequality in Modern Society, or Social Stratification Revisited." In *Social Stratification: Research and Theory for the 70s,* edited by Talcot Parsons and Edward Lauman. Indianapolis, IN: Bobbs-Merrill.

Posselt, Julie. 2016. *Inside Graduate Admissions: Merit, Diversity, and Faculty Gatekeeping*. Cambridge, MA: Harvard University Press.

Rosen, Robert, ed. 2013. *Class and the College Classroom: Essays on Teaching*. New York: Bloomsbury.

Rubin, Lillian. 1976. *Worlds of Pain: Life in the Working-Class Family*. New York: Basic Books.

Ryan, Jake, and Charles Sackrey, eds. 1984. *Strangers in Paradise: Academics from the Working Class*. Boston: South End Press.

Schmidt, Peter. 2007. *Color and Money: How Rich Kids Are Winning the War over College Affirmative Action*. New York: Palgrave Macmillan.

Sennett, Richard, and Jonathan Cobb. 1973. *The Hidden Injuries of Class*. New York: Knopf.

Shepard, Alan, John McMillan, and Gary Tate, eds. 1998. *Coming to Class: Pedagogy and the Social Class of Teachers*. Portsmouth, NH: Boynton/Cook.

Smelser, Neil, and Robin Content. 1980. *The Changing Academic Market*. Berkeley: University of California Press.

Sobel, Richard. 1989. *The White Collar Working Class: From Structure to*

Politics. New York: Praeger.

Steinberg, Jacques. 2002. *The Gatekeepers: Inside the Admissions Process of a Premier College*. New York: Viking.

Stetar, Joseph, and Martin Finkelstein. 1997. "The Influence of Faculty Backgrounds on the Motivation to Teach." In *Teaching Well and Liking It: Motivating Faculty to Teach Effectively*, edited by James Bess, 287–313. Baltimore, MD: Johns Hopkins University Press.

Stevens, Mitchell. 2007. *Creating a Class: College Admissions and the Education of Elites*. Cambridge, MA: Harvard University Press.

Strauss, Irving. 1975. *Stratification, Class, and Conflict*. New York: Free Press.

Terenzini, Patrick, Alberto Cabrera, and Elena Bernal. 2001. *Swimming against the Tide: The Poor in American Higher Education*. College Board Research Report No. 2001-1. New York: College Board.

Tesch, Renata. 1990. *Qualitative Research: Analysis Types and Software Tools*. New York: Falmer.

Tokarczyk, Michelle, and Elizabeth Fay, eds. 1993. *Working-Class Women in the Academy: Laborers in the Knowledge Factory*. Amherst: University of Massachusetts Press.

Townsend, Robert. 2005. "Privileging History: Trends in the Undergraduate Origins of History PhDs." *Perspectives*, September, 14–20.

Vander Putten, James. 2014. Review of *Faculty Identities and the Challenge of Diversity: Reflections on Teaching in Higher Education*, by Mark A. Chesler and Alford A. Young Jr. *Teachers College Record*, February 24. http://www.tcrecord.org/Content.asp?ContentID=17449

Walpole, MaryBeth. 2003. "Socioeconomic Status and College: How SES Affects College Experiences and Outcomes." *Review of Higher Education* 27 (1): 45–73.

Weber, Max. 1922. *Economy and Society*. New York: Bedminster.

Welsch, Kathleen, ed. 2005. *Those Winter Sundays: Female Academics and Their Working-Class Parents*. Lanham, MD: University Press of America.

Wright, Erik O. 1978. *Class, Crisis, and the State*. London: New Left Books.

Wright, Erik O. 1979. *Class Structure and Income Determination*. New York: Academic Press.

3

Culture Clash

A Working-Class Academic at a Liberal Arts College

Michelle M. Tokarczyk

In the many years since my co-edited volume *Working-Class Women in the Academy: Laborers in the Knowledge Factory* (1993) was published, I have become a tenured full professor at a small liberal arts college. I suspect that my position is somewhat unusual for someone of my class background; many of my colleagues in the Working-Class Studies Association teach at comprehensive state universities or community colleges. My position has distinct advantages, notably for the reasonable teaching load (3/3) and the small classes (usually 20 students or fewer) that my liberal arts college offers. Yet as working-class scholars such as Barbara Jensen (2012) have argued, class differences are cultural as well as economic. For me, adapting to a liberal arts college culture was disorienting and challenging, partially because I had no idea that I was entering a distinct culture. As I reflect on my experiences, I will highlight key moments of tension in faculty relations, teaching, and service. I will also offer some advice for working-class faculty at liberal arts colleges.

When I was writing the introduction to *Working-Class Women in the Academy*, I pondered women's ties to family and community, and I hypothesized that women are more reluctant than men to give up the comforts of proximity to family and friends in favor of upward professional advancement. Soon, I personally tested my hypothesis. After three years in full-time contingent faculty positions, in the spring of 1989 I received a tenure-track job offer in the English Department at The College (an appellation I have chosen to avoid naming my institution) near Baltimore. I was elated and accepted the offer. But as soon as I got past the initial joy of having a secure appointment, I recognized how difficult my transition would be. I'd grown up in New York City. I attended Herbert Lehman College, a CUNY institution, as an undergraduate, and SUNY at Stony Brook as a graduate student. In sum, my entire life had been lived in New York City and its environs. Although Baltimore is only a few hours away, I was afraid of losing touch with friends and family, and afraid of losing a part of my identity: that of the no-nonsense urban dweller. Little did I realize how difficult that identity would be to shed.

More problematically, my husband had a rewarding position as a vice president in a bank in New York—a true feat for a man from a working-class family. He had worked 30 hours a week as an undergrad to support himself in a state college before earning a doctorate at a New York State university. Joking that he was a better feminist than economist, he agreed to follow me to Baltimore, hoping for a lateral transfer. My elderly parents and my sister also lived in New York City. Two months before I moved to Baltimore, my sister, a DES daughter (a woman whose mother took DES, now known to be a carcinogen, during pregnancy), underwent surgery to have a large growth removed from her ovaries. Thankfully, the growth was benign, but the experience demonstrated how fraught my separation from my family might be.

Geographical mobility is essential in academia, especially given the incredibly tight job market. I am a proponent of national searches for tenure-track positions, as they lessen the possibility of local favoritism and cronyism that can especially affect small institutions. However, this imperative to relocate runs counter to the experience of many Americans, as noted in a *New York Times* article aptly titled "The Typical American Family Lives Only 18 Miles from Mom" (Bui and Miller 2015). Similarly, the Pew Center conducted a study finding that people with a college education or higher were more likely to move away from their families of origin; usually, people moved for employment opportunities, as I was about to do—or, if they stayed, did so because of family or community ties (Cohn and Morin 2008). For me, New York City was and is home. Yet my academic work was and is an intellectual home for me as well. I could try to maintain ties in New York even if I worked in Baltimore, but I could not remain in contingent faculty positions and have a stable, thriving academic career. So, I had no regrets about my decision.

However, I soon sensed that my spouse was second-guessing his agreement to relocate. Baltimore just did not have the opportunities in his field that New York did. Neither did Washington, DC. Not even close. When he finally secured a position, just about two weeks before I was to begin teaching, it was a disappointing one. He made the same salary, but the work was uninteresting, and, he thought, ethically questionable. So, when he was recruited for a position back in New York City, we decided to begin a commuter marriage. I didn't want to see him unhappy, and I didn't want to leave my position. Not only was I unwilling to give up a tenure-track appointment, I was unwilling to act in a way that suggested women could not balance family and career. I began my career at The College five short years after Geraldine Ferraro became the first female vice-presidential candidate; some people went so far as to question whether someone who probably experienced PMS was safe with nuclear codes. I did not want to behave in a way that suggested women were unreliable professionals.

Of course, I was nervous about shifting our 10-year-old marriage to a commuter basis. (We've now been commuting for 26 years and married for 37.) However, I was more nervous about informing my colleagues. Unlike faculties at many large public institutions, those at The College were expected to be part of the community. Indeed, the institution's name is seldom uttered by administrators or faculty without being followed by "community." As an untenured faculty member, I obviously wanted to earn my colleagues' approval. I was afraid that colleagues would question my commitment to the college if they thought I had an incentive to relocate, and would see my commuter marriage as detracting from my ability to be available to students—a primary responsibility in a liberal arts college.

Yet while I was extremely committed to all of my academic work—teaching, scholarship, and service—something about the construct of community and the way that faculty envisioned their role in it bothered me. The word suggested a cozy comfort and didn't acknowledge power dimensions between administrators and faculty or faculty and students. My colleagues identified with The College; they prided themselves (justifiably) on being fine teachers. The College's interests and their own seemed not just interrelated, but indistinguishable. As a (hopefully) permanent member of the faculty, I took seriously my obligations to serve on committees and participate in college-wide events. But I identified with the profession far more than I did with The College, or with the other two institutions where I previously had taught. At that time, I thought that academia was more ethical than other workplaces, and I was grateful to have found rewarding work—but I knew academic work was nonetheless work, and my employer's interests were not identical to mine.

As a contingent faculty member at my previous institutions, my status was so low and so precarious that I didn't have extensive interactions with tenured faculty. Once I began a tenure-track position, this situation changed. For someone from a working-class background, the structure of the academic hierarchy and decision-making is unfamiliar and sometimes counterintuitive. A working-class colleague at another college recounted an instance during which she had referred to her chair as her boss; the chair cringed and protested. However, my colleague had a point. In addition to heading the department, a chair has some control over faculty schedules, salaries, and tenure. Yet an academic who sees her chair as the equivalent of the blue-collar bosses her parents labored under may set herself up for failure. For instance, she may not demonstrate the trust (in the language of faculty reviews, "collegiality") that may ease the path toward tenure. While ethical chairs will not hold cool relationships against junior faculty, the latter may still lose valuable opportunities for mentorship.

Being an academic from the working class is lonely, especially in a liberal arts college. I did have a few colleagues who shared my background, and I couldn't help but notice how quick they were to express anger and frustration. Their reactions (and mine as well) likely resulted from exposure to colleagues who did not understand class migration and were often dismissive of the working class, sometimes using terms like "white trash" or stereotyping working-class people as ignorant bigots. Certainly, the institution could benefit from a more socio-economically diverse faculty. Some educators and policymakers have indeed argued that affirmative action should be based on class rather than race (see, e.g., Rosario 2014), but this idea has gained little traction in academia generally, and none at all at The College. Perhaps, as Lisa R. Pruitt (2015a, 2015b) has persuasively argued, academic institutions have bought into the false notion that they must choose between race-based and class-based affirmative action, or that race-based affirmative action will suffer if class is taken into account in hiring. As she also notes, we promote other forms of affirmative action—for LBGT faculty or faculty with disabilities—without fearing that hiring along these lines will endanger race-based affirmative action (2015b, 221). Without any acknowledgment of classism at The College, I was left to figure out whether to address it and, if so, how. Because class is not acknowledged, much less addressed, in academic institutions, faculty from the working class experience feelings of alienation and dislocation.

When I began teaching at The College, there were no assigned mentors or preparatory workshops for untenured faculty. Thankfully, this situation has since been remedied; I believe that tenure-track faculty at The College now have much better guidance and more clearly articulated requirements. I, however, had to decipher the college culture and teaching norms on my own. In retrospect, I see that some of my senior colleagues were very willing to mentor me in academic matters and to console me when I suffered personal losses, notably the death of my beloved father at the beginning of my second year at The College. But it didn't occur to me to approach my "bosses" in this manner. I was reluctant to ask for advice for fear of appearing underprepared, or to accept compassion for fear of seeming weak. Also, I knew that my class background had not prepared me for this profession as my colleagues' had, and I didn't want to display my ignorance. I was in the position of the quintessential working-class migrant at the dinner table: afraid to pick up the wrong fork, but equally afraid to ask which fork to use.

The only consistent support I had during this pre-tenure period was through an informal group of tenure-track faculty who met biweekly at a restaurant off campus. We shared some concrete information, such as what was required in a statement of teaching philosophy or how to interpret student evaluation numbers. But primarily we shared our fears. Most helpful was a session during which each of us revealed what about ourselves we feared would cause The College to deny us tenure: my commuter marriage, one colleague's two young children, another colleague's French citizenship. There was no mention of pedagogical or publication issues—or of class issues. Most of my colleagues were middle class. Yet this meeting showed me that others too had fears of being personally unacceptable to The College, and enabled me to feel less alone. I strongly encourage junior faculty at all institutions to join such groups or form them if they don't exist.

I did not interact with senior faculty as extensively as I now believe I should have. Yet in my early years at The College there were only about 80 full-time faculty members, and I was running the expository writing program, so I dealt with a number of faculty within and outside the

English Department. On the whole, I found The College faculty to be a friendly and inviting group. There was (until more recently) little of the backbiting competition that marks some research universities, though there were the seemingly inescapable departmental feuds. In contrast to the research university where I'd held a three-year non-tenure-track appointment, scholarship was relatively unimportant to the faculty and the administration. As someone who was passionately committed to my critical and creative writing, I found the publication requirements quite minimal, and soon realized that too much scholarly actively might be interpreted as a lack of interest in teaching. In my second year there, I was pleased to learn that I'd been listed in the reference work *Contemporary Authors*. When I informed the one department member with whom I'd developed a friendly relationship, he advised, "Don't tell anyone." In my over 25 years at The College, the prevailing attitude toward scholarship has not changed. While it was a relief not to have publication pressures, it was hard for me to envision myself as an academic if I didn't give some attention to research. Perhaps, as an academic from the working class, I felt a heightened need to prove myself in a national forum—not just in front of a small number of colleagues. Also, because so many of my friends who did very fine work did not get tenure-track positions, I wanted to hold myself to high standards.

Within a couple of years, I found a few faculty members who valued scholarship and had learned to assert its importance without rankling our colleagues. In one department, all the faculty were active and nationally recognized scholars. In an off-campus setting, one of these faculty members emphasized to me how essential it was that I make time for my research and myself. As a junior faculty member, I pondered her words, but did not yet look for ways to enact them. At the time, I was relatively silent about the merits of research and other controversial curricular and policy issues. Even after I gained tenure, it took me a few years to develop perspective on the issues facing The College; I had been so focused on my own portfolio, I hadn't devoted time to academic citizenship. Also, the cautious behavior I learned as an untenured faculty member took some time to unlearn.

One form of service was recommended to me as a junior faculty member—student advising—and I'm glad I listened. As an advisor, I got to know a number of students outside my classes and learned how the curriculum actually worked for students. I also worked with tenured faculty outside my department. A position such as this is ideal for faculty from the working class, as it can give them the opportunity to mentor working-class students. On the other hand, positions and committees that are more controversial should be deferred until tenure is achieved.

By the time I was a few years into my associate professorship, though, I fully appreciated the privilege of tenure. This privilege, I believe, comes with a responsibility to ensure the institution operates soundly and ethically. So, I began raising questions about the curriculum and college management. I took on major responsibilities—first, serving on the college's Reappointment, Promotion, and Tenure Committee, then chairing it. I took on this demanding position, in part, because some young, untenured women urged me to do so. For some of them, the issue was gender; for some, I believe, it was gender and class. When I was first elected to this committee, a woman coming up for tenure asked to meet with me. The chair of her department, she said, was biased against her because she had supported female students who complained that he was having an affair with a woman in their class. I advised her to make her portfolio as strong as possible so that any specious complaints he made would have no weight. That worked. (In fact, The College tried to remove the tenured department chair, but was unable to do so.)

For many years after I became an associate professor, I enjoyed the teaching and the ambiance at The College. Yet I regularly commuted to New York City on weekends, which was tiring and expensive. The expense was particularly trying, as The College's salaries were low compared to those of our peer liberal arts institutions, so I decided to go on the job market. Although I had a good publication record, I knew it was likely not stellar enough to earn me an appointment in the extremely competitive New York area. So, I decided to look for positions as department chair, where administrative ability would also be taken into account. Since I had several years of experience in running The College's freshman writing program, one of the largest programs in the college, my administrative experience was solid. Ultimately, I did not find another position. I cannot say this was because of my class and gender; I can, however, point to disturbing interactions that were classed and gendered.

At one point I was a finalist for a position in the English Department of a public Pennsylvania college. Both the department chair and the dean noted that the teaching load was 4/4, which, of course, I'd known. But the dean, familiar with my publications, volunteered that as someone who had grown up in the working class, I'd know how to roll up my sleeves and work. I didn't know what to say. I'd expected to be asked about my teaching style and pedagogical philosophy, my recent publications and work in progress. I didn't think I'd have to comment on my ability to work hard. Didn't the vast majority of faculty work hard?

I came very close to getting a position as the chair of the English Department in a private Long Island college. During my individual meeting with two middle-aged males in the department, I was repeatedly asked how tough I could be in negotiating with administrators. In fact, I am a consistently strong voice for faculty rights and am persuasive and forceful in negotiations. Yet my recently purchased pantsuit could not convince these men that my voice was strong enough. If the interview had occurred a few years later, I would have had a fine example to present to them, as I will relate below. At the time, however, my 4'10" petite stature spoke louder than my words. Still, I wondered what evidence of superior negotiating skills male candidates had presented.

In fact, one of my frustrations with The College faculty was that they did not fight. They complained about salaries, administrative changes without faculty consent, and the like. But even tenured faculty were reluctant to speak out at faculty meetings. Legally, the faculty were hampered by the Supreme Court's 1980 *NLRB v. Yeshiva University* ruling, which determined tenured and tenure-track faculty at private colleges could not unionize and bargain collectively because these faculty were, in effect, management. Unions are powerful vehicles for promoting workers' rights and well-being. As later events at The College would indicate, however, it is not impossible for faculty without unions to assert themselves.

My frustration was mitigated somewhat after I learned more about The College's history. The College faculty, I learned, were demoralized by the firing of tenured faculty in the 1970s, which caused the college to be on American Association of University Professors' (AAUP) list of censured institutions for years. This difficult period explained some of the faculty reticence, and it prompted me to wonder what role the institution's 100-year history as a women's college played in faculty culture. Anecdotes about The College indicate that women enrolled there to learn in a protected environment. In 1953, The College moved from an urban location to a suburban one situated on over 400 acres. The land had been purchased in the early 1920s, and The College's trustees began preparations to move the campus at that point. The move occurred, however, during the era of "white flight," when urban streets became equated with danger. I do not mean to suggest that The College did not offer quality education to women. It did. But I suspect that the faculty's nurturing stance, coupled with the campus's protected suburban locale, suggested safety to students and their families. I wondered if safety also became a core value for faculty, and thus made them averse to confronting the administration.

For many years, I have been active in the Working-Class Studies Association (WCSA), once serving as its president. Many members of WCSA were active in faculty unions and senates, as were some of their friends at city and state universities. As the 2011 rollback of collective bargaining rights for faculty in Wisconsin illustrates, not all their struggles over the years have been won. But some have. I saw the possibilities of faculty organizing, and again, regretted that there was no mechanism for it at The College. Then the 2008 financial collapse accelerated a financial crisis at my institution and created an opening for faculty organizing. In response to budgetary problems, the president, without consulting faculty officers, decided that the percentage that the college contributed to their TIAA-CREF retirement funds would be drastically cut. This move was extremely disturbing, but the administration had the legal right to make it. The issue was when the College began its cut. At The College, staff contracts run from July 1 to June 30; academic contracts run from September 1 to August 31. The College cut its contribution to faculty retirement accounts in July 2008, depriving faculty of two months' worth of contractually guaranteed contributions.

In response to this action, the faculty revived its long-dormant AAUP chapter, and I was elected president. With the help of the national AAUP organization and the Maryland State Committee of AAUP, we secured legal counsel. I made it clear to the president that the faculty would go to court if necessary, though this action was not our preference. Within a few months, the president agreed to reinstate the disputed funds. The college AAUP chapter could not have achieved this win without the support of a majority of The College faculty. Yet the AAUP action was contested, with many faculty unwilling to battle the administration.

As a woman from the working class and a scholar of working-class literature and history, I found it ironic and terribly sad that many tenured faculty in particular were so passive when they had so little to lose. I knew that no one would beat me up, or evict me from my home, or even fire me. My position, I knew, was an enviable one not only in academia but in the United States as a whole. To me, it seemed wrong not to fight when I held such privilege. As I progressed up the academic ladder, the words from one of my favorite texts, *The House on Mango Street*, echoed in the back of my mind: "When you leave you must remember to come back for the others, a circle, understand?" (Cisneros 1984, 105). I felt compelled to give back to women, the working class, and younger academics in particular. Part of giving back was and is standing up.

While the faculty had mixed feelings about the AAUP chapter, the Service Employees International Union's (SEIU) subsequent drive to organize contingent faculty provoked considerably more resistance. (According to the *NLRB v. Yeshiva* ruling, contingent faculty are not management and thus they can unionize.) As an officer in the Maryland State Committee of the AAUP, I was approached by the organizers for insight and support. This I was happy to provide, since my childhood had improved markedly when my father secured a union job—he repeatedly said, "Without a union, working people are nothing." Yet my colleagues, like many academics in institutions without a history of collective bargaining, thought of themselves as independent agents and perceived unions as vehicles for nonprofessional workers. Some reacted to being approached by union organizers with fear; the provost even sent an email stating that faculty should call security if the organizers frightened them. Faculty responses, I believe, reflected stereotypes of union organizers as agitators or, worse, "thugs," the word Mayor Bloomberg of New York City used to characterize transit workers during the 2005 Transport Workers Local Union strike. Ultimately, contingent faculty won the right to unionize; The College faculty will now deal with a new landscape in relations between faculty and administration, as well as in faculty–faculty relations.

As I stated earlier, my strongest loyalties have been to the institution of higher education rather than The College. This allegiance has only strengthened with time. As I got closer to retirement, I became more concerned with the next generation of academics, whose prospects were bleaker than my generation's had been—and our prospects were pretty bleak. I mentored female graduate students through the Shakespeare's Sisters Project of the Northeast Modern Language Association and less formally through the Working-Class Studies Association. In particular, I worked with an outspoken former graduate student from Stony Brook University who was the only person in her cohort to receive a tenure-track appointment. Her position was at a college in a southern rural area, and she experienced a great deal of culture shock. When I spoke with her, I recognized how her working-class values and determination could help her to connect with her students. To this end, she has incorporated community-based learning into her writing classes, even though doing so involved considerable work. She found working with many of the faculty members jarring, but working with the first-generation students rewarding.

In contrast to many faculty members, The College students showed little reluctance to speak up. Unlike the students at a private business-oriented college where I'd briefly taught, they were refreshingly non-careerist, interested in the arts (many students came to The College for its celebrated creative writing program), and concerned about social justice. An activist club stated its support for the contingent faculty union and volunteered to meet with interested faculty. The small classes enabled me to know my students, and I've kept in touch with a few for many years after their graduation. Yet as soon as I arrived at The College, whose reputation was lauded, I saw the students did not work as hard as those at state colleges and universities. When I taught at Rutgers, my syllabi stated that late papers would be penalized: my students, bleary-eyed and exhausted, would get their papers in on the due date. At The College, many students blithely handed in papers late and accepted deductions from their grades. Faculty from the working class, especially those who have attended public institutions, must keep in mind that students at liberal arts colleges may value their creative natures and rebel against deadlines. They may also expect more accommodations from faculty—especially in a time when many of these colleges are struggling to enroll enough students.

Probably the sharpest difference between my previous teaching experiences and those of my students at The College surfaced during my first year there. As an undergraduate I had worked part-time and appreciated having papers due after spring or fall break. Thus, my spring composition class's first paper was due the week after the break. To my shock, my students were outraged. One voiced their complaint: "How are we supposed to do this assignment? Some of us are going to the Caribbean." I postponed the due date and out of necessity redid my syllabus. Even at this point I did not realize that a few of the students would miss the Monday class after spring break. Like many peer institutions, The College has committed itself to increasing student diversity, and the population of first-generation students has gradually risen. Now many of my students do have to work; they have childcare issues or other family obligations. With such students, I often give extensions on due dates or make other accommodations (though in truth, many middle-class students require similar accommodations due to mental health problems or learning disabilities). It is gratifying for me to work with first-generation students, even as The College is very much in the process of learning to accommodate them.

While my institution is beginning to address microaggressions involving race and gender, it has no guidelines for microaggressions related to class. I am in the process of developing such guidelines based on my experiences, the experiences my former students have related to me, and the experiences of my colleagues at other institutions. I hope that my document will be the beginning of a dialogue.

As I reflect on my experiences of over 25 years in a vastly changing academic landscape, I come back to the question of what advice I would give to working-class academics teaching at liberal arts colleges. First of all, I'd note that in a small fishbowl your personality and temperament matter in a way that would be inconceivable in a comprehensive university. You need to get along with your colleagues, but remember that while you need to win your departmental colleagues' votes, you don't need their personal approval. The impostor syndrome often haunts academics from the working class; in my early years at The College I found it difficult not to be wounded by some colleagues' dismissal of my work. Now, I recognize that there is nothing to be gained by focusing on people who don't appreciate your research or your values. Undoubtedly, there will be some—if only a few—faculty who value your work. Seek them out.

Obligations such as faculty meetings may tax your patience. But service is important, so try to involve yourself in committees that you find meaningful. For example, I am resistant to the assessment movement promoted by Middle States (The College's accrediting agency)—as are many of my colleagues, regardless of class origin or gender—so I have scrupulously avoided this committee. Although being involved in and ultimately chairing The College's Reappointment, Promotion, and Tenure Committee involved an incredible amount of work, I thought it was crucial that tenure and promotion be awarded to faculty who earned them. It is extremely difficult to vote against someone's tenure; I didn't sleep the night before I did so for the first time. Yet if standards are not applied, tenure is meaningless. Other committees, such as those that write academic policies or review curricular requirements, can all be instrumental in promoting working-class students' success. Faculty who serve on hiring committees can speak up for working-class candidates who might otherwise be ignored.

It is entirely possible that despite the cultural differences between small liberal arts colleges and the public colleges and universities that many working-class students attend, working-class faculty will feel very much at home in a liberal arts college. To increase this possibility, I encourage newly hired faculty, through close examination of institutional websites and informal talks with colleagues, to learn about their institution's history. This knowledge will enable you to understand the institutional culture and adapt to it. Whatever your comfort level, focus on the aspects of your work that are most meaningful. My writing and teaching are very rewarding. In stressful times, I remind myself that I am doing what I'd wanted and trained to do.

In a small or isolated rural college especially, it is crucial to have a professional identity beyond the college. For years, I cultivated this identity not only through my publications, but also through my involvement in professional organizations—notably the Northeast Modern Language Association, the Working-Class Studies Association, and the American Association of University Professors. The latter two organizations in particular have an understanding of class, labor issues, and academic power dynamics that is mostly absent on my college campus.

Most importantly, I caution working-class academics not to fall into deficit thinking. Those of us from the working class who have earned doctorates and academic positions have incredible strengths. Maybe the schools we attended weren't as strong as our colleagues', but we learned to teach ourselves. Maybe our parents couldn't advise us on academic matters, but we found other mentors, located the information ourselves, or learned by trial and error. The culture of a liberal arts college and of academia as a whole is different from the culture of working-class communities, but it is not incomprehensible or unnavigable. We are in a unique position to understand liberal arts colleges as outsiders within. We can mentor first-generation students who are working to adapt to an unfamiliar environment in ways that our middle- and upper-class colleagues cannot.

Works Cited

Bui, Quoctrung, and Claire Cain Miller. 2015. "The Typical American Family Lives Only 18 Miles from Mom." *New York Times*, December 23. https://www.nytimes.com/interactive/2015/12/24/upshot/24up-family.html?_r=0

Cisneros, Sandra. 1984. *The House on Mango Street.* New York: Random House.

Cohn, D'Vera, and Rich Morin. 2008. "American Mobility: Who Moves? Who Stays Put? Where's Home?" *Pew Research Center Social and Demographic Trends.* December 17, updated December 29. http://www.pewsocialtrends.org/files/2010/10/Movers-and-Stayers.pdf

Jensen, Barbara. 2012. *Reading Classes: Class and Classism in America*. Ithaca, NY: ILR Press/Cornell University Press.

Pruitt, Lisa R. 2015a. "The False Choice Between Race and Class and Other Affirmative Action Myths." *Buffalo Law Review* 63 (4): 981–1060.

Pruitt, Lisa R. 2015b. "Who's Afraid of White Class Migrants? On Denial, Discrediting, and Disdain (and Toward a Richer Conception of Diversity)." *Columbia Journal of Gender and Law* 31 (1): 196–254.

Rosario, Adam. 2014. "Substituting Socioeconomic Status for Race in College Admissions." *Ramapo Journal of Law and Society* 1 (2): 56–64. https://www.ramapo.edu/law-journal/thesis/substituting-socioeconomic-status-race-college-admissions

Tokarczyk, Michelle M., and Elizabeth A. Fay, eds. 1993. *Working-Class Women in the Academy: Laborers in the Knowledge Factory*. Amherst: University of Massachusetts Press.

4

Working-Class Academics at Work

Perceptions of and Experiences within the Academy

Meghan J. Pifer and Karley A. Riffe

Working-class academics, like all academics, strive for employment opportunities and long-term careers that ensure access to and fit within academia. For faculty members from working-class backgrounds, however, the academy is not always the professional home they thought it would be, nor is it as welcoming an environment as it may be for others who seem to enjoy greater comfort or confidence in that context. There is the potential for a strong disconnect between these faculty members' cultural backgrounds, families, and communities of origin and their institutional, departmental, and disciplinary cultures and communities. This disconnect can be painful and unexpected, particularly following long efforts to enter the academy through graduate training, which frequently occurs without the financial, cultural, and other resources that often initiate and facilitate the professional experiences of academics from middle- and upper-class backgrounds.

Academics from the working class have often described the academy as a workplace, specifically within institutional and departmental contexts. This helps us to understand the challenges that scholars from working-class backgrounds encounter as they enact their careers and seek to construct meaning from their lives and work. Working-class academics' firsthand accounts of their experiences can also bring to light the previously unseen or unacknowledged barriers they face, enabling all members of the academy to become more mindful of the potential for class-based impediments to their professional success and satisfaction.

Although the scholarly literature does not offer much empirical knowledge about the experiences of working-class academics, there is a body of writing that provides rich insight into their work and lives. Through articles in scholarly journals and book chapters, some scholars have used the familiar tools of knowledge dissemination to share narrative accounts of their experiences as working-class academics.

Part of a larger study of the role of identity in faculty members' experiences in the academy, this chapter presents findings from a recently completed content analysis of the documented experiences of self-described working-class academics. By aggregating and considering this literature in a way that has not been done previously, we identify themes in these accounts and offer a resource for current and prospective members of the professoriate from working-class backgrounds. We focus on the ways in which the authors describe their perceptions of the academy as a workplace and community, and the ways in which class-based memories, experiences, and perceptions affect notions of access, community and friendship, collegial relationships, and fit within academic culture. We also discuss individual and institutional responses to challenges, as well as potential strategies for improved access to and practices within the academy.

Methods

To identify narratives of working-class academics' experiences in the academy, we reviewed books and academic journals from fields such as higher education, literature, sociology, labor studies, and women's studies. We focused on instances in which scholars relied on their class backgrounds to make sense of their experiences and careers. The final sample included 166 publications, most of which included individual narratives. Some publications were structured as reflective conversations between academics, and included several accounts within them. The majority of these publications were chapters in edited books (134), while the remaining sources were books (9) and journal articles (23).

We read each publication and entered it into a database that included the author(s), year of publication, name of the publication (e.g., journal title), publication type (book, book chapter, journal article), and whether each entry could be best described as a personal narrative, reflection, essay, or autoethnography. We also recorded key descriptors and exemplary quotes in the database for each source, to summarize the core concepts in each source and to facilitate analysis.

We then conducted content analysis to "identify core consistencies and meaning" across the narratives of class-based identity and experiences in the academy (Patton 2002, 453), and to identify trends and phenomena across the documents through unobtrusive analysis of previously published materials (Weber 1990). This method of analysis enabled a reduction of the data from a very large amount of text, allowing for a more thorough exploration of the literature and the generation of new knowledge about these publications in the aggregate (Schreier 2012). Each author independently read and coded a set of publications; we compared our coding schemes and interpretive processes throughout data analysis. We refined the initial list of codes to generate themes through inductive analysis that reflected the ways in which working-class academics described their professional experiences and the salience of their class identities in those experiences (Schreier 2012). We present these themes in the following section, relying on retrievals from the original texts to illustrate the findings (Weber 1990).

Working-Class Academics at Work

Our analysis generated several themes, all of which related to working-class academics' relationships and identities with their communities of origins and their academic communities, as well as the dissonance between the two. In this chapter, we narrow the focus to explore the themes related to these academics' efforts to understand colleges and universities as workplaces and whether it was possible for them to establish a sense of membership and belonging in those contexts. There are two related aspects of working-class academics' experiences in the academy that came through as strong themes across their narratives: their efforts to understand colleges and universities as workplaces and their efforts to see themselves as accepted members of those local contexts and the broader scholarly community.

Working-Class Understandings of Colleges and Universities as Workplaces

The theme of "academic workplaces" derived from our content analysis speaks to a common strategy used by working-class academics to understand academic culture as experienced within their institutions and, more specifically, the particular units in which they enact their careers, such as schools and departments. Included here are day-to-day routines and experiences with administrators, support staff, mentors and senior colleagues, peers, and students, occurring in offices, meeting spaces, hallways, and classrooms.

Many working-class academics have written about academic culture as something they did not understand. The perceived presence of a dominant, hierarchical, middle-class culture within the academy was clear in their narratives. Authors described not having the right cultural knowledge, what Naton Leslie referred to as "cultural anchors," such as habits of dress, jokes, familiarity with television shows—all of which negatively impacted their ability to fully participate in the informal conversations and social behaviors shared with ease among colleagues from other class backgrounds (1995, 73). As Constance Anthony describes it, working-class academics "find it more difficult to network in professional settings where their class background is underrepresented" (2012, 306). They write of their inability to read institutional culture, of not feeling adequately prepared by their graduate training for the social mores of the academy, and of experiencing the realities of academic culture as unwelcoming and alienating—all of which contrasted harshly with the idyllic environments they had long envisioned.

Some authors have written of rarely feeling comfortable within professional settings because of their understanding of the tangible consequences of the class-based differences between themselves and the academy, as experienced in the day-to-day interactions within their departments and institutions. Kim Clancy referred to her location in academia as a place where she was "creatively alive—if not completely comfortable" (1997, 51). A lack of comfort at work generates resistance toward what some authors perceive to be a hostile environment that houses elitism and classism, nepotism, unequal review processes, glass ceilings, and gatekeeping through "secret social norms and behaviors" (De la Riva–Holly 2012, 292). For some, this has led to feelings of distrust towards colleagues and to self-judgments of naiveté about academic practices such as tenure and promotion.

The authors surveyed located themselves within academic culture in terms of their class backgrounds, as they made sense of differences between their understanding and knowledge of academic work and those of their colleagues from higher social classes. Some responded to these pressures by working very hard to assimilate and to hide their class backgrounds, while others wrote of feeling most comfortable with secretaries and support staff, with whom they could easily relate and converse. As Milan Kovacovik writes, "Once poor, always poor—it's in your genes" (1995, 245).

For some of these authors, the academy had long stood as a vision of a home toward which they journeyed, where they would belong and be among like-minded others; for many, this stood in imagined contrast to the dislocation they recalled experiencing in their home communities and families of origin. As Jake Ryan and Charles Sackrey describe it, "the conditions of academic work, in themselves, are difficult enough. The workings of power within the university deliver their own alienating punch, indeed to everyone, but perhaps the blow is harshest on the interloper who likely enters with a marginal sense of membership" (1984, 123). After efforts to earn advanced degrees and obtain academic appointments that often required separation—both geographic and otherwise—from their families, working-class scholars recall feeling that their sacrifice was met with membership in a profession and work environment in which their legitimacy and right to membership were called into question by their peers and, sometimes, their students. Some authors describe being at once highly visible and unseen by colleagues, separated in both instances from group norms and behaviors by their class backgrounds.

These working-class academics' perceptions of their workplace environments point to an added layer of professional experiences and acculturation beyond the typical adjustment to new roles and responsibilities. For these academics, the most challenging aspects of their careers did not seem to be related to teaching, research, or service, but rather to learning how to enact those roles within the upper-middle-class socio-cultural norms of their departments and institutions. The authors reveal the effort required to negotiate these transitions and enactments without the same social and cultural capital as their colleagues who did not come from working-class backgrounds, while simultaneously engaging in private efforts to understand or hide their transitions. Such difficulties, along with concerns about their professional abilities and futures, relate to the second theme to emerge from our analysis: working-class academics' perceptions of self, their understanding of others' perceptions of them, and their efforts to cultivate relationships and a sense of community in their academic homes.

Working-Class Perceptions of (Mis)Fit in Academic Workplaces

Two key aspects of the challenges of membership in the academy present themselves in working-class academics' narratives. First, authors have described their efforts to determine for themselves whether they could secure a sense of belonging in their departments, disciplines, and institutions. Second, they have reflected on their efforts to make sense of others' interpretations of their right to and enactment of that membership.

Working-class academics' accounts of their struggles to understand academic culture betray an acute awareness of how their colleagues perceive them within that context, and of their hypervisible status as the other. They write of being characterized by peers as difficult, emotional, uncooperative, rude, blunt, uncultured, and overly passionate. Authors describe being judged for their "working-class personality traits," and determining that upholding their values would bring "potentially destructtive professional consequences in the academy" (Weaver 1993, 120). Some have written of being misinterpreted or mislabeled by their colleagues and of having their authenticity questioned in terms of both their academic abilities and their claims of working-class origins. Elvia Arriola (1997) described being mistaken for a staff member or student by fellow faculty. A powerful theme is the sense of being subject to discrimination, tokenism, silencing, and marginalization by colleagues. For example, Gerry Holloway writes of her concerns about academia:

> The main problem I still face is the silencing I often experience at work. Women I admire in other respects often operate unconscious gatekeeping processes which keep out women who "are not like them." Networks operate that I, and others, do not have easy access to and if we dare voice our views we are met by puzzled looks which silence us again, restating our Otherness and marginality. (1997, 198)

The surveyed authors also write of middle- and upper-class colleagues engaging in sense-making about them, treating them as the exception to the rule of what people from working-class backgrounds can achieve intellectually. Alternatively, they experience de-legitimization and questioning their scholarship and abilities at the hands of colleagues.

As a result of this deprivation of professional legitimacy and fit among colleagues, working-class academics often write of inner conflict and self-questioning. Bonnie Strickland writes of "life within the academy [as] pleasant but sometimes embarrassing as well," and recalls adjusting her spoken English to sound more academic (2008, 109). Authors have used words like *fictional, fraudulent, posing,* and *passing* to describe their feelings of inadequacy in response to their class-based exclusion from the scholarly community. Lyn Huxford describes feeling "as though I was an impostor who had somehow faked her way into the hallowed halls of academe" (2005, 207). Impostor syndrome and feelings of unworthiness are common in the authors' accounts, as illustrated by Louise Morley:

> Does this already sound too emotive, too rhetorical, too cathartic? Should I rapidly inject some references to research studies and critical social theories? How might I interrogate the subject in a disembodied, sanitized way, without activating my class distress? For the latter merely serves to remind the ruling class of my inferiority and unfitness to roam the corridors of academia. (1997, 109)

Some narratives reveal an attempt to hide one's class origins and pass as middle class in an attempt not to draw attention. For example, Deborah Piper describes the need to put on what she refers to as "the cloak of my education" to blend into the academic middle class during such occasions as professional meetings (1995, 295). The perpetual self-doubt described by some authors gives the lie to any semblance of belonging in their institutions and departments, or in the profession as a whole. These authors write of playing the part, masquerading, posing, and wearing a disguise, terms that suggest feelings of isolation and inauthenticity.

As Gabriella Gutiérrez y Muhs et al. (2012) have noted, working-class academics are likely to be aware of material differences from their peers. Several authors describe the inability to foster a sense of community, stemming from the lack of disposable income required for informal interactions, or the lack of free time to devote to recreational activities. Debt from graduate school, credit cards, prior periods of unemployment, financial responsibilities for relatives, and even debt accrued procuring attire needed to play the part of the academic were all mentioned by authors as ongoing barriers to financial comfort and the related sense of fitting in with the middle- and upper-class colleagues who populated their workplaces. Michael Schwalbe writes of these challenges to cultivating a sense of belonging in academic environments:

> Acquiring what's necessary to participate as an equal is expensive. But some people begin with enough resources to pay the price with no pain at all. Those of us who pay dearly, and perhaps can never buy all that we need, may always have mixed feelings about our

> purchase. Professors don't talk much about these matters, perhaps because they threaten the belief in achievement based on merit. (1995, 329)

Some authors, however, engaged in what Phyllis Baker referred to as "transformative microidentity management work," in order to balance the habits, norms, and behaviors of their class of origin with those of the professional environment they had joined. For example, to illustrate her own microidentity management, Baker writes, "There are not many things I like better than wine and classical music, though vodka and rock and roll are close seconds. This … is necessary to successfully continue in my upper-middle-class job" (2005, 204).

For many, the long-term ramifications of social-class difference, whether based on the self-perceptions of working-class academics or the perceptions of their colleagues, are exclusion from social participation, informal connections, and friendships; a deficit of mentoring and support; a lack of ease and comfort in professional interactions that others seemed to enjoy; and an absence of departmental and institutional allies. Many working-class academics' accounts are marked by a sense of loneliness perpetuated by existing on the fringes of academic life, alienated by colleagues and their own feelings of illegitimacy. It is important to note, however, that a few authors report both joys and challenges related to managing multiple class identities or to the experience of class mobility and their penetration of middle- or upper-class culture.

Moving Forward: Improving the Experiences of Working-Class Academics

Diane Reay writes, "the experiences of the working classes get left out because they have no constituency in academia" (1997, 26). Her statement may be less true today than when she wrote it in 1997, as we hope to show. The publishing of working-class academics' personal experiences, and the opportunities for research and dialogue about this population, increase the power and presence of those who seek to support students and scholars from working-class backgrounds.

Among the aims of the present volume is to facilitate research and practice that improves the experiences of working-class students and academics. This purpose aligns with many of the edited volumes reviewed in our analysis (see Table 4.1). While a minority of authors specifically invoke efforts to support other working-class students and academics as factors in their decisions to share their stories, several of the editors who invited

Editors	Year	Title
Dews and Law	1995	*This Fine Place So Far from Home: Voices of Academics from the Working Class*
Grimes and Morris	1997	*Caught in the Middle: Contradictions in the Lives of Sociologists from Working-Class Backgrounds*
Gutiérrez y Muhs, Niemann, González, and Harris	2012	*Presumed Incompetent: The Intersections of Race and Class for Women in Academia*
Muzzatti and Samarco	2005	*Reflections from the Wrong Side of the Tracks: Class, Identity, and the Working Class Experience in Academe*
Oldfield and Johnson	2008	*Resilience: Queer Professors from the Working Class*
Ryan and Sackrey	1984	*Strangers in Paradise: Academics from the Working Class*
Tokarczyk and Fay	1993	*Working-Class Women in the Academy: Laborers in the Knowledge Factory*
Welsch	2005	*Those Winter Sundays: Female Academics and Their Working-Class Parents*
Zandy	1990	*Calling Home: Working-Class Women's Writings*
Zandy	1995	*Liberating Memory: Our Work and Our Working-Class Consciousness*

TABLE 4.1. Edited Volumes of Working-Class Academics' Narratives

such narratives address this purpose. Our analysis of the literature by and about working-class academics has the potential to help others who may also feel isolated or excluded as they traverse the border that separates notions of the working class from notions of the academic.

While some authors have written passionately about the meaningfulness of their careers, their pride in their achievements, and their gratitude for membership in institutional communities, each of their stories is evidence of room for improvement in our understanding of and support for working-class academics. The themes in these accounts—whatever their variation across time, disciplines, institution types, appointment types, gender, race and ethnicity, nationality, sexual identity, and geography—suggest that class continues to be a point of differentiation in the experiences of members of the academy, and serves as a basis for insider-outsider status within the academic community. The experiences described here are in line with Rosabeth Moss Kanter's (1977) emphasis on the paradox of invisibility and hypervisibility among those who experience social isolation or underrepresentation.

These accounts and themes present several opportunities to improve institutional and disciplinary practice. First, as higher education continues to diversify and as we continue to engage in efforts to increase access and facilitate degree completion, this study can contribute to an understanding of the experiences of working-class students, including students from underrepresented populations, part-time and commuting students, returning adult students, community college students, and first-generation college students. Though not within the scope of this chapter, one finding of our larger study was that many working-class academics found meaningful opportunities to support students who were engaged in their own efforts to experience success and acceptance in higher education, whether the relevant axis of difference involved age, racial and ethnic background, family structure, or disciplinary interest. Working-class academics may provide similarly disadvantaged students with previously unavailable source of support and understanding. At the same time, such relationships can provide working-class academics with feelings of agency, inclusion, and contribution to their own communities of origin.

Second, class status is beginning to resurface as a socio-demographic characteristic of interest within higher education—an interest that might well extend to faculty selection, recruitment, and professional development efforts. Institutional leaders, faculty development professionals, and those with influence in disciplinary associations may consider how they might respond to the challenges experienced by working-class academics to alleviate the burden of membership and to promote class-based equity within academic departments, disciplines, and institutions. For example, applicants from working-class backgrounds may not have the disposable income to pay for the travel costs embedded in the academic interview process. A starting point would be to encourage clarity about costs related to on-site interviews and knowledge of the relevant procedures. Even when full reimbursement for expenses is not possible, clarity about the norms of academic searches may provide cultural knowledge to working-class applicants, fostering equity among applicants and alleviating one component of the stress of entering the academy experienced by those from working-class backgrounds.

Finally, the perspectives of working-class academics may be informative for graduate students considering academic careers, as well as those who seek to recruit and support talented students in graduate programs. Those who identify as working-class academics may garner a sense of support from knowing that they are not alone in experiencing the challenges we have outlined. At the same time, staff working in graduate recruitment, admissions, and counseling services—and of course, graduate faculty who serve in advising and instructional roles—have an opportunity to apply the knowledge presented here to their efforts to understand and support working-class graduate students striving to enter the academy. Such students are perhaps just beginning to reflect on the ways in which their class identities will shape their experiences of fit and membership in the community of scholars.

Conclusion

In this chapter, we have presented findings from our investigation of the ways in which members of the academy from working-class backgrounds have described their experiences in the colleges and universities within which they enact their careers. We have focused on the ways in which these scholars have described how their workplace contexts and relationships shape their self-perceptions. We have also summarized the ways in which these narratives address perceptions of membership in those workplace contexts and cultures, and the understanding of working-class academics of their own and others' perceptions about their relative worthiness as members of the academy. The efforts of working-class academics to understand academic culture, to interpret other academics' assessments of their right to membership in that culture and their ability to fit in, and to come to terms with both their class backgrounds and their potential for success in academic environments, serve as a starting point for understanding the lived experiences of working-class academics in a way that has not previously been explored.

Through this work, it is our aim to show strength in numbers by aggregating these stories and demonstrating the themes within them, so that current and future working-class academics may not feel isolated, but rather secure in their right to membership in the community of scholars. The potential for isolation, exacerbated by the invisibility of class background, easily leads to the masking of one's working-class identity when interacting with academic peers and operating within the daily locations of academic careers and professional experiences. It is particularly important to consider these narratives as a starting point for reducing isolation and encouraging full access to the rights and responsibilities of membership in the academy. Further, we remind working-class academics that they belong to another community as well—one established through the familiar values of persistence and hard work, and which adds richness and value to the academy through working-class perspectives, memories, knowledge, goals, and approaches to academic work and life.

Works Cited

Anthony, Constance G. 2012. "The Port Hueneme of My Mind." In *Presumed Incompetent: The Intersections of Race and Class for Women in Academia*, edited by Gabriella Gutiérrez y Muhs, Yolanda Niemann, Carmen González, and Angela Harris, 300–12. Boulder: University Press of Colorado.

Arriola, Elvia. 2009. "Welcoming the Outsider to an Outsider Conference: Law and the Multiplicities of Self." *Harvard Latino Law Review* 2:397–422.

Baker, Phyllis L. 2005. "Trajectory and Transformation of a Working-Class Girl into an Upper-Middle-Class Associate Dean." In *Reflections from the Wrong Side of the Tracks: Class, Identity, and the Working Class Experience in Academe,* edited by Stephen Muzzatti and Vincent Samarco, 197–206. Lanham, MD: Rowman & Littlefield.

Clancy, Kim. 1997. "Academic as Anarchist: Working-Class Lives into Middle-Class Culture." In *Class Matters: "Working-Class" Women's Perspectives on Social Class,* edited by Pat Mahoney and Christine Zmroczek, 44–52. London: Taylor & Francis.

De la Riva–Holly, Francisca. 2012. "Igualadas." In *Presumed Incompetent: The Intersections of Race and Class for Women in Academia*, edited by Gabriella Gutiérrez y Muhs, Yolanda Niemann, Carmen González, and Angela Harris, 300–12. Boulder: University Press of Colorado.

Dews, C. L. Barney, and Carolyn Leste Law, eds. 1995. *This Fine Place So Far from Home: Voices of Academics from the Working Class*. Philadelphia: Temple University Press.

Grimes, Michael D., and Joan M. Morris. 1997. *Caught in the Middle: Contradictions in the Lives of Sociologists from Working-Class Backgrounds.*

Westport, CT: Praeger.

Gutiérrez y Muhs, Gabriella, Yolanda Niemann, Carmen González, and Angela Harris, eds. 2012. *Presumed Incompetent: The Intersections of Race and Class for Women in Academia.* Boulder: University Press of Colorado.

Holloway, Gerry. 1997. "Finding a Voice: On Becoming a Working-Class Feminist Academic." In *Class Matters: "Working-Class" Women's Perspectives on Social Class,* edited by Pat Mahoney and Christine Zmroczek, 44–52. London: Taylor & Francis.

Huxford, Lyn. 2005. "Making the Grade: Impostors in the Ivory Tower." In *Reflections from the Wrong Side of the Tracks: Class, Identity, and the Working Class Experience in Academe,* edited by Stephen Muzzatti and Vincent Samarco, 197–206. Lanham, MD: Rowman & Littlefield.

Kanter, Rosabeth Moss. 1977. *Men and Women of the Corporation.* New York: Basic Books.

Kovacovic, Milan. 1995. "Working at the U." In *This Fine Place So Far from Home: Voices of Academics from the Working Class,* edited by C. L. Barney Dews and Carolyn Leste Law, 233–48. Philadelphia, PA: Temple University Press.

Leslie, Naton. 1995. "You Were Raised Better Than That." In *This Fine Place So Far from Home: Voices of Academics from the Working Class,* edited by C. L. Barney Dews and Carolyn Leste Law, 233–48. Philadelphia, PA: Temple University Press.

Morley, Louise. 1997. "A Class of One's Own: Women, Social Class and the Academy." In *Class Matters: "Working-Class" Women's Perspectives on Social Class,* edited by Pat Mahoney and Christine Zmroczek, 44–52. London: Taylor & Francis.

Muzzatti, Stephen L., and C. Vincent Samarco, eds. 2005. *Reflections from the Wrong Side of the Tracks: Class, Identity, and the Working Class Experience in Academe.* Lanham, MD: Rowman & Littlefield.

Oldfield, Kenneth, and Richard Greggory Johnson III, eds. *Resilience: Queer Professors from the Working Class.* Albany: SUNY Press.

Patton, Michael Quinn. 2002. *Qualitative Research & Evaluation Methods.* Thousand Oaks, CA: Sage.

Piper, Deborah. 1995. "Psychology's Class Blindness: Investment in the Status Quo." In *This Fine Place So Far from Home: Voices of Academics from the Working Class,* edited by C. L. Barney Dews and Carolyn Leste Law, 233–48. Philadelphia: Temple University Press.

Reay, Diane. 1997. "The Double-Bind of the 'Working-Class' Feminist Academic: The Success of Failure or the Failure of Success?" In *Class Matters: Working-Class Women's Perspectives on Social Class,* edited by Pat Mahoney and Christine Zmroczek, 44–52. London: Taylor & Francis.

Ryan, Jake, and Charles Sackrey, eds. 1984. *Strangers in Paradise: Academics from the Working Class.* Boston: South End Press.

Schreier, Margaret. 2012. *Qualitative Content Analysis in Practice.* Washington, DC: Sage.

Schwalbe, Michael. 1995. "The Work of Professing (A Letter to Home)." In *This Fine Place So Far from Home: Voices of Academics from the Working Class,* edited by C. L. Barney Dews and Carolyn Leste Law, 233–48. Philadelphia: Temple University Press.

Strickland, Bonnie R. 2008. "No More Rented Rooms." In *Resilience: Queer Professors from the Working Class,* edited by Kenneth Oldfield and Richard Greggory Johnson III, 101–14. Albany: SUNY Press.

Tokarczyk, Michelle M., and Elizabeth A. Fay, eds. 1993. *Working-Class Women in the Academy: Laborers in the Knowledge Factory.* Amherst: University of Massachusetts Press.

Weaver, Laura H. 1993. "A Mennonite 'Hard Worker' Moves from the Working Class and the Religious/Ethnic Community to the Academy: A Conflict Between Two Definitions of 'Work.'" In *Working-Class Women in the Academy: Laborers in the Knowledge Factory,* edited by Michelle Tokarczyk and Elizabeth Fay, 112–25. Amherst: University of Massachusetts Press.

Weber, Robert Phillip. 1990. *Basic Content Analysis.* Newbury Park, CA: Sage.

Welsch, Kathleen A., ed. 2005. *Those Winter Sundays: Female Academics and Their Working-Class Parents.* Lanham, MD: University Press of America.

Zandy, Janet, ed. 1990. *Calling Home: Working Class Women's Writings.* New Brunswick, NJ: Rutgers University Press.

Zandy, Janet, ed. 1995. *Liberating Memory: Our Work and Our Working-Class Consciousness.* New Brunswick, NJ: Rutgers University Press.

PART TWO

Stepping Up

Graduate Students and the Challenges of Academic Professionalization

5

First in Line

The Experiences of First-Generation, Working-Class Graduate Students

Kathleen Mullins

The challenges college students face when they are the first in their families to access higher education have been well researched. Scholars have called attention to the multiple identities inherent in first-generation status and to the significant cultural transitions and resulting marginality that first-generation undergraduate students often experience (London 1992; Orbe 2004; Terenzini et al. 1994). Student affairs professionals have responded by creating high school–to-college bridge programs, academic interventions, and mentoring projects designed to support first-generation undergraduate students and to ameliorate their disadvantages. In spite of these efforts, and even when controlling for other persistence and attainment factors, first-generation undergraduate students are more likely than non-first-generation students (those whose parents have a bachelor's degree or higher) to earn a college degree; 20% of first-generation students obtain bachelor's degrees compared to 42% of students whose parents hold bachelor's degrees (Redford and Hoyer 2017, 11). Even though a significant number of first-generation undergraduate students do persevere and obtain postsecondary degrees, they are again underrepresented at the graduate level, where only 3% of first-generation students will earn a master's degree or higher (Redford and Hoyer 2017, 11). As we will see, graduate programs typically offer fewer resources to help them with the continuing challenge of navigating cultural transitions and addressing issues of marginalization based on socio-economic class.

Statistically, first-generation, working-class students are underrepresented in graduate programs. This fact, when coupled with the high attrition rate for all graduate students, puts first-generation graduate students at a disadvantage when compared with their peers whose parents attended college. In terms of student growth and development, first-generation graduate students continue to face the same personal, interpersonal, social, and cultural issues that they grappled with as under-graduates. Multiple identity issues may become more salient as students integrate new identities, such as graduate student, teaching/research assistant, and scholar. Additionally, as the scale shrinks from large undergraduate courses to graduate seminars, and as relationships with faculty members become more intimate, the gap between the cultures of home and the university widens, cultural transitions may become more demanding, and feelings of marginality can become more pronounced.

In spite of the abundance of information on the experiences of first-generation college students during their undergraduate years, very little research has been done on the experiences of these students when they enroll in graduate programs. However, a wealth of first-person narratives provides a look into the personal and professional lives of first-generation academics, both Ph.D. students and professors. Much of this work focuses on issues of socio-economic status—particularly working-class status (Dews and Law 1995; Linkon 1999; Rose 1989; Ryan and Sackrey 1984)—and incorporates the voices of people of a wide variety of races, ethnicities, genders, abilities, sexual orientations, political beliefs, and religious practices. Present in many of these narratives are stories of cultural transitions and marginality that increase in complexity as the student's level of academic study becomes further removed from his or her family's educational experiences. These poignant narratives of working-class, first-generation doctoral students and academics supplement the research about first-generation undergraduates, highlighting the importance of providing ongoing support for these students. However, no one has collected the stories of first-generation college students who enrolled in terminal master's degree programs. This study begins that conversation.

Methods

In 2005, I conducted an applied research project as a requirement for my graduate program in Student Affairs Administration in Higher Education at Western Washington University (WWU). My qualitative study examined the experiences of nine students in masters' programs at WWU who were the first in their families to go to college. I identified the students through snowball sampling, using personal connections on campus who shared my call for participants with their students and colleagues, which led to a recruitment chain of study participants recruiting other students as well. The students were between the ages of 24 and 42; five were men, four women; seven identified as white or Caucasian, one as American Indian, and one as biracial. They are identified in this chapter with pseudonyms. Their graduate programs were primarily in the social sciences and humanities, including history, education, English, and psychology.

My interest in this topic was grounded in my own experience as a first-generation college student and my first graduate-school experience when I was completing a master's degree in English Studies in the mid-1990s. At the time, I had no name for the phenomenon, but I was consciously struggling to cross an ever-increasing cultural chasm between myself and my family and friends, and I sometimes felt out of place in the rarified academic environment where my fellow students seemed so comfortable. I found many of my personal experiences validated and reflected in the research and first-person narratives about first-generation college students.

After reviewing the literature and conducting a 90-minute, in-depth interview with each of the students in this study, I came to believe that the issues of cultural transitions and marginality do not disappear when students finish their undergraduate programs. It seemed logical to me that the dissonance and challenge may, in fact, increase with each progressive foray into higher education. I do, however, agree with Mark Orbe (2004) that some first-generation students have enough familial "cultural capital" (Bourdieu 1977) to lessen the impact of transitions and marginalization. For example, first-generation students who have the cultural capital of being white, male, of traditional age for their degree programs, and/or middle or upper class may have more advantages than other first-generation students.

As higher-education professionals, we know that first-generation college students are underrepresented in graduate programs. We also know from our experiences with first-generation undergraduates that college requires students to navigate cultural transitions to address marginalization. If we want to encourage the persistence and nurture the resilience of first-generation graduate students—particularly first-generation, *working-class* graduate students—we will need to listen and respond effectively to their stories. While first-generation students from all socio-economic backgrounds undoubtedly face challenges in higher education, working-class students often face particular challenges related to the cultural differences between their working-class family experiences and their new path to an ostensibly middle-class life as the result of post-baccalaureate education (Hurst 2012, 130). Susan Borrego reminds us that we have the ability and responsibility to "help students tap their unique class position as a source of power" (2003, 7). This power is not only an essential resource for students in their individual educational pursuits, it also allows them to make an important contribution to the academic learning community.

Resilience Factors

First-generation, working-class graduate students are higher-education success stories in many ways. They have defied the statistical odds not only by persevering to earn a bachelor's degree, but to join the ranks of the academic elite: scholars in pursuit of graduate degrees. Instead of focusing on the adversity that first-generation, working-class graduate students might face, this study looks at the strengths that they bring to universities. Borrego writes, "the idea of overcoming barriers falls short of embracing aspects of working-class culture that students bring with them to the academy" (2003, 5). Focusing on the need for services instead of the enriching contributions these students bring to higher education "reveals the class bias of those who conceive and carry out the research" (Borrego 2003, 5). With this critique in mind, I have chosen to focus on the strengths of these students instead of their challenges.

Crucial to this project is the concept of educational resilience, which focuses not on an individual student's abilities but on attributes or factors that can be encouraged in all students. Psychologists have studied the construct of resilience—a "dynamic process encompassing positive adaptation within the context of significant adversity"—since the 1970s (Luthar, Cicchetti, and Becker 2000), prompting educational researchers to start exploring the concept of "educational resiliency" (Wang, Haertel, and Wahlberg 1994). In their comprehensive review of several decades of research on educational resilience, Waxman, Gray, and Padron write that the construct of "educational resiliency" is "not viewed as a fixed attribute but as something that can be promoted by focusing on 'alterable' factors that can impact an individual's success in school" (2003, 1).

The students I spoke with shared several factors related to their K–12 education that contributed to their educational resilience: attending schools that offered Advanced Placement (AP) classes, challenging curricula, an affluent parent population, and teachers who expected *all* students to go to college. One student in my study attributed his decision to go to college to a family relocation. John said,

> We moved into a rich area.... We were a lower-, maybe lower-middle-class, blue-collar family, and we're surrounded by white-collar, upper-class people, and I think I really was influenced. Maybe not right away, but by junior high, definitely, I would have said college was in the picture. And then in high school it was sort of assumed. You have to go. If you want to make something of your life, you have to go to college.

In addition to the resilience factors that came from quality K–12 education, the majority of the first-generation graduate students I interviewed benefited from a tremendous amount of emotional support from at least one parent. However, this support was general, not specifically academic. These were not the highly pressured offspring of the middle and upper-middle class. For the most part, parents were proud of these students' accomplishments and pleased with their abilities, but they did not push their children to succeed academically. The support the participants described is more akin to encouragement than coaching. Parents of first-generation students who successfully navigate the narrowing pathway to the highest levels of higher education are fans in the bleachers rather than coaches signaling from third base. While the study participants often desired what parent-coaches have to offer, they were grateful for the encouragement and emotional support their parents provided. As Victor said, "They left it all on me. Everything was on me. I was in charge of my own destiny, and they pretty much said, 'Do what you can do ... and we'll support you as we can'." Jessica put it this way: "I didn't know how to play the game. My parents didn't know how to play the game. So it wasn't that they weren't supportive, but they just had no real practical support to offer."

Sometimes parental support came from a sense of missed opportunities. "They've been both very supportive," said Victor, "because they wanted to go to school but they couldn't." This particular family valued education so highly that they dedicated more than half their income to sending their children to a private elementary school. The tuition bill was prioritized over the basics, at times. Victor said, "I'll never forget.... There would be times we'd come home and the only thing we had was mustard and bread, so we'd have, you know, a mustard sandwich!" When asked why he thought education was so important to his parents, Victor replied, "They realized that they were working their tails off and not getting paid much, and they didn't want us to go through that."

Clearly, many of the students in my study had supportive family members. However, aside from general advice to "go to college," these parents did not have specific directions for their children. Several of the students recognized their family's inability to provide specific and knowledgeable advice about education long before they started the college admissions process. Two subjects described the challenge of getting help with homework. One joked that his mother was probably happy to get remarried because someone could finally help him with his math homework. Another participant, Sarah, said,

> Even in high school when I needed help with stuff like math or reading or, you know, writing a paper, I could never turn to my parents and ask them. If I did, there was sort of a blank look. And so that was always really difficult, so I always kind of figured stuff out by myself.

Many of the students in the study also described themselves as avid childhood readers, but there was a sense that they may not have read the "right" books. One subject, Cole, said, "My parents, I guess, weren't high culture or anything like that. Books that I should have read as a child.... I'm not saying that they didn't encourage me to read.... I'm just saying they might not have read X, Y, Z." Several participants wondered aloud during the interviews what it would be like to have parents who were well-educated professionals—particularly doctors, teachers, or professors. How would family discussions have been different? What books might they have read, or read with a richer understanding? Now in graduate school, these first-generation students have started to see and understand the advantages of students whose parents graduated from college.

Having a strong work ethic was a third resilience factor that the students in this study shared. One of the most compelling insights to emerge from the interviews was many of the students' adaptation of a working-class work ethic to an academic environment. For some participants, this was characterized primarily by their "in and out" approach to their studies at WWU. "I am the typical commuter student," related Victor. "I just show up to go to school, do what I need to do, go home to study and then do my job." Another interviewee had a similar experience in her undergraduate studies. Jessica said, "I didn't spend a lot of time socializing with the other students. I tried to be very efficient about getting in, getting my work done, and getting out on a daily basis." These attitudes are reflected in the literature as well. Terenzini and a team of researchers (1994) found that first-generation students might not become engaged academically or socially on campus because of family or work obligations, as well as a lack of familiarity or comfort with college culture.

Other study participants were more aware of their work ethic when they compared their own behavior to that of their peers, particularly in terms of responsibility. Jessica said, "I guess I see it as an inadequate work ethic [in other grad students]. Insufficient sense of responsibility." When asked about the differences between first-generation students and those whose parents went to college, Victor said, simply, "Hard work and discipline. That's about it, because I don't feel … I don't walk on campus going, 'I'm the first in my family.' I don't think like that. I just think, I work hard and am disciplined." Some interviewees identified graduate school as the first time they encountered equally hard-working peers; others maintained that they still noticed a difference between themselves and their non-first-generation peers in relation to a sense of responsibility and work ethic.

Several of the study participants related this sense of responsibility and personal work ethic to their socio-economic class background. Cole said, "I don't know if that has to do with class … but I think it's just a result of your upbringing. That's kind of how I was trained. I transferred how my father works into how I work in class…." He went on to make a possible connection between social class and college behavior:

> I think it's maybe an intellectual outlook, and it could be a result of upbringing or whatever, but when you see people skipping classes and you see all these people that are there [at school] to be there and their parents pushed them in because that's what's *expected.* There's an expectation to go to college. I mean, I wasn't expected to go to college.… I could have easily gone into college at … a technical school.… So I think there's an expectation there. I think students from working-class families … they kind of pull themselves up. They take initiative. They do all these things, because they know they have to work and work hard and things might not come easy for them.…

Finally, a work ethic and sense of initiative empower some students to take control of their education. Keenly aware of the financial sacrifices higher education entails, these students take graduate school very seriously. Jason observed,

> The working-class graduate students I've run into, we exert a lot more independence and self-reliance than the average student. We're not just going to be pushed in one direction. We're going to do this because this is what we're here to do. This is my graduate program, I'm spending my money, I'm doing this.... So I think we have a lot of independence compared to the other students.

My study tried to determine the factors that encourage the persistence in first-generation students who pursue master's degrees. Choy reports that the National Educational Longitudinal Study of 1988–2000 revealed that first-generation college students "tended to report lower educational expectations, be less prepared academically, and receive less support from their families in planning and preparing for college than their peers whose parents attended college" (2001, 10). What makes some of these students resilient and able to overcome the odds stacked against them as students whose parents have not graduated from college?

The interviews I conducted revealed that the resilience and persistence factors in the lives of first-generation students in master's programs are significant. Many of the study participants benefited from attending high-quality high schools and from having financial resources (whether in the form of family support, federal financial aid, or teaching assistantships) that made higher education a possibility. However, none of these advantages can completely account for their success against the odds. Central to their ability to persist in graduate school is their aptitude for academics, their love of learning, and their personal motivation to push ahead. Their motivations varied, from a desire to be of service to others, to a strong pull toward socio-economic upward mobility, to an insatiable intellectual curiosity. These motivations were powered by strong work ethics and nurtured by supportive family members. However, crossing over to graduate school required that these students to negotiate multiple identities, cultural transitions, and issues of marginality. All these complexities make the bridge from home to graduate school (and back again) a difficult one to cross.

Cultural Transitions

Like most graduate students, the participants in this study share a passion for learning and a great enthusiasm for their subjects. They enjoy discussing big ideas and concepts. Ironically, what they love results in an often unwanted distance from the family members who have encouraged them to attend college. The biggest cultural challenge facing the students in this study was that of bringing their identities as graduate students and scholars home. When describing her graduate student identity, Jessica said, "I think it's definitely more of an issue at home than it is here [at school]." For many participants in the study, bringing their intellectual identity home simply didn't happen. While they value the support and respect the intelligence of their family members, several of the subjects expressed disappointment about no longer being able to talk with their parents or other family members about issues or ideas that are important to them.

Talking about family members in a critical light was not easy for most of the interviewees; they were often quick to point to their family members' intelligence, skills, and wisdom. However, the intellectual distance between the participants and their family members is clearly a source of loss. The life of the mind is a central aspect of these students' identities, and not being able to share that with family members means that parents do not get to know the richness of their son's or daughter's life. Conversely, students who feel unable to bring their full self home miss an opportunity for potentially meaningful connection. The gulf between these students and their high-school-educated parents becomes even wider as they proceed through graduate programs. Victor described the phenomenon this way:

> When I'm at home, I've gotten to the point where I can't talk academically with my mom or one of my mom's best friends.... They're very intelligent and very well read for only having a high school education. There was a time when I could talk to them about literature and academic subjects, but now I've gotten to a point where I've eclipsed them. And I miss being able to talk intellectually with my mom's friend.... Very smart woman, and I remember last quarter telling her what I was studying and all she could say was, "Oh my." She couldn't *add* anything to it, whereas she used to be able to do that. And so I've eclipsed her in that regard. [In] lifetime wisdom, never.

Sarah expressed the same feelings of surpassing her family intellectually but honoring the differences in "lifetime wisdom" or "life knowledge":

> I go home, and I almost feel like I have to dumb myself down. I don't want to step on my mom's toes because I feel like she has a

> lot of life knowledge that I could never compare to, but there's a lot that she does as a parent or even as an individual that I feel like I've surpassed her on, and that's hard. Because how do you interact with a parent that's supposed to be on a higher level than you when you feel more intelligent than them sometimes?

Both of these students raise difficult questions about the intersections of personal and familial life. Their sense of loss highlights the challenges inherent in trying to negotiate this cultural transition. Rather than express frustration with their family's inability to "keep up," some participants in the study learned to limit academic talk at home, thus showing a reluctance to change family relationships or to find ways to invite parents and siblings into their new academic world.

One subject said that he noticed a shift in his at-home conversations once he started graduate school. Christian's anecdote below illustrates the difficulty first-generation graduate students face when they want to bring their new identities and ideas home.

> I guess I'm "smarter" than my parents, again in quotes, because my parents aren't dumb. They have very specialized professional knowledge, but coming home, you don't really come home and say, "Man, there's a Marxist dialectic going on in that right there" on the television, on *CSI* or whatever they're watching. They'd say, "*What* are you talking about, son?" And even if I'm not being really serious about it, it's fun to joke or just to talk like that. In the classroom we joke like that. With your peers, with my brother, I can joke like that because he's in college. But when I go to Mom and Dad's, I try to turn that off because I don't want to make them feel stupid. I don't think they necessarily will, but I don't want them to think I'm talking down to them.... Sometimes I might start a conversation and they just won't know so they can't really talk back. They just say, "Okay, that's nice, son. I don't know either."

What *do* these students talk about at home? "When I come home, I leave a lot of school behind," said Cole. Like other subjects in the study, he explained that going home was a vacation from graduate school. When Cole goes home, he talks about the things that "everybody talks about." He explained by adding, "I come from a very rural area, so I would probably be more apt to talk about if they saw elk or deer or something than how many term papers I did or what they were on." In a similar vein, Victor observed, "At home, the intellectual and educational level, I leave that behind. What I learned, yeah, I still use that, but I don't talk about that in specifics. At home, it's more about family. Family and work."

Clearly the biggest and most emotionally difficult cultural transition that these students make is between home or family and graduate school. The parents who have cheered from the sidelines have achieved their goal of higher education for their children. Their children are educational success stories. But, as Carolyn Leste Law wrote about her own transition from her working-class family to her doctoral program, many of these students have suffered a loss; their education has "destroyed something even while it has been re-creating [them] in its own image" (Dews and Law 1995, 1). No longer able to engage in fulfilling intellectual dialogue with family members, some first-generation students in graduate programs turn to faculty and fellow students, only to discover unexpected marginalization in the classroom.

Marginality

It is probably safe to say that graduate students, in general, are fairly comfortable with their academic abilities after having highly successful academic experiences as undergraduates. The students in my study did not express anxiety about competency or competitiveness; indeed, they seemed secure in their academic performance. Yet several participants described a discomfort with the culture of academia that they struggled to overcome (even to the point of abandoning plans to apply to doctoral programs), others shared stories of marginalization based on socioeconomic class or political affiliation, and many observed that their working-class background necessitated significant linguistic adaptations.

These experiences of marginalization may directly or indirectly influence students' decisions to move on to doctoral programs after completing a master's degree. At least one participant has found the culture of academia is so unwelcoming and undesirable that he has chosen not to pursue a career in higher education. "I don't want to get a Ph.D.," Jason said.

> Quite simply, I'm not like those people. And I just, I don't think like them, I don't... I certainly don't talk like them. I just feel uncomfortable with them.... I mean, they feel tangibly different than me, and certainly tangibly different from the people I usually associate with. Even if those people have gone to college and are working and things like this, they are fundamentally different. And whether or not that's due to economics—that probably has a lot to

> do with it—or whether or not they've just been out and seen more things than I have.... That's certainly true, too, but those two things certainly go together.

When describing a professor's regular queries about the world travel habits of the students in a particular class, Jason said, "You really get the distinct impression that you're not worldly enough."

Another classroom interaction left an indelible impression on Jason, who described his reaction to a professor's casual, offhand story about visiting what happened to be Jason's hometown. This incident captures not only the specifics of what marginalization *looks* like but also the powerful impact it can have on students.

> This little voice in the back of my head said, "You just described the vast majority of my entire family, and you just described them as beer-swilling, Republican-voting hicks." I didn't say anything. I just kind of sat there. I mean, what was I going to say to that? And ... that bothered me. I mean, it *still* does. Am I somehow separated from that just because I'm sitting here listening to you [the professor] talk about Marx and then I'm throwing in Derrida into this conversation? Is it because I'm conversant with these things that I'm somehow different? Or is there that possibility of me just backsliding into this beer-swilling, you know, gun-rack-havin' caste. I mean, that's exactly what it is, it's a caste.... And I think that's one reason I keep saying they're different than me. Is this something that they want to beat out of me or get out of me, somehow? Or is it something that I should let go myself? Or is it something I should hold on to?... That episode just hit me across the face.

Was this professor aware that students in his class might share the cultural background he was ridiculing? Was the attack intentional? Most likely not. Since class differences within the student population—and within the faculty ranks—are rarely addressed directly in higher education (Borrego 2003; hooks 2000), unconscious class bias comes as no surprise. Since higher education was historically limited to the country's elite (wealthy, white men) and since low-income and working-class students typically drop out of the educational system long before graduate school (Smith, Altbach, and Lomotey 2002), it may not occur to some that our graduate school classrooms are no longer exclusively populated with the offspring of the privileged middle and upper-middle classes. Later in the interview, the same student observed that first-generation students in his master's-level program were not planning to continue for the Ph.D.:

> It's like, is this [master's program] the final weedout? Obviously on some levels it is, but why?... It just struck me, why don't a number of us go the extra step? I can't speak for [a fellow graduate student], but I don't know of any of us here that are [going on for a Ph.D.], and it's not that we aren't capable. It's just there's something there that we don't want to go farther.... It's something that I'm starting to wrestle with, too. Why don't you want to do this? Are you afraid of doing this? Or you just don't want to be like those people?

These questions bring to light important issues for the academy to consider. We do not like to talk about class issues in higher education (Borrego 2003; hooks 2000), but clearly we need to examine the impact that class biases have on students and on the career aspirations of first-generation, working-class graduate students in particular. Regardless of this student's answers to his own questions—whether he decided not to pursue a doctoral degree out of fear or distaste for the typical professorial culture—his concerns are serious and illustrate the significant impact of marginalization.

Not every instance of marginalization borders on bigotry and prejudice as in Jason's example. Sometimes traditional academic culture is just at odds with the students' family backgrounds. While my subjects' stories were not identical, the overall tenor was similar. One interviewee objected to the formality of higher education and described an emotional distance that feels uncomfortable or unfamiliar. Cole identified non-first-generation students and professors as having limited worldviews. He felt that "students whose parents have gone to college and professors ... are kind of in this little bubble. They don't understand how the rest of the world, Middle America, works." One participant said that her biggest adjustment related to graduate school was encountering the socio-economic differences within the student population. For example, some graduate students talked about being able to purchase new furniture or mentioned that their parents paid their rent. Reflecting on these differences, Lisa mentioned that she had applied to a graduate program at an Ivy League school. "If I would have gotten into there," she said, "I don't know if I would have made it, because everybody would have been ten times worse. It would have been ... I would have felt *so* different than everybody else."

In response to these differences, some interviewees embraced their "real world" backgrounds or working-class perspectives and were reluctant to give them up. Christian said,

> A part of me doesn't want to become like one of those intellectuals that sits around in a black shirt and condescends to everybody and sees negativity in everything because it's all worthless. Be pervaded by cynicism because you know so much.... I'd like to be able to learn about it and be in control rather than becoming part of the intellectual system, I suppose. Does that make any sense?... I want to get inside, but I don't want to be consumed by them.

This desire to keep the culture of academia at arm's length and to maintain a connection to one's familial, cultural, or socio-economic background is at the crux of the dilemma for first-generation graduate students. As so many of the personal narratives of working-class scholars attest (Borrego 2003; Dews and Law 1995; hooks 2000; Rendón 1992; Rose 1989; Ryan and Sackrey 1984), many first-generation graduate students struggle to find a comfortable balance between identities and cultures. Like Collins (1999), hooks (1984), and Rendón (1996), these students want to exist on the margins by choice and from a position of strength rather than as the result of marginalization.

The experience of being "other" in relationship to academic discourse and the culture of academia is directly related to experiences of marginalization in the classroom. Many of the participants were highly aware of their cultural, political, and socio-economic differences. Christian remarked on the traditional liberalism of liberal arts departments:

> Some people are like, "Got to hate President Bush. Got to love Michel Foucault." This and that, you know, very left, intellectual things, which is fine if they believe that, but I feel, because I'm maybe not all the way over there with them, I might be kind of condescended to or marginalized a little bit, not by the professor necessarily but possibly by some of the other students.

Several times during the interviews, participants who criticized professors or other graduate students for being wholesale proponents of what they viewed as liberal political views backpedaled and suggested that perhaps these individuals knew something they did not. This phenomenon seemed to be partially motivated by social correctness and at times a genuine uncertainty about the value of their own beliefs and experiences.

This struggle with the cultural norms of the academic environment is exemplified by the linguistic adaptations that some first-generation students of lower socio-economic status or from working-class backgrounds make. Many are self-conscious about language, particularly in the classroom. "I'm quiet a lot of the time," said John. "For me to be articulate, and for me to sound like I know what I'm talking about, I have to think about things a lot. Get in that mindset." Another participant, Sarah, echoed this: "I have to be really careful about how I say things, what I say. I'm way more paranoid than anybody else about saying something wrong." Some subjects in the study described encountering unfamiliar terminology or academic concepts that their non-first-generation peers seemed already to know or understand. Others simply felt out of place. "Sometimes I think I am quiet," reported John, "because, maybe especially during some conversations, I feel like kind of an alien in academia." This subject chose the word "alien"—a word that is repeated many times in the literature on the first-generation experience (Chaffee 1992; Rendón 1992; Rose 1989)—without any prior reference to the concept during the interview. John went on to describe the importance of adapting to this alien environment. "You adapt to this special environment where you're supposed to say things a certain way," he said. To illustrate his point, John described his admissions interview for a highly competitive graduate program at WWU:

> When I was in my interview to get into this program, I thought I made a fatal mistake because I said something about coming from the "real world." [Academia is] sort of like a strange land. It's its own creation.... Maybe that's why I think very carefully, because you don't want to be the "stupid" person in the classroom, the "uncivilized" person. There's a certain kind of language you're supposed to learn. Like I'm using big words today [laughter]. When I say them, it surprises me. Even words like "academia." I remember I was reading a book, and I read "schism," and I thought, "How do I know that word?"

Language, and academic discourse in particular, is often the site where differences are highlighted in the classroom; it is also a primary marker of socio-economic class (Linkon 1999; Zweig 2004; Zwerling 1992). "Language is a very good example of how I've struggled," said Trisha.

> In the field I'm in [counseling] ... my background and language is *not* a deficit, but in college courses my background and language *is* a

> deficit. I have to struggle to find those right, exact-fit words. Where I don't need that in my [lower socio-economic] background, I need that in those college courses.

These particular examples of marginalization based on socio-economic class discrimination, discomfort with the culture of academia, and unfamiliarity with academic discourse were unique to the participants' *graduate-school* experience. Graduate school is designed to provide students with a taste of scholarly life, an introduction to the academic community. Faculty who see clear distinctions between themselves and undergraduates may have less rigid boundaries with graduate students. Indeed, they may perceive graduate students, even in master's programs, as future colleagues. Some may expect that all graduate students are—or should be—comfortable with academic discourse, academic culture, and the habits of a particular socio-economic class. Often, however, these expectations do not match the experiences of first-generation, working-class students.

While master's-degree-granting institutions ostensibly focus on the learning, growth, and development of *all* students, it is often the undergraduate experience that garners most attention. Colleges and universities that want to encourage the persistence of first-generation, working-class students in graduate programs will need to do more than usher undergraduates in the front door. We will need to understand the experiences of these students, provide appropriate and effective services, and help faculty to provide support at the departmental and graduate-school levels. These interventions need to focus on enhancing the strengths of first-generation, working-class graduate students and acknowledging and celebrating the cultural and socio-economic class richness that they bring to the university.

In sharing this research with others, I often hear the refrain, "This is my story!"—accompanied by gratitude, hugs, tears, or a plea to share our story with others. When I asked the students I interviewed what they would take away from our conversation, many of them indicated that this was the first time they had ever consciously examined the issues of first-generation status and social class. One participant said,

> I think just talking about it makes me realize just how much this has influenced my life. Whereas before, it was just sort of, "this is who I am." I didn't think that there was anything special about it.... And to think that there are other people out there like me, going through what I'm going through, is a *whole* new perspective.

A future counselor compared it to presenting a client with a diagnosis:

> Just making the [observation] that there are people out there that have shared this experience is really different. And, I mean, working in mental health, it's incredible ... when you present a diagnosis to somebody and they go, "Oh, my gosh. That's why I've been this way? My life makes so much more sense now." That's kind of how it feels. This really has had an influence on my life.

In the course of an hour-and-a-half conversation, these students came away saying, "it's not just me." One participant said, "Wow. It is surprising. I guess I've always felt like that was just my life. That's just how it is. I never really thought that there were other people that were going through that, ever. That's *really* interesting."

What I find noteworthy about these first-generation, working-class graduate students is their willingness to "go it alone." Strong familial support and academic preparedness is central to many of their stories, but what their narratives ultimately reveal is an intense desire to persevere in their studies in spite of a lack of understanding from their loved ones and the potential loneliness that can come from being the "first in line." Being the first person to do something implies privilege and opportunity. Being first often is related to being exceptional. Standing at the front of the line involves the responsibility of being an example and role model. It also evokes the excitement—and anxiety—of being first.

Works Cited

Borrego, Susan. 2003. *Class Matters: Beyond Access to Inclusion.* Washington, DC: National Association of Student Affairs Administrators in Higher Education.

Bourdieu, Pierre. 1977. "Cultural Reproduction and Social Reproduction." In *Power and Ideology in Education,* edited by Jerome Karabel and A. H. Halsey, 487–511. New York: Oxford University Press.

Chaffee, John. 1992. "Transforming Educational Dreams into Educational Reality." In *First-Generation Students: Confronting the Cultural Issues,* edited by L. Steven Zwerling and Howard B. London, 81–88. New Directions for Community Colleges, no. 80. San Francisco: Jossey-Bass.

Choy, Susan. 2001. *Students Whose Parents Did Not Go to College: Postsecondary Access, Persistence, and Attainment.* NCES 2001-126. Washington, DC:

National Center for Education Statistics.

Collins, Patricia H. 1999. "Reflections on the Outsider Within." *Journal of Career Development* 26 (1): 85–88. doi:10.1023/A:1018611303509

Dews, C. L. Barney, and Carolyn Leste Law, eds. 1995. *This Fine Place So Far from Home: Voices of Academics from the Working Class.* Philadelphia: Temple University Press.

hooks, bell. 1984. *Feminist Theory: From Margin to Center.* Boston: South End Press.

hooks, bell. 2000. *Where We Stand: Class Matters.* New York: Routledge.

Hurst, Allison L. 2012. *College and the Working Class: What It Takes to Make It.* Rotterdam, The Netherlands: Sense Publishers.

Linkon, Sherry L., ed. 1999. *Teaching Working Class.* Amherst: University of Massachusetts Press.

London, Howard B. 1992. "Transformations: Cultural Challenges Faced by First-Generation Students." In *First-Generation Students: Confronting the Cultural Issues,* edited by L. Steven Zwerling and Howard B. London, 5–11. New Directions for Community Colleges, no. 80. San Francisco: Jossey-Bass.

Luthar, Suniya S., Dante Cicchetti, and Bronwyn Becker. 2000. "The Construct of Resilience: A Critical Evaluation and Guidelines for Future Work." *Child Development* 71 (3): 543–62. doi:10.1111/1467-8624.00164

Orbe, Mark P. 2004. "Negotiating Multiple Identities within Multiple Frames: An Analysis of First-Generation College Students." *Communication Education* 53 (2): 131–49.

Redford, Jeremy, and Kathleen Mulvaney Hoyer. 2017. "Stats in Brief: First-Generation and Continuing-Generation College Students: A Comparison of High School and Postsecondary Experiences." NCES 2018-009. Washington, DC: National Center for Education Statistics.

Rendón, Laura. 1992. "From the Barrio to the Academy: Revelations of a Mexican American 'Scholarship Girl'." In *First-Generation Students: Confronting the Cultural Issues,* edited by L. Steven Zwerling and Howard B. London, 55–64. New Directions for Community Colleges, no. 80. San Francisco: Jossey-Bass.

Rendón, Laura. 1996. "Life on the Border." *About Campus* 1 (5): 14–20.

Rose, Mike. 1989. *Lives on the Boundary: A Moving Account of the Struggles and Achievements of America's Educational Underclass.* New York: Penguin.

Ryan, Jake, and Charles Sackrey, eds. 1984. *Strangers in Paradise: Academics from the Working Class*. Boston: South End Press.

Smith, William A., Philip G. Altbach, and Kofi Lomotey, eds. 2002. *The Racial Crisis in American Higher Education: Continuing Challenges for the Twenty-first Century*. Albany: SUNY Press.

Terenzini, Patrick. T., Laura I. Rendón, M. Lee Upcraft, Susan B. Millar, Kevin W. Allison, Patricia L. Gregg,andn Romero Jalomo. 1994. "The Transition to College: Diverse Students, Diverse Stories." *Research in Higher Education* 35 (1): 57–73.

Wang, Margaret C., Geneva D. Haertel, and Herbert J. Wahlberg. 1994. "Educational Resilience in Inner Cities." In *Educational Resilience in Inner-City America: Challenges and Prospects*, edited by Margaret C. Wang and E. W. Gordon, 45–72. Hillsdale, NJ: Erlbaum.

Waxman, Hersh C., Jon P. Gray, and Yolanda N. Padron. 2003. *Review of Research on Educational Resilience*. Research Report, no. 11. Santa Cruz: Center for Research on Education, Diversity, and Excellence, University of California, Santa Cruz.

Zweig, Michael, ed. 2004. *What's Class Got to Do with It? American Society in the Twenty-first Century*. Ithaca, NY: Cornell University Press.

Zwerling, L. Steven. 1992. "First-Generation Adult Students: In Search of Safe Haven." In *First-Generation Students: Confronting the Cultural Issues*, edited by L. Steven Zwerling and Howard B. London, 45-54. New Directions for Community Colleges, no. 80. San Francisco: Jossey-Bass.

6

Narrating, Understanding, and Reflecting on the Experiences of Working-Class Graduate Students in Rhetoric and Composition Programs

David Marquard

I am a self-identified member of the working class. I am also a first-generation academic, having recently (2011) graduated with my doctoral degree in rhetoric and composition from a Research-1 university. The coupling of my socio-economic background with the rigors of graduate school is not entirely uncommon. However, while scholars have collected and published an abundance of data and research on the working-class undergraduate student, very little has been researched in regard to the working-class graduate student. Beginning with this observation of a gap in the literature, this study offers a collection of voices from three self-identified working-class graduate students; such voices speak to the lived experience of those from a working-class background as they enter into and engage with the professional discourse of graduate school. While all of these students are pursuing degrees in rhetoric and composition, the insights deriving from their experiences are largely applicable across disciplines. Their various impressions and feelings cast the experience of graduate school in a distinctly nonacademic light. The chapter concludes by arguing for the inclusion of more socio-economic, class-based scholarship in TA training texts, calling for more research into the experiences of working-class graduate students, and offering key functions for a rhetoric of listening in regard to understanding and nurturing working-class students.

Rationale for the Study

As teachers, scholars, writing program administrators (WPAs), and members of the rhetoric and composition community, we have seen a growing awareness of pedagogy regarding working-class undergraduate students. This correlates with the continued emergence of research dedicated to the linguistic acquisition and performance of working-class students. From the early quantitative studies conducted by Basil Bernstein (1971) and Pierre Bourdieu (1977) to recent work like Irvin Peckham's *Going North, Thinking West* (2010) and Elizabeth Armstrong and Laura Hamilton's *Paying for the Party: How College Maintains Inequality* (2013), researchers have continued to examine the linguistic effects, successes, and failures of working-class students. Additionally, there have been anthologies and other published accounts by and about established working-class academics (Dews and Law 1995; Muzzatti and Samarco 2005; Ryan and Sackrey 1984; Shepard 1998; Tokarczyk and Fay 1993; Zandy 1995), as well as notable autobiographical/autoethnographic texts by Mike Rose (*Lives on the Boundary*, 1989), Richard Rodriguez (*Hunger Memory*, 1982), and Victor Villanueva (*Bootstraps*, 1993).

Alongside this growing body of notable publications, there has been a steady stream of scholarship dedicated to examining and critiquing the professional discourse of graduate school. Research in this vein has addressed the systemic isolation of graduate students (Damrosch 1995; Golde and Walker 2006), as well as the oppressive and often violent nature of graduate school and institutional hegemony (Hinchey and Kimmel 2000).

In addition, we have witnessed a growing body of research focusing on graduate students' participation in rhetoric and composition programs throughout the country. Generally speaking, during the 1990s scholars recognized a need to evaluate and publish detailed information on and accounts of our graduate rhetoric and composition programs (Brown, Meyer, and Enos 1994; Chapman and Tate 1987; Miller 2001; Miller et al. 1997). There has also been scholarship dedicated to graduate students as WPAs and to graduate student training.[1] In addition, two primary studies that examine disciplinary literacies and writing at the graduate level are Paul Prior's extensive ten-year case study, *Writing/Disciplinarity: A Sociohistoric Account of Literate Activity in the Academy* (1998) and Berkenkotter, Huckin, and Ackerman's article, "Conventions, Conversations and the Writer: A Case Study of a Student in a Rhetoric Ph.D. Program" (1998).

Rhetoric and composition graduate students express the value of their positions as developing and emerging experts in the field in the volume *In Our Own Voice: Graduate Students Teach Writing* (Good and Warshauer 2007), the sole text to draw directly from the knowledge and experience of the graduate students in our writing programs.

Lastly, Amy Rupiper Taggart and Margaret Lowry (2011) address Kathleen Blake Yancey's (2002) assertion that we think little about TA instruction in proportion to the amount of time we spend teaching undergraduates how to write. Rupiper, Taggart, and Lowry surveyed graduate student TAs attending teacher preparation programs at the University of Texas at Arlington and North Dakota State University, reporting that graduate student TAs struggle or are concerned mostly with "grading, classroom management, and developing a teacherly *ethos*" (98).

Despite the growing body of research on language acquisition, writing, and academic access for the working-class undergraduate student, research on graduate students lags behind. Furthermore, while we have seen a growth of working-class narratives written primarily by established professors and educators, there are no published narratives focusing on working-class graduate students. This study addresses that gap with respect to rhetoric and composition graduate programs, while furthering the literature on both working-class/first-generation students and the current overall climate of graduate education.

Study Design and Participants

This study examines the experiences of working-class graduate students in rhetoric and composition programs. Three participants, all of whom self-identify as being from the working class and are enrolled in rhetoric and writing programs in the United States, were asked to write narrative accounts of their experiences with graduate work, and to be interviewed shortly after composing their narratives. Throughout below, all proper nouns, including the personal names of the three participants and the names of institutions they have attended, have been rendered pseudonymously per the study's terms of consent.

The participants bring to light the overarching theme of experiencing graduate school as an outsider, witnessing a sense of deep frustration on the part of working-class graduate students. More specifically, this study reveals how graduate students 1) experience a sense of anger and frustration that relates specifically to differences in social class; 2) experience anger and frustration toward navigating the professional discourse of graduate school while balancing the discourse of the home; and 3) experience anger and frustration related to financial difficulties and insecurities.

Here follows a brief narrative introduction to each of the pseudonymous participants, capturing various themes that were discovered through my reading of the narratives and our conversational interviews.

William

William is in the third year of his Ph.D. program in English composition studies at Northeast University. He served initially as a graduate assistant. He has recently completed his coursework and has commenced work on his dissertation, but has moved away from the university where he is pursuing his Ph.D., due to his wife having taken a job. William is currently teaching as a part-time instructor while writing his dissertation.

William's narrative focuses primarily on his entrance into graduate school, when he considered an M.F.A. but decided to pursue composition studies. This decision was influenced by the readings he discovered within the latter discipline. He reveals a sense of difference between students who have working-class social values and students rooted in more middle- to upper-class values. He also reveals anger at having to deal with various social realities within his family, as well as frustration at such graduate school challenges as the high level of weekly reading. William discusses his anger at the religious views held by many of his family members, and he implies a sense of anger about having his worldviews challenged. Early on in William's narrative, he makes very clear that he comes from a working-class background; his father is a union plumber and his mother ran a cleaning business. Only one family member has gone to college: his brother, who continues to occupy working-class jobs, currently working "with fire systems and construction sites."

Leanne

Leanne comes from what she calls a poor upbringing. She admits in her narrative that her family could have qualified for welfare, but due to their family pride they never asked for it. While growing up, Leanne's mother and father failed in running a graphic design business, leaving her family in a very difficult economic situation. Her mother and father value the arts and both have associate degrees in art. Leanne's mother is currently on disability and her father is a factory laborer. Leanne has one sister, who lacks insurance and is struggling to pay for her own education.

Leanne is currently finishing up her coursework at Midwestern University, pursuing a Ph.D. in English composition studies. She previously earned an M.A. in linguistics from East Coast University on Long Island and a B.A. in networking and data communications. Prior to graduate school she spent a brief time in the workplace, earning $160,000 per year. Her early interest in English led her to linguistics—despite her passion for art, in which she saw little economic promise. Leanne currently maintains the English Department website at Midwestern University.

Jennie

Jennie is in her second year of her Ph.D. at Southwest University. She began her undergraduate work at a "premier higher education institution" in the Northeast. Halfway through, she transferred to a university in Puerto Rico, where she obtained her B.A. in English and an M.A. in linguistics. While Jennie was growing up, her parents worked in factories. Neither attended college. Her mother died while she was in high school, and her father is retired. Jennie has four siblings, none of whom have attended college.

In the home, Jennie's parents participated little in her schoolwork. Her father held the belief that some folks were meant for college, while others were not. It was his firm belief that their family, and specifically her brother Peter, who was constantly failing in school, was simply not meant to go to college. Jennie does not recall ever being read to at an early age, although her father was an avid reader (this she credits nonetheless for her early love for reading). She admits that her parents did little to encourage her to attend college.

Early in her narrative, Jennie writes that her father considered the family to belong to the lower class. She, on the other hand, was comfortably in denial in habitually describing her family as working class. She writes: "As young adults, we do not want to be singled-out for being different from the images we see in the media (i.e., middle class) or from our classmates." Her early understanding of her family background influences Jennie's sense of the working class, which she equates with working for an hourly wage and forming part of the lower socio-economic strata.

Results

The primary theme to emerge from the narratives and interviews was that of experiencing graduate school from an outsider's perspective. This theme has several dimensions, including anger and frustration toward social-class differences, the need to balance the professional discourse of graduate school with the discourse of the home, and financial difficulties and insecurities. A sampling of the participants' comments on these matters is given in the chapter appendixes, which aggregate salient qualitative data related to the overarching theme and subthemes and may perhaps serve as a stimulus to future research.

All three participants document a sense of anger and frustration toward social class differences in a way that creates a sense of direct opposition to many of their peers. William expresses this experience throughout his narrative. As presented in Appendix 6.1, he addresses shifts in cultural practices within the English Department. He observed, upon arriving in graduate school, that many of the social functions had a very working-class atmosphere. William conveys frustration that, over the course of two years, these functions shifted from "a working-class way of socializing" to an "upper-middle-class way of socializing." This experience resonates throughout Jennie and Leanne's narratives as well. While she is just in the second year of her graduate program, Jennie notes at the end of her narrative: "I have days that I say, 'Why am I here?' This question stems from, not doubt about my abilities, but perhaps reflects my working-class background." And as is documented throughout Appendix 6.1, Leanne expresses anger and frustration by positioning herself against her upper-class peers. Toward the end of her narrative, Leanne writes, "I try to live my life peacefully and do not believe that violence solves any problems, but to deny the anger I expressed over distinctions between the classes would have been to misrepresent myself."

The overarching theme that captures how these participants experience graduate school from an outsider's perspective is further documented by how these three participants struggle with balancing the professional discourse of graduate school with the discourse of the home. Leanne and William expressed their difficulties with maintaining a sense of social acceptance in graduate school while still maintaining positive relations with others outside the professional discourse of graduate school. For example, as is captured in Appendix 6.2, William discusses both his anger toward his family and his fears about acceptance among his graduate student peers. He notes that he was very angry during his first year of graduate school, finding "cause to get angry at family gatherings" where "things that didn't bother me before really began to get under my skin." He also relays how uncomfortable he felt speaking out during graduate seminars, for fear that he might not be right about what he was saying.

Similarly, Leanne addresses the difficulties she has with "fitting in" within the discourse of graduate school, while, like William, she is concerned with being accepted socially within her graduate program. In Appendix 6.2, she poignantly captures this balancing act, outlining how members of her home community struggle to relate to or even understand what she is doing in her graduate studies. She expresses how difficult it is to witness her family's struggles with very practical issues like finances and jobs, while at the same time she has to study "high theory" in "a postmodern class," which, for her, seems "frivolous." Regarding such difficulties, she notes, "these worlds are so far apart and I just don't know where I fit. And I don't know if I'm ever going to fit." Nor are the strains on family relationships simply a matter of discourse. Jennie notes that due to job constraints she had to live away from her husband while she was working on her master's degree, a situation she refuses to bring forward into her Ph.D. program.

The final subtheme that affirms how these participants bring to graduate school an outsider's perspective is highlighted through financial difficulties and insecurities. This subtheme resonates through both Leanne and Jeannie's graduate experiences, as shown in Appendix 6.3. For example, Leanne repeatedly asserts how upper-class incomes equate with easier educational access, citing the "luck" of many of her graduate-school peers in having their incomes supplemented by large amounts of money from their parents. Jennie makes much the same observation, noting how many of her graduate school peers did not have to pay for their education and that "their parents provided them with a stipend or allowance for monthly spending." Meanwhile, lack of money was the deciding factor as to where she could attend school, and created high levels of stress throughout her academic endeavors. Leanne, too, references how financial difficulties within the working class inhibit "access to a good education, access to reasonable health insurance, access to networking to allow one to climb the social ladder—access, even, to a comfortable life." In addition, Leanne expresses anger and resentment toward the upper class in general, sarcastically noting how people with large amounts of money can purchase "dog insurance" while her father and sister live without any insurance.

Analysis and Discussion

The differences described above regarding academic and social outlooks between the working class and the middle to upper classes create an outsider sensibility among working-class graduate students. This shows how the working-class graduate student lacks symbolic capital within what Pierre Bourdieu might call the *habitus* of higher education. As Bourdieu theorizes, habitus is a system of

> durable, transposable dispositions, structured structures predisposed to function as structuring structures, that is, as principles which generate and organize practices and representations that can be objectively adapted to their outcomes without presupposing a conscious aiming at ends or an express mastery of the operations necessary to attain them. (1977, 72)

Furthermore, for Bourdieu, "habitus is the background of and resource for playing the social game. Habitus is interior to history, yet as a general environment for practice, pervades or saturates social processes" (Foster 1986, 105). Translated into the present context, working-class graduate students feel like they are impostors who do not fit within academia. This is a direct result of their lack of symbolic capital, or a lack of insider knowledge of how to properly "play the game."

The participants' narratives frequently exhibit an "us versus them" mentality, as with Leanne's questioning of where her "allegiances lie": whether to side with the academy or the home (see Appendix 6.2). Balancing the discourse of the academy with that of the home is nothing new for working-class academics; it is featured in a number of published narrative anthologies (Huxford 2005; LeCourt 2005; Sowinska 1993). However, the notion of separation and differences based on financial insecurities, as evident in these graduate students' comments, is relatively neglected within previously published narratives of working-class academics. Jennie's account not only addresses her struggles with financial insecurities, but also speaks to her identification with peers who are also struggling with financial concerns. Jennie felt out of place during her elite undergraduate education, despite being in the ethnic majority. Yet at the University of Puerto Rico, where she completed her M.A. as an ethnic minority, she felt comfortable because she could identify with her peers' financial struggles. I suggest that the disinclination within published working-class academic narratives to engage with this issue, as well as Jennie's ability to identify more closely with peers who are struggling financially than with those of similar ethnic background, may be related to degrees of shame. The relative inattention within previously published narratives (e.g., Dews and Law 1995; Muzzatti and Samarco 2005; Ryan and Sackrey 1984; Shepard 1998; Tokarczyk and Fay 1993; Zandy 1995) to the issue of financial insecurity may have to do with the contributors' fear of being judged for their lack of financial acumen during their time in graduate school.

I offer this speculation partly because of the anger toward financial insecurity manifest in the participants' narratives and interviews. Anger tends to surface in the presence of fear or shame, as the participants' narratives demonstrate. For example, in Appendix 6.3, Leanne describes her financial situation as "well below the poverty line" and refers to her lack of finances as an "economic hardship." She notes how she will only admit—in her narrative, but not elsewhere—her "anger and hatred" toward these socio-economic differences. The willingness to express such anger may be attributed to the anonymity of the present study's participants. The authors of previously published narratives may have imagined they were writing for a primarily middle- to upper-class audience, where such anger might not be fully understood or accepted. As established career academics, they may have distanced themselves from the experiences of graduate school, enabling them to write from their new socio-economic class positions.

In contrast, because the participants in this study were promised anonymity, they were allowed to freely narrate both their experiences and their emotions. The fact that they were expressing their experiences as they lived them (absent the safety of hindsight), and that they were part of a study and not writing as named authors for a contributed volume, may have helped to create a safe place for them to fully express their outlooks and experiences with the academy and social class. They were not writing their narratives with an editor in mind, or with the idea of drafting and redrafting their narratives for the sake of molding them in a way that would meet an editor's needs.

The sheer display of anger and frustration toward financial differences and insecurities, as well as toward social class differences, shows a divide between the working-class graduate student and the middle- to upper-class student. I use the word "divide" because of the anger and frustration revealed in the participants' tone. Differences are to be expected and are understandable; the intensity of anger and frustration at such differences is surprising and alarming.

Conclusions and Suggestions

First, I think that if we in composition studies pedagogically value the writing and experience of working-class students at the undergraduate level, we need to extend this value to the graduate level. For example, after having surveyed many of the more common teacher-training texts used to guide our graduate students entering rhetoric and composition, I have discovered little to no concern for the working-class student.[2] In light of this absence, coupled with the ample scholarship relating to race and gender included in our teacher-training texts, I suggest that more scholarship on teaching working-class students be included in such publications. Given the ongoing concern we have for teaching writing in diverse classrooms, it can only be beneficial to further strengthen our pedagogical practices by including scholarship that relates to teaching the working-class student. The inclusion of scholarship more sensitive to socio-economic and class-based differences will extend our pedagogy and commitment to diversity as we train future scholars and teachers within our field.

I also suggest further research, not just on how working-class students approach writing, but on how socio-economic class differences may help or hinder the process of entering into the communities of the composition classroom and the academy. We should welcome research that focuses on exploring questions related to ways we can better understand why and how working-class students experience socio-economic and class differences within the writing classroom. Such research can further help us on many pedagogical fronts—classroom management, student resistance, creating writing prompts, writing assessment, and student conferencing—while advancing our understanding of the early developmental stages of working-class writing students. It will also help us understand the overarching academic endeavors of these students, and to move toward building more harmonious writing classrooms and communities. By facilitating a better understanding of our differences, such research will help us grasp our own socio-economic backgrounds and ideologies in relation to the ideologies of working-class students, helping writing teachers understand how such students learn and approach writing, as well as how they navigate through the academy.

Moreover, I think it would be beneficial to the academy and the field of composition studies if there were more narratives written by working-class graduate students and faculty. Given the predominance of anger and frustration expressed by the participants in this study, further narrative exposition regarding the emotion of anger as it is felt within the academy would aid our understanding of such an emotion. Additional attention is due to the potentially oppressive nature of graduate school, as explored by Hinchey and Kimmel (2000) in response to several incidents of violence by graduate students across the country—most notably at the University of San Diego where, in 1996, an M.A. student shot three committee members during his thesis defense). The more recent shooting rampage by faculty member Amy Bishop at the University of Alabama highlights the need for further research into the underlying role of anger and frustration in precipitating such acts.[3]

I now turn to a final suggestion that relates to the overarching theme of experiencing graduate school as an outsider. Because class differences are so prominent for the working-class graduate student (and for established working-class academics, as noted in many of the published working-class narratives mentioned above), I suggest we continue to try to understand these differences, applying a sense of *rhetorical listening*, as described in Krista Ratcliffe's book of that name (2005). Ratcliffe offers four functions whereby rhetorical listening may emerge as a means to better understand our differences.

The first function, a rhetoric of listening that focuses openly on *terms* (both positive and negative), creates a space that will allow us to engage both sides' views of the differences: "instead of reading the terms only as negative, listeners might also hear the terms as offering honest and painful claims that deserve further consideration" (94). For example, when considering such negative terms as "white trash" or "redneck," Jennifer Beech, in her article, "Redneck and Hillbilly Discourse in the Writing Classroom" (2004), makes a point to refer to herself as a "scholar and a redneck" (173). She argues that such pejorative and painful terms need to be confronted, researched, and interrogated in all their complexities.

The second function proceeds via a cultural logic that recognizes simultaneous commonalities and differences. This approach to listening rhetorically, Ratcliffe asserts, "interrupts the emphasis of Western logic to perpetuate either-or reasoning, for instance, to recognize commonalities or to recognize differences. Such simultaneous recognitions are important because they afford a place for productively engaging differences, especially those differences that might otherwise be relegated to the status of 'excess'" (Ratcliffe 2005, 95). This second function can be of use when responding to how the working class creates a sense of divisiveness between itself and the upper class. As has been noted throughout this chapter, the three participants imply an "us versus them" stance throughout their narratives. Ratcliffe's second function would entail transcending the socio-economic differences between the upper and lower classes, enabling us to find commonalities between the two and thus to interrupt the either-or dichotomy.

The third function of rhetorical listening offers listeners three functional rhetorical stances: recognition, critique, and accountability. In our present circumstance, separations and differences most often function as independent silences—we are not functioning together to better understand our differences. Yet, to first recognize that differences do exist, and by way of this recognition, we can offer the opportunity for merging reflection with praxis—"in hopes of not only reinforcing the positive personal and cultural functions but also revamping the dysfunctions" (96). The notion of critique is also important: critique "affords opportunities for negotiation, for questioning not just others' claims, assumptions, and conclusions but also our own" (97). Doing this sort of critique opens up the existence of numerous questions as well as "multiple answers to each questions, and multiple places from which to speak and listen" (98). It assumes places of identification, disidentification, and nonidentification, wherein subject and cultural positions are always already in play just as they are always already weighted within history and culture. The third aspect of this function of rhetorical listening is accountability. For Ratcliffe, accountability creates a space where listening is not couched in the "backward-looking stance of guilt/blame" but instead "offers forward-looking ways to address not just individual errors but also unearned structural privileges" (98).

These three functional rhetorical stances are responses to the inherent silences that often accompany social and cultural separations and differences. They offer a way to strengthen our understandings of the inherent silences and divisions between social classes. Specifically, my hope is that readers from all social backgrounds will recognize the divisions, separations, and differences expressed by the participants. Recognizing these divisions is a crucial step toward overcoming them. It is also my hope that all readers will pause and reflect on their own accountability, and not rush to impose blame on others.

The last function that Ratcliffe offers is a rhetoric of listening that proceeds via the interpretive trope of listening "metonymically," as opposed to listening by way of generalities and absolutism. As Ratcliffe writes,

> the trope of listening metonymically assumes that a text or person does not share substance with all other members of its/his/her cultural group but, rather, is associated with them. In other words, this trope invites listeners to assume that one member of a group (say, one woman) does *not* speak for all other members (say, all

women); as such, this trope helps listeners avoid the trap of unfair generalizations and stereotyping. (98–99)

In other words, if we were to listen to Leanne, William, and Jennie metonymically, we would not quickly conclude that their voices represent the entirety of the working class—or even the "working-class graduate student." To do so would be unfair both to the larger population of working-class graduate students (in composition studies or other fields) and to the research participants in this study.

Ultimately, by understanding and employing these functions of rhetorical listening—recognizing obvious divisions but also overlaps; listening without blame; listening to oneself and to the other; listening in a way open to numerous questions and answers; and listening so as to forge connections while maintaining a respect for differences—we can understand and move forward in the face of the divisions and separations that exist within graduate education, the working class, the academy, and society at large.

Notes

1. On the former, see Brown 1999; Duffey et al. 2007; Edgington and Taylor 2007; Jukuri and Williamson 1999; and Mountford 2002. On the latter, see Covino, Johnson, and Feehan 1980; Mack 2009; and Ohmann 1990.

2. The teacher-training texts I surveyed are based on a compilation of "the top listed books for TA training" conducted on the Writing Program Administrators listserv by Susan McLeod. McLeod asked WPAs to state which texts they use in their writing programs, and ranked them in order of responses received.

3. Amy Bishop was an assistant professor at the University of Alabama in Huntsville, where she was denied tenure in March of 2009 and was terminated in February 2010. Her termination was effective on February 12, the day on which she attended a faculty meeting where she shot and killed three faculty members and injured three others.

Works Cited

Armstrong, Elizabeth, and Laura Hamilton. 2013. *Paying for the Party: How College Maintains Inequality*. Cambridge, MA: Harvard University Press.

Beech, Jennifer. 2004. "Redneck and Hillbilly Discourse in the Writing Classroom: Classifying Critical Pedagogies of Whiteness." *College*

English 67 (2): 172–86.

Berkenkotter, Carol, Thomas Huckin, and John Ackerman. 1998. "Conventions, Conversations, and the Writer: A Case Study of a Student in a Rhetoric Ph.D. Program." *Research in the Teaching of English* 22:9–44.

Bernstein, Basil. 1971. *Class, Codes, and Control.* 3 vols. London: Routledge.

Bourdieu, Pierre. 1977. *Outline of a Theory of Practice.* Translated by Richard Nice. Cambridge, UK: Cambridge University Press.

Brown, Johanna Atwood. 1999. "The Peer Who Isn't a Peer: Authority and the Graduate Student Administrator." In *Kitchen Cooks, Plate Twirlers and Troubadours: Writing Program Administrators Tell Their Stories*, edited by Diana George, 120–25. Portsmouth: Boynton/Cook Press.

Brown, Stuart, Paul Meyer, and Theresa Enos. 1994. "Doctoral Programs in Rhetoric and Composition: A Catalog of the Profession." *Rhetoric Review* 12 (2): 240–389.

Chapman, David, and Gary Tate. 1987. "A Survey of Doctoral Programs in Rhetoric and Composition." *Rhetoric Review* 5 (2): 124–86.

Covino, William, Nah Johnson, and Michael Feehan. 1980. "Graduate Education in Rhetoric: Attitudes and Implications." *College English* 42 (4): 390–98.

Damrosch, David. 1995. *We Scholars: Changing the Culture of the University.* Cambridge, MA: Harvard University Press.

Dews, C. L. Barney, and Carolyn Leste Law, eds. 1995. *This Fine Place So Far from Home: Voices of Academics from the Working Class.* Philadelphia: Temple University Press.

Duffey, Suellynn, Ben Feigert, Vic Mortimer, Jennifer Phegley, and Melinda Turnley. 2001. "Conflict, Collaboration, and Authority: Graduate Students and Writing Program Administration." *Rhetoric Review* 21 (2): 79–87.

Edgington, Anthony, and Stacy Hartlage Taylor. 2007. "Invisible Administrators: The Possibilities and Perils of Graduate Student Administration." *WPA: Journal of the Council of Writing Program Administration* 31 (1–2): 150–70.

Foster, Stephen. "Reading Pierre Bourdieu." 1986. *Cultural Anthropology* 1 (1): 103–10.

Golde, Chris M., and George E. Walker, eds. 2006. *Envisioning the Future of Doctoral Education: Preparing Stewards of the Discipline.* San Francisco:

Jossey-Bass.

Good, Tina Lavonne, and Leanne B. Warshauer, eds. 2007. *In Our Own Voice: Graduate Students Teach Writing.* New York: Longman.

Hinchey, Patricia, and Isabel Kimmel. 2000. *The Graduate Grind: A Critical Look at Graduate Education.* New York: Falmer.

Huxford, Lyn. 2005. "Making the Grade: Impostors in the Ivory Tower." In *Reflections from the Wrong Side of the Tracks: Class, Identity, and the Working Class Experience in Academe,* edited by Stephen Muzzatti and Vincent Samarco, 207–20. Lanham, MD: Rowman & Littlefield.

Jukuri, Stephen Davenport, and W. J. Williamson. 1999. "How to Be a Wishy-Washy Graduate Student WPA, or Undefined but Overdetermined: The Positioning of Graduate Student WPAs." In *Kitchen Cooks, Plate Twirlers and Troubadours: Writing Program Administrators Tell Their Stories,* edited by Diana George, 105–19. Portsmouth: Boynton/Cook Press.

LeCourt, Donna. 2005. "Making Class Matter: My Life as a Semi-Earhole." In *Reflections from the Wrong Side of the Tracks: Class, Identity, and the Working Class Experience in Academe,* edited by Stephen Muzzatti and Vincent Samarco, 83–100. Lanham, MD: Rowman.

Mack, Nancy. 2009. "Representations of the Field in Graduate Courses: Using Parody to Question All Positions." *College English* 71 (5): 435–59.

Miller, Scott, Brenda Jo Brueggemann, Bennis Blue, and Deneen M. Shepherd. 1997. "Present Perfect and Future Imperfect: Results of a National Survey of Graduate Students in Rhetoric and Composition Programs." *College Composition and Communication* 48 (3): 392–409.

Miller, Thomas. 2001. "Why Don't Our Graduate Programs Do a Better Job of Preparing Students for the Work That We Do?" *WPA: Journal of the Council of Writing Program Administration* 24 (3): 41–58.

Mountford, Roxanne. 2002. "From Labor to Middle Management: Graduate Students in Writing Program Administration." *Rhetoric Review* 21 (1): 41–53.

Muzzatti, Stephen L., and C. Vincent Samarco, eds. 2005. *Reflections from the Wrong Side of the Tracks: Class, Identity, and the Working Class Experience in Academe.* Lanham, MD: Rowman & Littlefield.

Ohmann, Richard. 1990. "Graduate Students, Professionals, Intellectuals." *College English* 52 (3): 247–57.

Peckham, Irvin. 2010. *Going North, Thinking West: The Intersections of Social Class, Critical Thinking, and Politicized Writing Instruction.* Logan: Utah State University Press.

Prior, Paul. 1998. *Writing/Disciplinarity: A Sociohistoric Account of Literate Activity in the Academy.* Mahwah: Erlbaum.

Ratcliffe, Krista. 2005. *Rhetorical Listening: Identification, Gender, Whiteness.* Carbondale: Southern Illinois University Press.

Rodriguez, Richard. 1982. *Hunger of Memory: The Education of Richard Rodriguez: An Autobiography.* Boston: Godine.

Rose, Mike. 1989. *Lives on the Boundary: A Moving Account of the Struggles and Achievements of America's Educationally Underprepared.* New York: Penguin.

Rupiper Taggart, Amy, and Margaret Lowry. 2011. "Cohorts, Grading, and Ethos: Listening to TAs Enhances Teacher Preparation." *WPA: Journal of the Council of Writing Program Administration* 34 (2): 89–114.

Ryan, Jake, and Charles Sackrey, eds. 1984. *Strangers in Paradise: Academics from the Working Class.* Boston: South End Press.

Shepard, Alan, ed. 1998. *Coming to Class: Pedagogy and the Social Class of Teachers.* Portsmouth: Boynton/Cook.

Sowinska, Suzanne. 1993. "Yer Own Motha Wouldna Reckanized Ya: Surviving an Apprenticeship in the 'Knowledge Factory.'" In *Working-Class Women in the Academy*, edited by Michelle Tokarczyk and Elizabeth Fay, 148–61. Amherst: University of Massachusetts Press.

Tokarczyk, Michelle, and Elizabeth Fay, eds. 1993. *Working-Class Women in the Academy.* Amherst: University of Massachusetts Press.

Villanueva, Victor, Jr. 1993. *Bootstraps: From an American of Color.* Urbana, IL: NCTE.

Yancey, Kathleen Blake. 2002. "The Professionalization of TA Development Programs: A Heuristic for Curriculum Design." In *Preparing College Teachers of Writing: Histories, Theories, Programs, Practices*, edited by Betty Pytlik and Sarah Liggett, 63–74. New York: Oxford University Press.

Zandy, Janet, ed. 1995. *Liberating Memory: Our Work and Our Working-Class Consciousness.* New Brunswick, NJ: Rutgers University Press.

Appendix 6.1: Anger and Frustration toward Social-Class Differences

William

- Our writing program potlucks and department picnics were casual gatherings. We drank beer out of kegs and played softball or tennis. But toward the end of my time there, department picnics were held at a manor owned by the college. Instead of softball, we stood around and talked. Instead of beer, there was only wine and only what people brought themselves. People wore suits and business clothes, whereas before it was shorts and t-shirts.
- Our Friday night gatherings didn't disappear; however, they were held at a coffee shop instead of a bar. Darts and pool became Scrabble or sitting around talking. Cheese sticks, fried mushrooms, and Buffalo wings became coffee or tea and biscotti. And it's not important that we weren't drinking alcohol at social functions anymore or playing sports or anything like that. Instead, I think the changes were important because it showed an evolution from a working-class way of socializing to a middle-class or upper-middle-class way of socializing.
- The students accepted to the English Department's graduate programs were no longer people who liked to play softball and drink beer while they talked about how to get a paper accepted to the CCCCs [Conference on College Composition and Communication]. Instead, they wanted to stay home on Wednesday and Friday nights and read and write. People entered the department who seemed a little harder for me to approach, I guess.

Leanne

- Sometimes I wake up in a sweat at night thinking I won't finish my dissertation and will be forced to live as an adjunct for the rest of my life. I don't think these kinds of feelings are shared by the bulk of my graduate student colleagues.
- It is also hardly surprising to me that of the three working-class students in my year in the program, all of us are working on very

practical, pragmatic issues dealing with student success in their dissertations, not working in high theory spewing Derrida from their butts.

- I am frustrated and sometimes angered to see those people who do half the work or slack off still get A's in the graduate classes, still graduate on time with me. To me, I feel they haven't worked hard enough.
- Just last week, I had a rather heated discussion with a friend about a particular instructor we both currently have, and our perceptions of him. My friend, coming from an upper-class background, didn't see a problem with him being a lazy slacker and pushing off work that he should be doing on his students. The course we are taking is a mentoring course, but instead of him teaching us and mentoring us about how to be better instructors, he is having us write grants and work on projects that would benefit him. I have serious problems with the instructor and his ethics. My friend sees no problem with what he is doing and thinks it is understandable. I think that this issue, and our discussion, ultimately comes down to a working-class issue.
- I try to live my life peacefully and do not believe that violence solves any problems, but to deny the anger I expressed over distinctions between the classes would have been to misrepresent myself.

Jennie

- I have days that I say, "Why am I here?" This question stems from, not doubt about my abilities, but perhaps reflects my working-class background.
- I realized after taking a critical race theory class out here for my Ph.D., I realized that by doing the process, that I really identified with *Bootstraps* … and the idea that I really did feel like I belonged in Puerto Rico and that's why I stayed. I never felt like "I'm the white girl," and that class, for me, was primary over all the other differences.… Everyone I met was like me.… They were working, trying to pay for college, they didn't have a lot of extra money to spend … like at [my first undergraduate institution] … like my roommate [had]. Her father was a lawyer and she had a monthly

stipend. She really didn't care too much about her studies, to tell you the truth. She was heavily involved with the Greek system … and I really do think it was an issue of class at [that school] … and that's why I felt more comfortable [in Puerto Rico].

Appendix 6.2: Anger and Frustration about the Need to Balance the Professional Discourse of Graduate School with the Discourse of the Home

William

- Despite being drawn to this field over my first couple of years in graduate school, I remember being angry a lot that first year—angry at the things I was reading and angry at the things people were saying, I think, but the specifics are gone now.
- I do remember, though, that once I entered graduate school, I had more cause to get angry at family gatherings. I started to see a clash between the things that I was learning in graduate school and my family life at home. Things that didn't bother me before really began to get under my skin.
- Before I went to grad school, it didn't really bother me all that much that my brother and my sister-in-law believed things like being gay is a sin and abortion should be illegal. I didn't agree with what they said, but I just didn't really care one way or the other about it.
- After a few months in grad school, though, I found myself getting really angry when my brother would say things like "you can't help being homosexual, but you have to be aware that being a practicing homosexual is a sin." I overheard one of these comments when I was reading a book to my nephew (their son) one day, and it made me so angry.
- I felt a little uncomfortable speaking out … because I was never sure if I was ever going to be right about what I was saying. Even though I read everything that I needed to read for that day … for the assignment … I still wasn't sure—what if I'm misunderstanding it or what if it's not quite the way I'm supposed to be thinking about it?

Leanne

- Another thing that affects me strongly is the gap between what I am doing here in the academy and the rest of my home life: my family, working-class friends, the town I grew up in. I often feel like I am an imposter, like I shouldn't be here studying these things, like I don't belong.
- But other times I relish our academic-happy-closed world where we have the intellectual freedom to pursue what interests us, and where we can help shape our students' lives in meaningful ways. Each time I go home, however, that split is so apparent to me, it's shocking. The gap between these worlds is too much to traverse at times.
- How could I tell [my best friend from home] that I probably will never come home? That my education has given me so much and shifted me so that I no longer feel that I fit in? That I am in between the world of the academy and my home world and feel like an alien in both places?
- It gets so overwhelming at times. It's to the point that when I go home it literally is like two different planets … and it's not even a matter of understanding what I'm doing or what rhetoric and composition is … [N]obody understands that. It's just that, it's the mindset that we are privileged to take in academia. Like we get to sit around all day and we get to think. And we get to study things and we get to learn and grow and we don't really worry about finances…. I mean we do as graduate students, but the general mentality is that we sit around thinking great thoughts … in the ivory tower and all these different concepts…. [T]his mentality is still there and anyone who denies it … well, they're not keeping their eyes open when they go to like a faculty meeting, and this idea that we're improving democracy and all of this, and then I get home and I drive around and see all my old friends and my family and see my father making tanks right now because he can't find a job and hates every bit of it right now because he doesn't believe in war but he does it because he needs health insurance, and I get so frustrated…. [I]t's like I don't know which group I should be in or where my allegiance should lie … and I feel like I'm strained between the two and they don't really allow either…. [I]t's like, I took this postmodernism class … and we're

talking about Heidegger and Derrida and Deleuze … and I know that theory has its place but it just seems so frivolous to me…. I go to this class, and my mom calls me on the phone before I go, and she's talking about how she's worried about how to pay for my sister's education … and I go to this class and we're talking about all of this high theory…. [T]hese worlds are so far apart and I just don't know where I fit. And I don't know if I'm ever going to fit.

Jennie

- Although my husband supported me and thought it would be possible to travel back and forth, I was tired of being separated from him and didn't want to move around anymore.

Appendix 6.3: Anger and Frustration about Financial Difficulties and Insecurities

Leanne

- [Growing up,] everybody was poor, and being poor didn't matter. But on Long Island, I was in one of the wealthiest areas of the country. Nobody was poor. Even most graduate students had their parents sending substantial amounts of money to them each month to supplement our well-below-the-poverty-line incomes.
- This economic hardship certainly affected my work in the program, my desire to stay, and even my future plans for academia.
- To me, being part of the working class is a way of seeing. When I see the world through my working-class lens, I am angered by the frivolous amounts of money people who have it spend on things like "dog insurance" when my own parents and sister go uninsured.
- My working-class lens makes me a frugal shopper, never wasting and saving what I can in case something happens at my current job. I'll admit here, but not elsewhere, that sometimes my working-class lens leaves me full of anger and hatred for those who live in places like the Hamptons or Fifth Avenue—because in most cases, their success was earned on the backs of my working-class people.

- And many of those who are "lucky" get additional funding from parents, relatives, grandmothers, who have it to send. The rest of us are stuck with what we get and have to say "no" to going on the spring break trips or out to eat every night of the week.
- Being in the working class also has a lot to do with access, or perhaps lack of access: access to a good education, access to reasonable health insurance, access to networking to allow one to climb the social ladder—access, even, to a comfortable life.

Jennie

- In the end, I chose to attend the state university not because I wanted to be close to home, but because financially, I did not think it possible to go out of state.
- I found myself living among students from the middle or high socio-economic groups from out of state. Most did not have to work to pay for college and their parents provided them with a stipend or allowance for monthly spending.
- I don't recall the classes as being difficult, but the stress of paying for college and understanding the new culture I was immersed in was overwhelming.
- Again, this was due to having to work in order to pay for school as well as adjusting to lecture hall classes of 200+ where professors only knew your student number.
- But now, after reading *Bootstraps*, by Victor Villanueva, I realize that I stayed in Puerto Rico because I no longer felt like the "other." Even among the differences of language, culture, and food, I still felt I was among people like me. The majority of the students (80% at least) were on financial aid in the University of Puerto Rico. Those that lived in the dorms were no better off than anybody else; they chose to live there because of the difficulty of traveling to and from their hometown. Everyone I met, everyone I roomed with, had the same financial difficulties that I did.

7

Navigating Positive and Hostile Department Climates

Experiences of Latino/a Doctoral Students

Elvia Ramirez

According to the Pew Research Center, the nation's Latino/a population has long been characterized by its rapid growth and wide dispersion to parts of the country that historically have had little Latino/a representation (Stepler and Lopez 2016). More recent data, however, indicate that the growth and dispersion of the U.S. Latino/a population has slowed since 2007, largely as a result of reduced immigration from Latin America and declining fertility rates. On the other hand, data indicate that Latino/a student enrollment in higher education institutions has been steadily increasing. As of 2012, almost 69% of Latino/a high school graduates enrolled in college, compared to 67% of their white counterparts (Fry and Taylor 2013). Still, Latino/as remain less likely than white students to enroll in a four-year college/university, attend a selective college, enroll in college full time, or complete a bachelor's degree (Fry and Taylor 2013). At the doctoral level, Latino/a enrollment has been steadily increasing, as evidenced by an increase of over 100% in the number of doctorates awarded to Latino/as over the past 20 years (NSF 2015). Nevertheless, Latino/as remain dramatically underrepresented in doctoral education. For example, in 2015, Latino/as represented 17% of the entire U.S. population but just 10% of all first-time enrolled graduate students (Okahana, Feaster, and Allum 2016) and 6.2% of all doctoral degree recipients (NSF 2016).

Among Latino/as, Mexican Americans are the largest subgroup but are the least likely to obtain doctoral degrees (Huber et al. 2015).

Because doctoral education represents the primary gateway to research careers and the professoriate, scholars investigate Latino/as' graduate school experiences in order to understand the causes of this gap in representation. Since the department constitutes the focal point of doctoral students' experiences (Solem, Lee, and Schlemper 2009), it is imperative that researchers examine Latino/a—particularly Mexican American—doctoral students' perceptions of and experiences with departmental climate. Concomitantly, because first-generation doctoral students experience unique and added barriers compared to their non-first-generation doctoral student peers (Gardner 2013), examining how first-generation doctoral student status impinges on Latino/a doctoral students is critical. This chapter presents findings of a study examining the experiences of Latino/a doctoral students, most of whom are first-generation college students, with departmental climate. The central research question guiding the present study is: How do race, class, and gender inequalities shape Latino/a doctoral students' perceptions of and experiences with department climate?

Literature Review

Research suggests that campus climate is inextricably linked to racial/ethnic minority student educational outcomes (Hurtado 1994). For example, studies of minority undergraduate students find that positive (i.e., non-discriminatory) campus climates are associated with higher grade point averages, retention, and student involvement on campus (Hurtado 1994). In contrast, hostile racial climates have a negative impact on minority students' sense of belonging on campus (Hurtado and Carter 1997). In a study of Latino/a undergraduate students, Hurtado, Carter, and Spuler (1996) found that Latino/as who perceived a hostile campus climate "expressed more difficulty adjusting academically, socially, and emotionally as well as more difficulty building a sense of attachment to the college" (summarized in Hurtado and Ponjuan 2005, 237).

There is thus a clear link between campus climate and student educational experiences and outcomes. However, because most of the research on campus climate has focused on undergraduate students, less is known about graduate students' perceptions of and experiences with their campuses and, more specifically, their departments (Griffin, Muñiz, and Espinosa 2012; Hirt and Muffo 1998; Hurtado 1994; Solem, Lee, and

Schlemper 2009; Ward and Zarate 2015). Because departments assume almost full responsibility for the socialization and education of graduate students (Hirt and Muffo 1998), the department (or discipline) is the locus of the graduate student experience (Gardner 2010). Analyzing department climates is thus critical for understanding graduate students' experiences. Research on graduate students' perceptions of and experiences with departmental climate is still relatively uncharted scholarly terrain, however. In one of the few studies examining this issue, Solem, Lee, and Schlemper (2009) found that students of color, women, international students, and doctoral (versus master's) students in geography programs perceived their departments as less tolerant, equitable, and diverse than did study participants overall; the authors also found that these students experienced the greatest amount of social isolation in their graduate programs.

How Latino/a doctoral students, specifically, perceive department climate has not been the subject of much scholarly investigation. In fact, only a few scholars have examined the experiences of Latino/a students in doctoral programs (e.g., Achor and Morales 1990; Bañuelos 2006; Cuádraz 1993; Espino 2014; González 2006; Ramirez 2014, 2017; Solorzano 1998; Solorzano and Yosso 2001). Overall, research finds that Latino/a doctoral students encounter systemic race, class, and gender inequalities in the form of "low faculty expectations, stigmatization, alienation, racial isolation, tokenism, stereotyping, lack of faculty mentorship and support, hostile departmental and institutional climates, and racially biased epistemologies and Eurocentric curricula" (Ramirez 2014 170). Research also finds that Latino/a doctoral students often experience racist, sexist, and classist microaggressions in the form of *microassaults* (i.e., subtle or explicit derogations against marginalized groups), *microinsults* (i.e., communications that convey stereotypes, rudeness, and insensitivity towards marginalized groups), and *microinvalidations* (i.e., communications that exclude, negate, or nullify the thoughts, feelings, or lived realities of marginalized groups) (Ramirez 2014; Sue 2010).

Notwithstanding the valuable insights and contributions of the existing literature on Latino/a doctoral students, more research is clearly needed and warranted. For example, no research studies of Latino/a doctoral students have placed the issue or question of department climate at the center of analysis. Furthermore, the literature rarely examines how class background generally, and first-generation college student status in particular, impinges on Latino/a doctoral students' experiences (Ramirez 2014). The general lack of class analysis in the study of Latino/a doctoral students is especially problematic in light of the predominantly low-income, working-class roots of the U.S. Latino/a population (Chapa and De La Rosa 2004). Furthermore, as of 2014, more than 40% of Latino/a doctorate recipients came from families in which neither parent had been awarded a college degree; in comparison, approximately three-fourths of white doctorate recipients come from families with at least one college-graduate parent (NSF 2015). Latino/a doctoral students are thus significantly more likely than white students to be first-generation college students.

According to Gardner (2013), first-generation doctoral students tend to have unique characteristics and challenges that sent them apart from non-first-generation students. For example, first-generation students face greater financial constraints and extended time-to-degree, experience feelings of otherness, are less likely to understand the system of graduate education, and are more likely to suffer from "impostor syndrome" (Gardner 2013). First-generation college student status clearly has a significant impact on doctoral students' experiences and educational outcomes. Yet, relatively little is known about first-generation doctoral student experiences (Gardner and Holley 2011), including their experiences with department climate. In order to fill existing empirical gaps in the literature, this study analyzes the experiences of a sample of Latino/a doctoral students, most of whom are Mexican American and first-generation college students, regarding department climate.

Theoretical Framework

This study is grounded in intersectionality theory, a conceptual framework pioneered by women of color feminists (e.g., Baca Zinn and Thornton Dill 1996; Collins 2000; Crenshaw 1991) that interrogates multiple and interlocking structures of inequality. Emerging as a critique of essentialist and unitary theories of inequality, intersectionality theory problematizes race, class, and gender inequalities. Though each of these systems of inequality is analytically distinct, they all intersect and influence one another. Intersectionality theory also argues that although one or another system of inequality may be salient in an individual's experience and/or consciousness, all three major forms of inequality are structured into society. "At any moment," Andersen and Collins (2001) note, "race, class, or gender may feel more salient or meaningful in a given person's life, but they are overlapping and cumulative in their effect on people's experience" (3).

Intersectionality theory also rejects the "ranking of oppressions" and refuses to privilege one system of inequality over another, especially because these systems of inequality are interconnected and collectively configure the structure of our society (Andersen and Collins 2001). Furthermore, intersectionality theory illustrates that intersecting forms of inequality produce both oppression and privilege. "At the same time that structures of race, class, and gender create disadvantages for women of color, they provide unacknowledged benefits for those at the top of these hierarchies—whites, members of the upper classes, and males" (Baca Zinn and Thornton Dill 1996, 327). These inequality regimes thus simultaneously produce structures of oppression and privilege that affect all individuals.

Intersectional analysis also is guided by standpoint epistemology, a philosophy and methodology that calls attention to "social location in the production of knowledge" (Baca Zinn and Thornton Dill 1996, 328). Intersectional analysis is grounded in the assumption that "marginalized locations are well suited for grasping social relations that remain obscure from more privileged vantage points" (Baca Zinn and Thornton Dill 1996, 328). As this study will elucidate, the graduate education experience, viewed from the standpoint of Latino/a students, looks decidedly different from—and, I argue, more comprehensive and complex than—institutional accounts (i.e., "master narratives") of the same experience.

In short, I employ intersectionality theory in order to examine the departmental climate as perceived and experienced by Latino/a doctoral students, most of whom are first-generation college students. Using an intersectional framework, this study analyzes how Latino/a doctoral students are impacted by the racialized, classed, and gendered dimensions of department climate. Such an intersectional analysis will contribute significantly to the body of campus/department climate studies, which typically interrogate just one system of inequality.

Research Methods

Data for this paper stem from a larger case study examining the graduate school experiences of Latino/as at a doctorate-granting public research university located in the western United States. The larger study examined how public and institutional policies, as well as race, class, and gender inequalities embedded within the graduate schooling process, impact Latino/as' access to and experiences in doctoral degree programs. The study is based on in-depth, semi-structured qualitative interviews conducted with Latino/as who had completed, or were in the process of completing, their doctoral (Ph.D.) degrees at the time of the study.

A total of 24 respondents—12 men and 12 women—were recruited for the study. Prospective interviewees were identified through an official list of enrolled Latino/a doctoral students at this institution. All enrolled Latino/a doctoral students were sent a letter that both explained the nature of the study and requested their participation. Individuals who agreed to participate were also asked to refer potential recruits for the study. All interviewees were asked to fill out a written questionnaire, which documented their background and family characteristics, as well as answer open-ended questions from an interview guide. Interviews lasted approximately two to four hours each, and were conducted face-to-face and via telephone. Each interview was tape recorded and transcribed verbatim.

The respondents span all major disciplinary groupings, including natural sciences (n = 3), social sciences (n = 16), education (n = 3), and humanities (n = 2). Nineteen respondents were enrolled in the university at the time of the study and were at various stages of their graduate program, ranging from the first year to the dissertation stage. Five interviewees had already obtained their Ph.D.'s, having completed their programs between 1990 and 2005. The vast majority (n = 22) of respondents are of Mexican American descent; two interviewees are of non-Mexican Latino/a origin. Additionally, most respondents are first-generation college students (n = 19) and from working-class backgrounds (n = 15). Four respondents reported having one parent who had obtained a bachelor's degree, and one had two parents with a bachelor's degree or higher. Respondents who are the first in their families to obtain a bachelor's degree are identified as "first-generation," while those who have at least one parent who has obtained a bachelor's degree are identified as "second-generation." All study participants have been assigned a pseudonym in order to protect their confidentiality.

To analyze the data, the interview transcripts were read several times, common themes in the narrative transcripts were identified, and the most theoretically relevant data were extracted for analysis. The goal of data analysis was to identify patterns in Latino/a students' descriptions of the departmental climates they encountered. I employed intersectionality theory to further understand how the multiple and interlocking dimensions of race, class, and gender inequality shaped Latino/as' perceptions of departmental climate.

Results

When queried about their departmental climates, respondents offered either positive or negative appraisals; that is, they either "loved" the department climate or they "hated it." Approximately one-third of respondents described the department climate as positive, while two-thirds characterized it as negative or hostile. Furthermore, most respondents felt that the lack of demographic diversity among graduate students and/or faculty negatively impacted their graduate studies. These findings are further delineated below.

Positive Departmental Climates

Respondents who described their department climate as positive reported that faculty and/or fellow graduate students were generally supportive, friendly, and collegial. For example, Xavier (first-generation) described graduate students in his department as "helpful," "friendly," and "easy to get along with." Susana (first-generation) also characterized her department as "pretty supportive," and she felt "welcomed" by department faculty. Similarly, Emilio (second-generation) stated that he "loves" his department because faculty are approachable and because faculty and fellow graduate students are supportive of his research endeavors. He contrasts his experience with those of graduate students enrolled at a nearby institution:

> I love [my department]. In the sense that the [department] is very encouraging and nurturing towards its graduate students. And when I say that, I am making comparisons to, let's say, the [department] over at [a nearby research-intensive university]. I know a lot of people in that department and I've talked to them about their experiences and I've heard nothing but horror stories, as if it were boot camp. I really didn't have that experience here. I've always felt encouraged. I've always felt like I can approach the professors. I've always felt that my fellow graduate students and cohort, that whenever I had a question or problem or comments, they would always offer constructive criticism or they would always take into consideration my point of view. So it's been more of a nurturing and encouraging environment than anything.

Patricia (second-generation) also felt her department was supportive of students. She described her graduate program as "small, flexible, supportive … and cooperative.” Furthermore, Patricia believed the small size of her department afforded students an opportunity to interact closely with faculty and fostered a collegial atmosphere among students, since fewer graduate students meant less competition for resources.

> From what I hear, at bigger universities I know, like the sister school at [a nearby research-intensive university], their [graduate] program is twice as big as the one here.… And that would definitely be more competitive because [a] bigger [graduate student] population [makes it] more competitive for the finances, more competitive for the teaching positions. But here it’s definitely more cooperative.

Ana (first-generation) also described the climate in her department as positive. She noted that although “there’s a lot of competitiveness” and “politics” in her program, she had received substantial support from, and had forged strong bonds with, faculty in her program. When she first entered her doctoral program, Ana felt “so different” and isolated as a Latina and as a first-generation doctoral student; growing up, she had no knowledge of doctoral education and had never envisioned herself as a scholar doing academic work. Ana thus experienced feelings of otherness at the intersections of her race, class, and gender identities. However, Ana felt socially and academically integrated into her department, largely as a result of the mentorship she had received from department faculty.

> I now have wonderful relationships with the professors, most of them, in my department. I’m actually working with them in a research project, and so I have a good relationship. I mean, they’ve been to my house, I go to their house. We meet in different places. We go out. I mean, now I can’t believe what I’m doing, because I felt like none of that was a part of who I would be, and this is what I do. I work with them. And so we, my advisor and I, are very close.… I like her a lot. And I know she respects me for what I do and who I am. And the other professors, I feel like I’ve gotten to know a lot of people very well.

Similarly, Cassandra (first-generation) expressed positive feelings toward her department. As a first-generation doctoral student, Cassandra initially felt academically underprepared for graduate school and experienced some difficulty relating to graduate students in her department due to class differences. “I was really faced by class differences,”

Cassandra reflected. "A lot of [graduate students] came with their privileged backgrounds, coming from private schools. They were children of educators, or two or three generations of educators," she explained. Despite feeling alienated from her peers, Cassandra felt she had found "a place in [her] department" due to the intensive mentorship she had received from her faculty mentors. Moreover, she related well to most of the faculty in her department, many of whom often invited her to their homes. "In the department," Cassandra noted, "I think I'm a very liked person. I also make an effort to like them, take an interest in what they do."

In short, respondents' narratives and standpoint reveal that supportive and collegial relationships with faculty and/or fellow graduate students help foster positive departmental climates. Although some respondents initially felt isolated and "different" because of their working-class roots, racial/ethnic background, and/or first-generation doctoral student status, intensive faculty mentorship facilitated respondents' social and academic integration into their doctoral programs. Finally, respondents' narratives also suggest that smaller departments help foster collegial relationships among graduate students.

Hostile Departmental Climates

Respondents who described their department climate in negative terms, on the other hand, consistently characterized their programs as "divided," "conflicted," "hostile," "racially polarized," and/or "dysfunctional," and department faculty as "unapproachable." These respondents felt their department was divided along racial and/or ideological lines, and these divisions negatively affected relationships among and between students and faculty. Moreover, respondents felt the ideological divisions entrenched in their departments' academic culture negatively impinged on their academic freedom. For example, some study participants reported feeling "attacked" by faculty for expressing interests in such areas as critical theory; race, class, and gender studies; qualitative research methodology; and/or social justice activism. Alberto (first-generation), for example, stated,

> I didn't like [the department]. I didn't like it because it wasn't open to the things that I believed in. I couldn't do qualitative [research]. I felt like doing qualitative work was maligned. I felt like doing critical theory was challenged. I was challenged for that. Not only

> challenged—it's good to be challenged. I felt like I was *attacked* for that and attacked for doing qualitative work, as if it were non-scientific.

Respondents in this department also described some of the faculty as "elitist" and remote. "They're very standoffish," Anthony (first-generation) remarked. "They wouldn't say hi to me, any of the white professors.... It was culture shock, coming here from [my undergraduate college]."

Twelve respondents from one department reported that graduate students had been involved in a dispute with faculty over the graduate school curriculum. In this department, all graduate students who had not yet reached ABD (all but dissertation) status were required to attend colloquia for academic credit. Various graduate students had been concerned that certain colloquia, particularly those concerned with social inequality or that were presented by scholar-activists, were not deemed "legitimate," since students attending these colloquia were not given credit. When students from the department's graduate student association expressed concerns about these disparities to the graduate advisor and faculty in the department, the graduate students were stigmatized and reprimanded for their actions. For example, four respondents reported hearing at second hand that a tenured faculty member openly referred to some of these students, particularly the men of color, as "thugs" during a faculty meeting. Additionally, some faculty attempted to delegitimize these students' concerns by suggesting that the graduate student association in the department was an "illegitimate" and nonrepresentative body.

Interviewees within this department thus felt very marginalized. Several of them noted that while their own research interests were maligned, those of their white graduate student peers were validated and supported. Furthermore, several respondents noted that some of their white male peers would make racist and sexist comments inside and outside the classroom setting, and respondents felt perturbed that faculty in this department would allow such problematic behavior to continue. Thomas (second-generation), for instance, described newcomers to his graduate program in these terms:

> This first-year cohort that came in, they're very, very, very Eurocentric.... They're saying comments out in public and in class, with nothing done about it. [They're] saying things like, "I piss on feminist theory," "Race, class, and gender gives me [an] allergic reaction," that kind of thing.

According to respondents, a few white male graduate students had been harassing and bullying women of color in the department. Thomas explained, "They've taunted and provoked a lot of women of color.... A woman of color was followed out of her department and yelled at by a white male. That would have been very much a racial thing if [it had been] a Latino or a Black man." Interviewees in this department found it quite ironic that at the same time, minority male graduate students in the department were being stigmatized. "They tried to say that I was a thug," Anthony (first-generation) wryly remarked, "but there's this guy who's going around and attacking [a woman of color], literally attacking her in front of her peers." Still other respondents highlighted the simultaneously racialized and gender-based dynamics of the situation, suggesting that these white male graduate students, guided by patriarchal presuppositions concerning the emotional and/or physical weakness of women, felt more comfortable attacking women, rather than men, of color. For example, Beto (first-generation) pointed the way to an intersectional analysis of the incidents, pondering, "How come they don't [harass] the men of color? It's an obvious point.... They are confronting *women* of color."

Although the situation in that department represented an extreme example of racial and gender conflict, other respondents also felt their departmental climates were relatively hostile. For example, Leticia (second-generation) shared that although her department is on the "cutting edge" of theory and encourages students (particularly students of color) to pursue minority-themed scholarship, it is nonetheless elitist and unwelcoming. She felt her "very conservative, apolitical" department

> tokenizes students like myself or other students who have certain politics ... because they seem to actively want to recruit students—minorities, or students of color—but then discourage you.... They don't really permit you to express your culture in the classroom.... There seems to be a lot of intellectual censoring that occurs there ... in terms of how you can approach certain discussion in seminars.... I would say that it's a very unwelcoming and exclusionary department.

Leticia also noted that "much of the time, the [department] staff seems to carry out unfair practices toward students of color, like undergrad students."

In short, hostile department climates were characterized by the intersections of racial, gender, and/or ideological conflicts between and among graduate students and faculty. Lack of faculty support and validation for respondents' research interests and standpoint, "unapproachable" and "elitist" faculty, tokenization of students of color, staff mistreatment of students of color, and racist and sexist microaggressions from faculty and/or graduate student peers all contributed to respondents' feelings of marginalization and alienation in their graduate programs. Race, class, and gender inequalities and conflicts were clearly salient, overlapping factors in these respondents' narratives, foregrounding the intersectional nature of their experiences as Latino/a doctoral students.

"The department is very white and very male": The Lack of Demographic Diversity

Regardless of how they described their graduate programs, most study participants felt that the lack of demographic diversity among graduate students and/or faculty negatively impacted their doctoral education experiences. For example, some interviewees felt they were perceived as members of their department's "Latino/a experiment"; that is, they felt their departments were only minimally, superficially, and temporarily invested in diversifying the graduate student population, as Victoria (first-generation) commented:

> The department is very white and continues to be very white.... There were seven of us that were Latinos. And all of a sudden it was just very diverse [laughs], because there were the seven of us. But we were concerned that once we finished, once we left the place, that there weren't going to be enough students of color. And I think that's been the case.... I mean, it became again this white place.

Furthermore, across fields, respondents felt their departments lacked adequate representation of faculty of color, and they felt this under-representation was especially problematic in light of the significant racial/ethnic diversity of the student population on campus and of the surrounding community. Respondents were also concerned that the lack of representation of faculty of color in their programs would result in reduced access to faculty mentorship, including both career/instrumental (i.e., mentorship that helps advance a mentee's career) and emotional/psychosocial (i.e., counseling, acceptance, and friendship) support (Kram 1985; Ramirez and Mirandé 2015). Yesenia (first-generation), for example, was concerned about the lack of women of color faculty in her program. She remarked:

> The department overall … I would describe as very white and very male. You can easily see that most of the tenured professors are white males. If not [white], then males. There are very few women of color, which is really problematic for me because there's no mentor. There's no opportunity for mentorship by a woman of color in my own department. I feel like that would be very helpful in me getting through this program and being successful at what I do.

Other interviewees also felt that the underrepresentation of faculty of color impacted them negatively, both in personal and professional terms. Xavier (first-generation), for example, was concerned about not being able to relate to faculty in his program: "There's no diversity [laughs]. It's bad, actually. It's bad because you can't relate to anybody. If I have problems … I can't just go to [faculty], especially in this department." Jessica (first-generation) also lamented the lack of faculty diversity, particularly in regard to her dissertation committee:

> I struggled [over] who's going to be on my committee.… I don't have a single person of color on my committee.… I think that they would have offered me a perspective that would have only strengthened my work.… So I think that was really hard, not having mentorship and also guidance in terms of my intellectual development around the issues that I was studying. So I had to seek it elsewhere, outside of the department.

Similarly, Susana (first-generation) felt that her white male advisor could not provide her with the type of career/instrumental and emotional/psychosocial support that a Latino male or female professor could have offered:

> I think everyone, depending on their ethnic background, has different things that they can share from their perspective because as faculty, when you're in grad school, they're not just your academic advisors. In some cases, you're asking them [for] advice about jobs and professionalism.… In my case, the Chicano/Latino professor, female professor, for example, could offer a very different set of things than my advisor can offer. My advisor's an incredible person, but you know, he's a white man. So there are things that are not going to occur to him that are challenges that I might face.

Overall, respondents' narratives and comments revealed that the lack of compositional diversity among the faculty and/or graduate student population was a problematic feature of their graduate programs. Respondents felt tokenized as graduate students of color, and they were concerned that the underrepresentation of faculty of color would result in reduced access to both career/instrumental and emotional/psychosocial support. Lack of demographic diversity thus had a negative impact on respondents' experiences with department climate.

Conclusion and Implications

This study has analyzed Latino/a doctoral students' perceptions of and experiences with the department climate. Findings reveal that Latino/a doctoral students perceive their graduate department climates as either welcoming or hostile. Positive department climates were generally characterized by supportive and collegial relationships with graduate students and/or faculty. While some respondents initially felt "different" and isolated because of their first-generation college student status, race/ethnicity, and/or their working-class roots, they eventually became socially and academically integrated into their departments, largely as a result of intensive faculty mentorship. Respondents' relationships with faculty were thus central in their assessment of the department climate, a finding consistent with previous literature. Hirt and Muffo (1998) conclude that the most influential factor in graduate students' perceptions of and experiences with department climate is their relationship with faculty, and that faculty expectations are an incredibly important factor in shaping the academic climate for doctoral study. Meanwhile, respondents in the present study voiced the belief that small departments help foster a collegial atmosphere, since a lower number of graduate students reduces the competition for resources.

Findings also revealed that hostile department climates were characterized by systemic racial, gender, and/or ideological conflicts between and among graduate students and faculty. Respondents noted that their graduate programs were polarized along these lines, and the entrenched divisions in their department's culture impinged on their academic freedom. They felt stifled in their scholarly pursuits, and "attacked" for expressing interest in race, class, and/or gender studies. Study participants in these programs also felt that some of the faculty in their departments were elitist, unapproachable, and unwelcoming. Additionally, respondents' narratives and experiences clearly revealed the salience of racist and sexist attitudes and behaviors among fellow graduate students and faculty. Overall, these findings are consistent with existing studies of Latino/a doctoral students (e.g., Achor and Morales 1990; Bañuelos 2006; Cuádraz 1993; Espino 2014; González 2006; Ramirez 2014, 2017; Solorzano 1998; Solorzano and Yosso 2001), which find systemic race, class, and gender inequities in graduate programs.

Furthermore, the lack of demographic diversity among graduate students and/or faculty negatively impacts the quality of the graduate school experience for Latino/a doctoral students. As campus climate scholars note, when demographic diversity among students is low, students of color may be perceived as tokens and subject to negative stereotypes and increased visibility; on the other hand, graduate programs with higher proportions of students of color are often perceived as more welcoming to students of color and are better able to signal that diversity is important (Ward and Zarate 2015). Respondents in the present study felt the lack of faculty diversity negatively impacted their opportunities for accessing both career and personal support mechanisms.

Overall, the study underscores the importance of intersectionality theory, a central tenet of which is that multidimensional social inequality and stratification processes cannot be reduced to just "one fundamental type" of oppression (Collins 2000). The findings clearly reveal that race, class, and gender inequalities simultaneously structure the experiences of Latino/a doctoral students. Respondents felt "different" and isolated due to their first-generation college student status and/or working-class background. Class-based inequalities, however, were not experienced in isolation from other vectors of inequality (Ramirez 2014). As individuals situated at the confluence of multiple, interlocking systems of oppression, respondents also experienced racism and sexism. Thus, the experiences of Latino/a doctoral students, including those who are first-generation, cannot be comprehensively understood or analyzed by single-axis theoretical frameworks that focus on just one system of inequality. As this study illustrates, race, gender, *and* class matter.

Finally, from a policy standpoint, the findings indicate the need to address and reform graduate department climates, particularly as a way of improving the graduate school experiences of doctoral students of color. The first step for improving department climates is diversifying the graduate student and faculty populations. Diversifying the graduate student population would help minimize Latino/a doctoral students' feelings of isolation and tokenization, while increasing faculty diversity would provide these students with greater access to mentorship opportunities and role models. However, as campus climate researchers (e.g., Hurtado 1994; Hurtado and Carter 1997; Hurtado, Carter, and Spuler 1996) suggest, increasing the demographic diversity of students and faculty is a necessary but not sufficient step for improving campus/departmental climates. Doctoral programs must do more than simply increasing the numbers of doctoral students of color and minority faculty. Findings from this study suggest that intensive faculty mentorship, relatively small graduate cohorts, support for graduate students' research interests, and collegial and supportive relationships among graduate students and faculty would go a long way toward improving the departmental climate for Latino/a doctoral students.

Works Cited

Achor, Shirley, and Aida Morales. 1990. "Chicanas Holding Doctoral Degrees: Social Reproduction and Cultural Ecological Approaches." *Anthropology and Education Quarterly* 21:269–87.

Andersen, Margaret, and Patricia Hill Collins, eds. 2001. *Race, Class, and Gender: An Anthology*. 4th ed. Stamford, CT: Wadsworth.

Baca Zinn, Maxine, and Bonnie Thornton Dill. 1996. "Theorizing Difference from Multiracial Feminism." *Feminist Studies* 2:321–31.

Bañuelos, L. Esthela. 2006. "'Here They Go Again with the Race Stuff': Chicana Negotiations of the Graduate Experience." In *Chicana/Latina Education in Everyday Life: Feminista Perspectives on Pedagogy and Epistemology*, edited by Dolores Delgado Bernal, C. Alejandra Elenes, Francisca E. Godinez, and Sofia Villenas, 95–112. Albany: SUNY Press.

Chapa, Jorge, and Belinda De La Rosa. 2004. "Latino Population Growth, Socioeconomic and Demographic Characteristics, and Implications for Educational Attainment." *Education and Urban Society* 36: 130–49.

Collins, Patricia Hill. 2000. *Black Feminist Thought: Knowledge, Consciousness, and the Politics of Empowerment*. New York: Routledge.

Crenshaw, Kimberlé. 1991. "Mapping the Margins: Intersectionality, Identity Politics, and Violence Against Women of Color." *Stanford Law Review* 43:1241–99.

Cuádraz, Gloria. 1993. "Meritocracy (Un)Challenged: The Making of a Chicano and Chicana Professoriate and Professional Class." Ph.D. diss., University of California, Berkeley.

Espino, Michelle. 2014. "Exploring the Role of Community Cultural Wealth in Graduate School Access and Persistence for Mexican American PhDs." *American Journal of Education* 120:545–74.

Fry, Richard, and Paul Taylor. 2013. "Hispanic High School Graduates Pass Whites in Rate of College Enrollment." Washington, DC: Pew Hispanic Center. http://www.pewhispanic.org/files/2013/05/PHC_college_enrollment_2013-05.pdf

Gardner, Susan K. 2010. "Contrasting the Socialization Experiences of Doctoral Students in High- and Low-Completing Departments: A Qualitative Analysis of Disciplinary Contexts at One Institution." *Journal of Higher Education* 81:61–81.

Gardner, Susan K. 2013. "The Challenges of First-Generation Doctoral Students." *New Directions for Higher Education* 163:43–54.

Gardner, Susan K., and Karri A. Holley. 2011. "'Those Invisible Barriers are Real': The Progression of First-Generation Students through Doctoral Education." *Equity and Excellence in Education* 44:77–92.

Gonzalez, Juan Carlos. 2006. "Academic Socialization Experiences of Latina Doctoral Students: A Qualitative Understanding of Support Systems that Aid and Challenges that Hinder the Process." *Journal of Hispanic Higher Education* 5:347–65.

Griffin, Kimberly A., Marcela M. Muñiz, and Lorelle Espinosa. 2012. "The Influence of Campus Racial Climate on Diversity in Graduate Education." *Review of Higher Education* 35:535–66.

Hirt, Joan B., and John A. Muffo. 1998. "Graduate Students: Institutional Climates and Disciplinary Cultures." *New Directions for Institutional Research* 98:17–33.

Huber, Lindsay Pérez, Maria C. Malagón, Brianna R. Ramirez, Lorena Camargo Gonzalez, Alberto Jimenez, and Verónica N. Velez. 2015. "Still Falling through the Cracks: Revisiting the Latina/o Education Pipeline." Los Angeles: UCLA Chicano Studies Research Center. http://www.chicano.ucla.edu/files/RR19.pdf

Hurtado, Sylvia. 1994. "Graduate School Racial Climate and Academic Self-Concept among Minority Graduate Students in the 1970s." *American Journal of Education* 102:330–51.

Hurtado, Sylvia, and Deborah Faye Carter. 1997. "Effects of College Transition and Perceptions of the Campus Racial Climate on Latino College Students' Sense of Belonging." *Sociology of Education* 70:324–45.

Hurtado, Sylvia, Deborah Faye Carter, and Albert Spuler. 1996. "Latino Student Transition to College: Assessing Difficulties and Factors in Successful College Adjustment." *Research in Higher Education* 37:135–57.

Hurtado, Sylvia, and Luis Ponjuan. 2005. "Latino Educational Outcomes and the Campus Climate." *Journal of Hispanic Higher Education* 4:235–51.

Kram, Kathy E. 1985. *Mentoring at Work: Developmental Relationships in Organizational Life*. Lanham, MD: University Press of America.

National Science Foundation, National Center for Science and Engineering Statistics [NSF]. 2015. *Doctorate Recipients from U.S. Universities: 2014*. Special Report NSF 16-300. Arlington, VA: author. http://www.nsf.gov/statistics/2016/nsf16300

National Science Foundation, National Center for Science and Engineering Statistics [NSF]. 2016. *Doctorate Recipients from U.S. Universities: 2015*. Special Report NSF 17-306. Arlington, VA: author. http://www.nsf.gov/statistics/2017/nsf17306

Okahana, Hironao, Keonna Feaster, and Jeff Allum. 2016. *Graduate Enrollment and Degrees: 2005 to 2015*. Washington, DC: Council of Graduate Schools.

Ramirez, Elvia. 2014. "*¿Qué Estoy Haciendo Aquí?* (What Am I Doing Here?): Chicanos/Latinos(as) Navigating Challenges and Inequalities During Their First Year of Graduate School." *Equity and Excellence in Education* 47:167–86.

Ramirez, Elvia. 2017. "Unequal Socialization: Interrogating the Chicano/Latino(a) Doctoral Education Experience." *Journal of Diversity in Higher Education* 10:25–38.

Ramirez, Elvia, and Alfredo Mirandé. 2015. "Autoethnography, Insider *Testimonios*, Common Sense Racism, and the Politics of Cross-Gender Mentoring." In *Modeling Mentoring Across Race/Ethnicity and Gender: Practices to Cultivate the Next Generation of Diverse Faculty*, edited by Caroline Sotello Viernes Turner and Juan Carlos Gonzalez, 161–78. Sterling, VA: Stylus.

Solem, Michael, Jenny Lee, and Beth Schlemper. 2009. "Departmental Climate and Student Experiences in Graduate Geography Programs." *Research in Higher Education* 50:268–92.

Solorzano, Daniel. 1998. "Critical Race Theory, Race and Gender Microaggressions, and the Experience of Chicana and Chicano Scholars." *International Journal of Qualitative Studies in Education* 11:121–36.

Solorzano, Daniel, and Tara Yosso. 2001. "Critical Race and LatCrit Theory and Method: Counter-Storytelling." *International Journal of Qualitative Studies in Education* 14:471–95.

Stepler, Renee, and Mark Hugo Lopez. 2016. "U.S. Latino Population Growth and Dispersion Has Slowed Since Onset of the Great Recession." Washington, DC: Pew Research Center. http://assets.pewresearch.org/wp-content/uploads/sites/7/2016/09/PH_2016.09.08_Geography.pdf

Sue, Derald Wing. 2010. *Microaggressions in Everyday Life: Race, Gender, and Sexual Orientation.* Hoboken, NJ: Wiley.

Ward, Kelly Marie, and Maria Estela Zarate. 2015. "The Influence of Campus Racial Climate on Graduate Student Attitudes about the Benefits of Diversity." *Review of Higher Education* 38:589–617.

8

Working-Class Graduate Students and the Neoliberalization of Higher Education

A Collaborative Autoethnography

Aaron Hoy, Marcus Bell, Selene Cammer-Bechtold, and Mauricio Torres

Introduction and Literature Review

"Neoliberalism," as many now observe, is a contested term. Although many definitions exist, two in particular have gained the most traction. According to David Harvey's widely cited definition, neoliberalism, at the level of politics and the economy, "proposes that human well-being can be best advanced by liberating individual entrepreneurial freedoms and skills within an institutional framework characterized by strong private property rights, free markets, and free trade" (2005, 2). First elaborated by Mont Pelerin Society figures like Friedrich von Hayek and Milton Friedman, neoliberalism advocates a crucial, though highly circumscribed, role for the state: its objective should remain limited to creating and sustaining the conditions that allow markets to function without restriction (Peck 2013). Although this often involves a rhetoric of individual freedom and responsibility, neoliberalism is ultimately about reassembling the deep economic and power inequalities that were characteristic of pre-Keynesianism and were curbed by embedded liberalism (Duménil and Lévy 2004; Harvey 2005). Importantly, though, neoliberalism is also a mode of rationality that can move between the economic and other spheres (Brown 2005). Foucault argues that this rationality is now deployed as a technology of governmentality, inducing the return of *homo economicus*, who is "an entrepreneur of himself" (2008, 226). Neoliberal rationality remakes individuals into calculating and self-sufficient actors who are unburdened by the controls of collective life and are thus free to compete in highly marketized environments. Such actors choose their actions and value all of their accomplishments in strictly economic terms. Education, for instance, is instrumentalized and untethered from curiosity and personal or intellectual growth, becoming instead an investment in one's human capital (Becker 1975).

In the United States and other Western countries, the principles of the market have extended far beyond the economy, reaching into the heart of nearly every institution, including higher education. To be sure, such principles were in effect on most college and university campuses at the time of their founding (Leslie and Slaughter 1997; Saunders 2010), and the development and implementation of neoliberal policies has been uneven and widely challenged (Gaffikin and Perry 2009). Even so, neoliberalism continues to reshape the landscape of higher education in consequential ways. As part of the neoliberal restructuring of state budgetary decisions, funding for higher education has steadily declined in recent years, leaving many colleges and universities in search of economic support (Aronowitz 2000; Leslie and Slaughter 1997). This has led to dramatic increases in the cost of tuition and, for many institutions, an overhaul of their financial aid systems (Slaughter and Rhoades 2004; Winston 1999). Furthermore, as state funding has shifted from block grants to student loans, the financial burden of higher education has been passed from the state to individual students (Slaughter and Rhoades 2004). Colleges and universities now prioritize generating revenue. Since the passage of the Bayh–Dole Act in 1980 and the National Cooperative Research Act in 1984, this has been accomplished largely through an increased emphasis on applied research, the results of which remain the intellectual property of colleges and universities and, in some instances, investor companies (Saunders 2010; Slaughter 1998; Slaughter and Rhoades 2004). Exemplifying both the material realities of austerity under neoliberalism and the neoliberal logics of privatization and instrumentality, neoliberalization has been enabled by the diversion of funding from liberal arts disciplines to those that produce more immediately commodifiable knowledge, including most notably, the sciences (Mignolo 2000; Olssen and Peters 2005; Powers 2003; Slaughter and Leslie 1997; Slaughter and Rhoades 2004). Similarly, many colleges and universities have instituted policies and practices that maximize economic efficiency (Aronowitz 2000; Saunders 2010). While it remains questionable whether such efforts effectively streamline costs, institutional cultures that stress the value of auditing and self-governance make colleges and universities more readily manageable and facilitate their partnership with private enterprises (Bansel and Davies 2005; Davies and Bansel 2010; Davies, Gottsche, and Bansel 2006; Gumport 2000). Broadly, these trends signal that the goals of higher education are now oriented less toward the free and open exchange of ideas for society's benefit and more toward the production of knowledge that can be commodified and sold (Aronowitz 2000; Giroux 2008; Kezar 2004).

The consequences of neoliberalization have been profound for faculty. Dwindling state support for higher education has led to, or at least been used to justify, a dramatic increase in adjunct and part-time labor (Aronowitz 2000; Slaughter 1998; Slaughter and Rhoades 2004). Between 1975 and 2011, the number of faculty members working as adjuncts increased by 300% (AAUP 2011). According to a report by the American Federation of Teachers, of the 1.5 million undergraduate classes that were taught at public colleges and universities in 2008, 49% were taught by contingent faculty (JBL Associates 2008). On average, faculty earn $2,700 for teaching a three-credit course, and as a result, many adjunct faculty members live at or below the federal poverty line (House Committee on Education and Workforce Democratic Staff 2014). The growth of adjunct labor within higher education, which has recently come into the public spotlight, mirrors the growth of contingent labor across a wide array of industries. Increasingly, employers avoid unionized labor and rely instead on contingent or "flexible" workers who can be let go of more easily, who receive few if any benefits, and who have little leverage with which they can initiate collective bargaining (Rachleff 2006).

For those faculty who remain tenured or on the tenure track, neoliberalism has meant, among other things, a compromised sense of autonomy in relation to their research goals and curricular decision-making processes (Archer 2008; Hammersley-Fletcher and Qualter 2009; Rhoades 2006; Slaughter and Rhoades 2004). As colleges and universities are restructured to serve the needs of business and the economy more generally, many faculty members report feeling compelled to pursue a research agenda that is financially profitable, sometimes to the detriment of their other responsibilities, including teaching (Archer 2008; Lee and Rhoads 2004). Many find themselves subject to administrative decisions made without faculty input (Rhoades 2006). Such difficulties are often compounded by an overwhelming workload that can threaten a faculty member's professional career, family life, and even his or her physical and mental well-being (Archer 2008; Bansel and Davies 2005; Wills 1996). Despite this, many remain committed to and even satisfied with academic labor, which demonstrates the pervasiveness of the neoliberal logic of individual responsibility. This logic promotes an academic subjectivity through which faculty members are self-governed (Archer 2008; Bansel and Davies 2005; Davies and Bansel 2010; Dowling 2008).

Neoliberalism has also reshaped how students experience higher education; students now understand themselves as consumers entitled to the same services and protections guaranteed in any other exchange relation (Aronowtiz 2000; Baldwin 1994; McMillan and Cheney 1996; Slaughter and Rhoades 2004; Titus 2008; Wellen 2005). As Titus explains, education has become less of a "process" and more of a "product," and students therefore expect that colleges and universities will respond to their preferences and desires (2008, 398). For many, higher education's value is primarily, if not exclusively, monetary. Financial rewards, rather than learning, have become students' strongest incentive (Astin 1998). Thus, students have also come to see education instrumentally, reframing the collegiate experience as an investment in their human capital (Becker 1975). While neoliberalization in graduate education is comparatively understudied, many graduate students appear to be no less instrumentalist in their pursuits, often stressing the importance of professionalism, productivity, and marketability in one's training and scholarship (Vander Kloet and Aspenlieder 2013). As with faculty, graduate students often feel overburdened by the demands of their education, especially when it is coupled with professional development work and independent research, but many persist in performing the role of the diligent or "responsible" graduate student because doing so is demanded by increasingly competitive academic labor markets (Vander Kloet and Aspenlieder 2013).

Importantly, there may be class differences in terms of whether, to what extent, and for what reasons students embrace the neoliberalization of higher education. Students from poor and working-class backgrounds are especially likely to see higher education as a path toward upward mobility (Armstrong and Hamilton 2013). Coming to campus from conditions of economic disadvantage, they work hard to maximize the opportunities they are given in order to escape those conditions. Thus, many enter higher education with instrumental motivations, and they may accept professionalization, even absent a fully formed neoliberal subjectivity, given that escaping economic disadvantage is at stake. By comparison, students from middle- and upper-middle-class backgrounds tend to see higher education as a means of reproducing their class position (Armstrong and Hamilton 2013). Because of their economic advantage, they may have already learned the values and norms of professionalism. It is also possible that for some, their class privilege allows them to resist instrumentality and professionalism altogether, since their families are relatively secure economically.

Even further, there may be class differences in terms of how students pursue the improvement of their human capital. Lareau (2011) describes class as a dividing line on how to engage with figures of authority, such as college professors. Her work demonstrates that students from a middle-class upbringing feel a higher sense of entitlement and willingness to engage with authority figures and institutional representatives to advocate for their own interests. Conversely, children from a poor or working-class background do not demonstrate the same level of entitlement and are often averse to engaging with those who hold institutional power (Lareau 2011). While working-class students no doubt also see higher education as instrumental to improving their human capital, their ability to actively engage in this exchange relationship as a demanding consumer is hamstrung. Middle-class students are advantaged by the neoliberalization of higher education in their ability to be the consumer comfortably and consequently to access advantageous relationships such as asking faculty for mentoring.

To date, the literature on the neoliberalization of higher education has not paid sufficient attention to the possibility that class differences exist in how students, both undergraduate and graduate, experience and make sense of higher education. In this chapter, we contribute to this literature by drawing upon our personal experiences to show that working-class graduate students sometimes have a conflicted relationship with the ongoing processes of neoliberalization. To be clear, because our approach is not comparative we cannot speak directly to the experiences of middle-class graduate students. However, given that our experiences are rooted in our shared class position, one might expect those from a middle-class background to have different experiences.

Methods and Overview

In this chapter, we rely on collaborative autoethnographic methods, which allow us to use our intimate knowledge of life as working-class graduate students to describe and analyze the complex meanings associated with neoliberalism in the context of higher education. Collaborative autoethnography is a method that combines ethnography, autobiography, and researcher collaboration, and in contrast to the positivism characteristic of so much in this body of literature, it assumes that experience is a valid form of knowledge (Chang, Ngunjiri, and Hernandez 2012). Importantly, the focus is on a deep understanding of those experiences.

Therefore, comparisons to experiences of others may or may not be applicable. Entering our Ph.D. program in sociology at the same time, we came to this paper through our shared experiences of disappointment, frustration, and stress. As we moved through our program together, we often reflected on the themes of this chapter in private conversations before and after class and on weekends. Despite differences in gender, race, sexuality, ethnicity, and rurality/urbanness, we four were drawn into a supportive relationship with each other due to our experiences of being raised in working-class homes, and identifying as working-class today, despite the prestige that is sometimes linked to our positions within the academy. Over time we discovered that we felt similarly out of place in academia. Like Vander Kloet and Aspenlieder (2013), we engaged in a pattern of analytic autobiographical writing and collaborative reflections, attempting to make sense of how our shared socio-economic background impinges on our experiences of the institutional circumstances in which we work and learn. Each of us would write in vivid and honest detail about our first two years in graduate school, focusing in particular on the aspects that we had attributed to neoliberalism, before coming together as a group to read through and collectively code our writings. We also supported and pushed one another to explore our experiences and the meanings we had attached to them in greater depth; to do this, we often asked probing questions based on our own experiences in an effort to highlight the similarities and differences among us. We then used these as prompts for further writing, which were also coded before we agreed upon the most significant themes within and across our personal accounts, as well as the ways in which they align with and depart from existing knowledge on the neoliberalization of higher education.

Our analysis is divided into two sections. In the first, we show how we approach our educations professionally and instrumentally, a method that feels necessary given the material constraints that we confront as working-class graduate students. We have families in poverty and economic hardship who depend on our incomes, and we are burdened by student loan and other forms of debt that are sometimes overwhelming; in these circumstances, academic labor presents itself as the surest opportunity to secure a middle-class income. Thus, we argue that our efforts to become professionals and to perform at a high level while in graduate school are motivated by the disadvantages that we have accrued as people from working-class backgrounds. In the second section, we describe how, because of our previous experiences with or conceptions of work and labor as working-class graduate students, we accept the demanding working conditions that have become common under neoliberalism. Even the most taxing requirements or responsibilities often seem manageable when compared to the low-wage, often physical labor that we have performed and that our families continue to perform. These experiences have instilled in us a perspective that can sometimes inhibit our willingness to describe academic labor as unfairly burdensome or problematic, even as it can overstress key personal relationships and personal stability that are necessary to persevere through a doctoral program. Importantly, the compulsion to work and learn in these ways, which might be interpreted as an internalization of neoliberal principles, stems more directly from the material conditions of economic desperation that we face. We argue against a strain of the existing literature on the neoliberalization of higher education by showing that the compliance of educational actors with neoliberalism sometimes has less to do with their passive acceptance and more to do with conditions of economic need. Overall, we attempt to illustrate how working-class graduate students confront neoliberal colleges and universities.

Material Constraints, Professionalization, and Instrumentality

As working-class graduate students, we face a variety of material constraints that constantly call for our attention, even as we work and learn. One of these constraints is the immediate and persistent needs of our families. For instance, in describing how he spends his stipend, Mauricio writes, "the little I earn … already has claims to it.… [I]t comes down to my mother and I pooling our resources to help my brother finance his schooling." Mauricio's stipend goes not only toward the quotidian expenses that are shared by all graduate students but also toward helping his mother bear the costs of his brother's education. He continues: "Last year, I consistently sent money home to my mother who herself was cutting whatever corners she could to ensure that my brother could stay in school. I offered to pay for my brother's books to alleviate the load my mother carries, but even then, it wasn't always enough." Sending money home is necessary, he explains, because these costs have become so burdensome that his mother chose to forgo the electric bill for several months in order to make sure that his brother can remain in school.

In fact, for all of us, the stipends that we receive as teaching or research assistants are among the greatest sources of income in our families, and sometimes it is necessary that we use these to help our families bear the hardships that they face. Marcus, for example, describes five of his six siblings as "stuck in the race–class grind, fighting through dead-end minimum wage jobs," with the sixth struggling to make ends meet in college. As such, Marcus' family often looks to him for assistance during times of financial stress. Like Mauricio, Marcus wants to help meet the needs of his siblings, both those living paycheck to paycheck and his sister, who is pursuing an undergraduate degree. His family and their material needs occupy the forefront of his mind as he progresses through graduate school, and they figure prominently in the decisions that he makes, shortening the time he feels he can spend in graduate school in order to more quickly solve what he calls their "material deprivation."

We also carry debts that necessarily affect the decisions we make as graduate students. These debts come primarily from student loans, but also from credit cards and other forms of debt. For instance, Selene accumulated over $80,000 in student loan debt financing her prior education, but she has taken on further debt to pay for graduate school. Initially the loans were to cover living expenses. However, it did not spread out as much as intended. She writes:

> I made the choice to take out more loans so I can concentrate only on school and get out of here as soon as possible instead of having to take time off to make survival money. I just didn't know I would have to spend so much of that borrowed money on technology, books, and trying to fund conference expenses.

Aaron also has debts, mostly from student loans, as does his wife. Together, they are approximately $120,000 in debt, which has prevented them from taking on additional loans while Aaron is in graduate school. Aaron's student loans are currently in deferment, but his wife is in the process of repaying hers. This monthly expense has, at times, cut considerably into their household income. In this sense, the material constraints that affect students from working-class backgrounds—particularly those who have taken on a considerable amount of debt—constitute a present *and* future financial burden that contributes to the already burdensome emotional and intellectual labor that comes with being a graduate student.

Thus, the needs of our families and the debt we have accrued are two of the most important material constraints that we have brought with us to graduate school, and we have responded to these constraints by embracing, sometimes reluctantly, the instrumentality and professionalization that are frequently characterized as the keys to success in graduate school and in the academic labor market. In the terms of neoliberalism, we have come to see our doctoral program as an investment in our human capital (Becker 1975). Its value for us has become almost exclusively economic, as the possibility of a tenure-track position is now identified as the most realistic opportunity we have to ensure a middle-class income. Mauricio describes this as a zero-sum game, one in which the only avenue to financial security is to earn his doctorate. As he succinctly states: "now my schooling has become my career." The pressure of an all-or-nothing mentality towards graduate school adds fear and anxiety about the possibility of failure, which would represent the squandering of his only opportunity for upward mobility. Selene forcefully illustrates this point: "This Ph.D. program is my last resort. I have to get this degree. I am so incredibly in debt that I need to have the highest credentials I can get because my social capital isn't going to help." For all of us, graduate school has become valuable precisely because it will enable us to compete for tenure-track positions at colleges and universities throughout the country, positions that we need because of the income and the benefits that they carry.

Interestingly, all authors identified tenure track jobs as the only viable successful outcome, which might be attributable our working-class background. Earning a bachelor's degree enabled us to see the professoriate as a means of achieving social mobility, but none of us had a sense that alternative career paths are possible for someone with a Ph.D. Our working-class upbringing provided many models of employment, most of which we regard as undesirable. However, our upbringing also precluded us from seeing different examples of employment that would utilize a Ph.D.

Given the processes of neoliberalization that higher education has undergone, securing such a tenure-track position will likely require that we approach our graduate school experiences with the type of professionalism and instrumentality valued under neoliberalism. Indeed, as Vander Kloet and Aspenlieder explain, graduate school has been reconfigured as career training, and graduate students are now expected to "[self-actualize] a career by adhering" to neoliberal rationalities (2013, 294). Because our shared goal is to become viable candidates for faculty positions, we need to prepare ourselves for the competition that lies ahead, and this involves becoming more professional and instrumental in our orientation to graduate school.

We learned this during the first year of our program through the professional development seminar required of all graduate students in our department. Led by a different faculty member each week, it centered on teaching us the skills that we would need in order to make ourselves intelligible to our colleagues in sociology and to position ourselves for the tenure-track job market. In addition to being forewarned about the difficulty of earning a tenure-track job, we learned how to write a grant proposal, the components of a curriculum vitae, and how to deliver a successful job talk in order to enhance our marketability as a successful tenure-track candidate capable of getting grants, and to a lesser extent, good student evaluations. All of this, Aaron writes, "seemed then, and especially now, like sound advice, but it was also difficult to hear." He continues: "Suddenly, I was up against the harsh reality that I would someday need a job and that jobs are increasingly hard to come by—especially those that offer a livable salary, health insurance, and the promise of a shot a tenure." The message that we took from this seminar was that successful academic careers are difficult to obtain and that we should therefore make every decision in graduate school based on how it could prepare us for the job market.

As a consequence, we have begun to approach graduate school with professionalism and instrumentality, conceiving of every task as an opportunity to make ourselves stronger candidates for tenure-track jobs. For example, Mauricio describes "being told to be entrepreneurial," and trying to "find some kind of use value in every term paper," including serving as the basis for conference presentations and publications. Similarly, Aaron describes his preoccupation with adding lines to his CV:

> I wanted to build the very best CV that I could, and when I looked at the CVs of the best, most accomplished academics, I noticed that many of them began professional work very early in their careers as graduate students. And so it seemed as though the only surefire way to get a tenure-track job—and the only thing that would make graduate school financially cost-effective and the only way that I could honestly expect to pay off my student loans—I

> had to take the advice I was being given whether I liked it or not. That meant attending conferences, writing for publication, and forging professional relationships that would one day prove beneficial on the job market. Everyone else seemed to be doing the same, and this created an environment in which to opt out of such professionalism seemed like a sentence to the swelling ranks of the adjunct class. For me, that wasn't an option. It was a constant threat, of course, but I had to do everything I could to prevent it from happening.

For both Mauricio and Aaron, the need to achieve professionally at an early stage in their academic careers was difficult because it was not what either initially expected, or wanted, out of graduate school. Both came to graduate school eager to study and learn without the constant worry of building a career. As Aaron explains, "I wanted to think of my graduate education as an opportunity to learn deeply, to follow my curiosities wherever they led me. I recall that as part of the application process, I wrote a personal statement in which I claimed that I was motivated by the desire to know more." Both Mauricio and Aaron describe feeling an intense pressure during their first years of graduate school to produce new and useful knowledge while still insecure and unsatisfied with their own knowledge. Because neither *wanted* to be considered a sufficiently professional sociologist at that point to try to publish, their productivity was a mostly involuntary effort to strengthen their eventual job prospects that they did not feel confident in pursuing at that moment in their program.

In addition to working toward professional achievements, Selene also changed the focus of her methodological training. Selene's interests lie in poverty and rural sociology, among other things. Both are topics that she believes are best explored through qualitative methods, which allow her to see the richness and complexity of people's lived experiences. Only qualitative methods, she explains, can "expose what rural poverty is and does to people." But she also suspects that quantitative methods will better allow her to maximize the financial return from earning her degree. Quantitative methods are more highly valued within sociology, and expertise in research methods more generally will likely make her a competitive applicant for tenure-track positions by qualifying her to teach classes in both qualitative and quantitative methods. As she notes, "I'm nowhere near good at it yet, but if I could learn enough about quantitative methods, I might be able to market myself as someone who can teach undergraduate methods and statistics when I look for a job." For Selene, being professional in her orientation to graduate school translates into learning the skills for which there is the strongest demand on the job market. If this involves setting aside some of her more genuine interests, she feels compelled to do so by the looming threat of failing to escape the tight, and sometimes unrelenting, grip of her working-class background.

For Marcus, professionalism entails a responsibility to move quickly through graduate school. Like all of us, he works to accomplish as much as he can professionally, but he is also committed to graduating as soon as possible. In an effort to curb the hyper-professionalization that many graduate students seem to exhibit, a professor once told him that students should remain in their respective programs for as long as possible. For Marcus, however, staying in graduate school "as long as possible" is anathema. As he writes, "my desire to streamline graduate school in the most effective and efficient way possible … [stems] from the reality that I have multiple loved ones who both look up to and to some extent depend on me to succeed." Marcus readily acknowledges that graduate school *should* be a rewarding experience in and of itself, a challenge to the now-pervasive sense that it can only serve instrumental ends. Yet he also acknowledges that this is not an experience in which he can indulge. For him, professionalization means expediting his graduate career, which will in turn ensure that he can better and more quickly support his family financially.

Like so many graduate students, then, we pursue an involved and often stressful set of professional activities that we hope will one day allow us to secure the increasingly few tenure-track positions available. The neoliberal context of higher education today has informed our sense of how to succeed as graduate students and hopefully as academics, but it has done so in part because of the material constraints that we face as working-class graduate students. Indeed, neoliberalism promotes a professional approach to graduate school that our shared working-class background has compelled us to accept. We have families at home that continue to experience poverty and economic hardship; any possibility that their lives can improve seems largely contingent on our success. We are also personally burdened by crushing student loans and other forms of debt; paying these off seems to depend on whether we can find positions as tenure-track faculty members. Both are reasons that we try to approach graduate school with the professionalism and instrumentality necessitated by the neoliberal regime of higher education.

This, we think, stands in stark contrast to much of what has been argued in the existing literature on higher education's ongoing processes of neoliberalization (for example, Bansel and Davies 2010; Davies and Bansel 2010; Dowling 2008; Vander Kloet and Aspenlieder 2013). Using Foucault (2008) to highlight neoliberalism's capacity to produce subjectivities, some scholars argue that it controls the "hearts and minds" of those who work at colleges and universities (Davies and Bansel 2010). For instance, Davies and Bansel write that we "take up … institutional ambitions as [our] own" and become "neoliberal [subjects] whose morality is intimately muddled with that of the entrepreneurial institution whose project is a pragmatic one of survival within the terms of government" (2010, 9). To the extent that we self-regulate according to the instrumental rationality of neoliberalism, the same rationality that we acknowledge increasingly guides institutional practices and opportunities, it is not because we are convinced of its virtue but rather because of the material constraints that we face. Thus, we join Archer in questioning the pervasiveness of neoliberal subjectivities within higher education (2008). At the very least, people who share our working-class background may be compelled to perform the role of the "responsible" educational actor less because they passively accept the values of the neoliberal university and more because the university represents the only economic opportunity that is possibly within our reach. Our motivations to pursue professional activities make us instrumental in relationship to our graduate school experiences, but they hardly come from a set of "ambitions" that we share with our educational institution; rather, they come from the need to overcome the material constraints that we and our families share.

Working-Class Histories and the Negotiation of Academic Labor

Throughout our graduate school experiences, we have often felt overwhelmed by the work that is required of us in our roles as students, teaching or research assistants, and aspiring professionals. Like many others who currently work and learn within neoliberal educational institutions, the amount of work that we are expected to accomplish is frequently a source of emotional or even physical distress. Our coursework requires that we read several hundred pages and write papers of various lengths on a weekly basis. As teaching assistants, we are contractually obligated to work an additional twenty hours per week. These hours are usually spent preparing lectures, grading, managing class logistics, holding office hours, meeting with students, and responding to e-mails. For Mauricio, who also works as a research assistant, his additional responsibilities include reading, preparing annotated bibliographies and literature reviews, and meeting with his advisor. Furthermore, as we described in the previous section, the need to build a strong CV in preparation for the job market encourages us to take on other tasks, including writing for publication and attending conferences and workshops. We estimate that these responsibilities add up to an average of 75 hours per week, although this number can increase at various times throughout the semester. With such demands on our time and energy, we are often exhausted but must remain productive. As Mauricio describes it, "I convince myself that if I can just down one more chapter or spend a few more hours in my office or in the library, then maybe I can be more productive and maximize my use of time."

The consequences of such a workload are sometimes detrimental to our psychological well-being, our physical health, and the strength of our personal and romantic relationships. For instance, in describing the intimacy with his wife that he has had to sacrifice for productivity, Aaron notes that even though they "always knew that it would be hard," they "underestimated just how much work it would be." As a result, according to Aaron, "there was a lot of tension in our new apartment.... I think [my wife] was upset, and even somewhat resentful, that I had so much to do with my time." Aaron's unexpectedly demanding workload created hostility between them. His wife struggled to understand why he needed to work so much, while his work caused Aaron to withdraw from the relationship, often against his will. The cycle of Aaron's retreat into his work and his wife's perceived neglect was a significant emotional burden on both of them during Aaron's first year of graduate school.

In addition to sacrificing time with his loved ones, Mauricio also found himself forced to abandon "basic necessities" for his emotional and physical health:

> I realized that I couldn't manage the load without in some way cutting corners. I had to scale back my personal life, which meant taking fewer trips to New York City or Philadelphia to see friends and family. It meant fewer hours on the phone or Skype with my partner, who was in Italy at the time. It meant less time for hobbies like reading (for fun), wrestling, and shooting. It even meant less time for basic necessities like eating a home-cooked meal.... There were weeks where if I didn't prepare a week's worth of meals (usually some kind of CrockPot meal), I would relegate myself to Hot Pockets and take-out or forego eating altogether in an effort to keep working.

For Mauricio, the demands of graduate school have put such pressure on his time that he is often unable to do the things that bring him personal satisfaction, including visiting with his family and friends. Furthermore, he is sometimes unable to cook for himself, compromising his physical well-being. The immediate answer was to just keep working and accept the consequences instead of renegotiate the intensity, or the eventual exhaust-tion, of the work ethic demanded of the current and future job market expectations of the neoliberal institution.

Indeed, as these consequences illustrate, the requirements of academic labor have intensified under neoliberalism (Bansel and Davies 2005; Wills 1996). This has been driven in part by the competition of academic labor markets and also by the prevalence of neoliberal rationalities, which insist that students, faculty, and administrators always use their time in the most productive way possible. Although we have also felt the psychological and sometimes physical consequences of this intensification, our previous experiences with and conceptions of work have convinced us that only manual or service-oriented work can legitimately exhaust our bodies and deplete our faculties. In turn, this makes neoliberal working conditions within higher education appear favorable to the most immediate alternative: the working-class jobs that we once held and that our families hold onto desperately.

For instance, before entering graduate school, Aaron held more physical jobs, working alongside his father in a lumberyard and occasionally paving driveways. Likewise, Marcus worked in a factory before deciding to pursue higher education. We have also held jobs in the service sector; Aaron and Selene both worked in restaurants while Mauricio worked in a retail outlet. These experiences were mostly physical and directed by standardized corporate directives, requiring us to use our bodies, rather than our minds, to accomplish our assigned tasks. As such, our previous work experiences were characterized by a necessity to adhere to standardized policies and a physical exhaustion that differs from the routine mental exhaustion that we now experience as graduate students. During his first year, Aaron was "constantly exhausted, suffering from a mental fatigue that contrasted sharply with the aches and pains I had felt as a manual laborer." In fact, he was surprised to find that academic labor sometimes "felt more strenuous or taxing" than physical labor. Thus, the differences between our previous and current work experiences are dramatic, and they center mostly on the extent to which they demand that we use our bodies or our minds.

Moreover, it is often difficult for us to appreciate that academic labor can also be taxing. In comparison to the labor that we once performed with our bodies in factories, restaurants, and elsewhere, the labor involved in reading, writing, and research seems less intense and therefore more manageable. In other words, precisely because it is *not* physical, academic labor, by comparison, seems like it should be incapable of exhausting us. As Selene explains, she is "*just* emotionally exhausted, and it kills [my] spirit. I keep chastising myself: if this isn't physical, then it isn't hard—then why the hell am I have such a fucking hard time doing this work and convincing myself that I really belong here?" For Selene, her struggles to keep up with her responsibilities as a graduate student suggest to her that she is better able to perform manual labor and is therefore less capable of succeeding academically. The differences between her previous and current work experiences create for her a sense of emotional turmoil because she feels unable to accomplish all that is required of her in graduate school without becoming exhausted, even though these new requirements expend only her mental and not her physical energy.

Similarly, many people in our families hold the types of jobs that we left before entering graduate school, and the comparison between their work responsibilities and ours makes what we do seem somehow more achievable. For instance, many in Aaron's family hold working-class jobs, including his father, who "is 61, and he still works as a maintenance man for his landlord repairing rental properties.... On the weekends, he takes odd jobs for the extra money; these usually involve roofing, and paving in the summertime." Mauricio's brother "is a kind soul who has battled addiction and depression" and who now "cuts tile at Lowe's to pay his bills." His grandmother works informally as a babysitter, and his cousin sells drugs. But the manual or service-oriented work that our families constantly perform makes visible for us not only the work that we once performed ourselves but also the work that we would likely return to should we fail in our program. Our families, in other words, perform the labor that seems the most realistic alternative to the academic labor that we now perform. This labor is what we see and know. The logic that only physical work can exhaust us and that our work as graduate students is therefore easier causes us to reimagine our current work as preferable. As Mauricio explicitly states: "when I start to think that this shit is unbearably hard, I remember that compared to slinging rocks and working custodial jobs, life in the academy, even when you occupy its lowest rungs, is really cushy compared to the labor members of my family engage in to make sure they eat, keep their power, and don't get evicted."

In short, what often compels us to work through the difficulties that we encounter in graduate school is our shared sense that these difficulties are more manageable than the difficulties that we once faced, and that our families continue to face, in conventional working-class jobs. For us, this turns largely on the distinction between physical and mental labor. However burdensome the working conditions of neoliberal universities are, they nevertheless seem more desirable than the working conditions that we have experienced and that our families still experience.

This contrasts with the image portrayed in the literature on academic workers who embody neoliberal subjectivities. For us, the motivation to work as graduate students comes less from a deep-seated belief in our accountability and more from the realization that academic labor is more desirable than other types of labor. If bearing the working conditions imposed by the academic labor system is, according to some scholars, a sign that graduate students in neoliberal colleges and universities have become subjects of neoliberalism by performing the role of the "responsible" student (see Vander Kloet and Aspenlieder 2013), we find ourselves performing the same role as a result of the perspective that we have gained through our previous experiences with, and our families' continued reliance on, manual or service-oriented labor. Keeping up with the demands that these conditions impose is not, for us, a matter of accountability; rather, it is about the recognition that other conditions are far more demanding and that these are the likeliest alternatives to the labor we currently perform.

Conclusion

Our personal experiences as working-class graduate students in a neoliberal educational context illustrates the complex relationships that we have with the processes of neoliberalization currently underway throughout the higher education landscape. Such relationships have been produced in part by our shared position within the prevailing system of socio-economic stratification. Because of the material constraints that we face, including the financial struggles that our families experience and the debt that we have accumulated, higher education represents economic opportunity. We therefore approach graduate school in an explicitly professional and instrumental way by trying to develop the skills and credentials that we will need to succeed on an ever more competitive academic job market, especially the tenure-track one. This means that we are complicit with the processes of neoliberalization that have recently transformed graduate school and higher education more generally. To be sure, the cutbacks in educational funding from the federal and state governments, as well as the proliferation of neoliberal values like instrumentality and accountability, have fueled the growing emphasis within higher education on career training and professionalism. But our participation in these processes has been rooted in our material need rather than our agreement with or even an acceptance of neoliberalism. Similarly, if neoliberalism has intensified the work expectations that academics face, we have acquiesced to this, often to our detriment—not because we believe in the version of accountability that neoliberalism espouses, but because we have seen and experienced more trying alternatives. For us, this has to do with the manual and service-oriented labor that we have performed and that our families continue to perform. Although we may vehemently oppose neoliberalism on principle, we also find ourselves acting out some of its aspects in the face of our knowledge of the few middle-class options we had originally been exposed to.

These conclusions are important, we think, for multiple reasons. First, higher education in the United States has expanded dramatically throughout its history, especially in the years immediately following World War II, and this has led to an increased number of students who were once excluded (Brint and Karabel 1989; Doughtery 1994; Rosenbaum 2001). Although disparities in access remain for people from poor and working-class backgrounds (Karen 1991), a considerable number of students who share our socio-economic status are currently enrolled at colleges and universities across the country, and it is probable that they also share our experiences. Indeed, working-class students are generally more likely to regard higher education as a path toward upward social mobility, and many work hard to take advantage of the opportunity it provides (Bergerson 2007; Armstrong and Hamilton 2013). However, as our analysis reveals, researchers should not assume that these students prefer to approach their educations in this way. It is possible that they are also motivated to see higher education instrumentally because of their material circumstances, not because they are passive subjects who have learned, and accepted, the values and logics of neoliberalism. Our conclusions might also take on added significance as the neoliberalization of higher education continues and as conflicts over this process become more intense. Mounting student debt and the working conditions faced by adjunct faculty members are among the most visible signs of neoliberalism's take-over of higher education, but other issues, including graduate student unionization and declining support for the arts and humanities, might also enter the public's consciousness in the years ahead. In these disputes, activists and commentators should seek out and appreciate the complexity of what appears to be collusion with neoliberalism.

Works Cited

Archer, Louise. 2008. "The New Neoliberal Subjects? Young/er Academics' Constructions of Professional Identity." *Journal of Education Policy* 23 (3): 265–85.

Armstrong, Elizabeth A., and Laura T. Hamilton. 2013. *Paying for the Party: How College Maintains Inequality*. Cambridge, MA: Harvard University Press.

Aronowitz, Stanley. 2000. *The Knowledge Factory: Dismantling the Corporate University and Creating True Higher Learning*. Boston: Beacon Press.

Astin, Alexander W. 1998. "The Changing American College Student: Thirty-Year Trends, 1966–1996." *The Review of Higher Education* 21 (2): 115–35.

Baldwin, Gabrielle. 1994. "The Student as Consumer: The Discourse of 'Quality' in Higher Education." *Journal for Higher Education Policy and Management* 9 (2): 131–39.

Becker, Gary S. 1975. *Human Capital: A Theoretical and Empirical Analysis, with Special Reference to Education*. Chicago: University of Chicago Press.

Bergerson, Amy A. 2007. "Exploring the Impact of Social Class on Adjustment to College: Anna's Story." *International Journal of Qualitative Studies in Education* 20 (1): 99–119.

Brint, Steven, and Jerome Karabel. 1989. *The Diverted Dream: Community Colleges and the Promise of Educational Opportunity in America, 1900–1985*. New York: Oxford University Press.

Brown, Wendy. 2005. "Neoliberalism and the End of Liberal Democracy." In *Edgework: Critical Essays on Knowledge and Politics*, edited by Wendy Brown, 37–59. Princeton, NJ: Princeton University Press.

Chang, Heewon, Faith W. Ngunjiri, and Kathy-Ann C. Hernandez. 2012. *Collaborative Autoethnography*. Walnut Creek, CA: Left Coast Press.

Davies, Bronwyn, and Peter Bansel. 2010. "Governmentality and Academic work: Shaping the Hearts and Minds of Academic Workers." *Journal of Curriculum Theorizing* 26 (3): 5–20.

Davies, Bronwyn, and Peter Bansel. 2005. "The Time of Their Lives?

Academic Workers in Neoliberal Time(s)." *Health Sociology Review* 12 (1): 47–58.

Davies, Bronwyn, Michael Gottsche, and Peter Bansel. 2006. "The Rise and Fall of the Neoliberal University." *European Journal of Education* 41 (2): 305–19.

Dougherty, Kevin J. 1994. *The Contradictory College: The Conflicting Origins, Impacts, and Futures of Community Colleges*. Albany: SUNY Press.

Dowling, Robyn. 2008. "Geographies of Identity: Labouring in the 'Neoliberal' University." *Progress in Human Geography* 32 (6): 812–20.

Duménil, Gérard, and Dominique Lévy. 2004. *Capital Resurgent: Roots of the Neoliberal Revolution*. Translated by Derek Jeffers. Cambridge, MA: Harvard University Press.

Foucault, Michel. 2008. *The Birth of Biopolitics: Lectures at the Collège de France, 1978–1979*. London: Picador.

Gaffikin, Frank, and David C. Perry. 2009. "Discourses and Strategic Visions: The US Research University as an Institutional Manifestation of Neoliberalism in a Global Era." *American Educational Research Journal* 46 (1): 115–44.

Giroux, Henry A. 2008. "Academic Unfreedom in America: Rethinking the University as a Democratic Public Space." *Work and Days* 26 (1/2): 1–27.

Gumport, Paricia J. 2000. "Academic Restructuring: Organizational Change and Institutional Imperatives." *Higher Education* 39 (1): 67–91.

Hammersley-Fletcher, Linda, and Anne Qualter. 2009. "From Schools to Higher Education: Neoliberal Agendas and Implications for Autonomy." *Journal of Educational Administration and History* 41 (4): 363–75.

Harvey, David. 2005. *A Brief History of Neoliberalism*. New York: Oxford University Press.

House Committee on Education and the Workforce Democratic Staff. 2014. *The Just-In-Time Professor: A Staff Report Summarizing eForum Responses on the Working Conditions of Contingent Faculty in Higher Education*. Washington, DC.

JBL Associates. 2008. *Reversing Course: The Troubled State of Academic Staffing and a Path Forward*. Washington, DC: American Federation of Teachers.

Karen, David. 1991. "The Politics of Class, Race, and Gender: Access to Higher Education in the United States, 1960–1986." *American Journal of Education* 99 (2): 208–37.

Kezar, Adrianna J. 2004. "Obtaining Integrity? Reviewing and Examining the Charter Between Higher Education and Society." *The Review of Higher Education* 27 (4): 429–59.

Lareau, Annette. 2011. *Unequal Childhoods: Class, Race, and Family Life.* Berkeley: University of California Press.

Lee, Jenny J., and Robert A. Rhoads. 2004. "Faculty Entrepreneurialism and the Challenge to Undergraduate Education at Research Universities." *Research in Higher Education* 45 (7): 739–60.

Leslie, Larry A., and Sheila A. Slaughter. 1997. "The Development and Current Status of Market Mechanisms in United States Postsecondary Education." *Higher Education Policy* 10 (3/4): 239–52.

McMillan, Jill J., and George Cheney. 1996. "The Student as Consumer: The Implications and Limitations of a Metaphor." *Communication Education* 45 (1): 1–15.

Mignolo, Walter D. 2000. "The Role of the Humanities in the Corporate University." *PMLA* 115 (5): 1238–45.

Olssen, Mark, and Michael A. Peters. 2005. "Neoliberalism, Higher Education, and the Knowledge Economy: From the Free Market to Knowledge Capitalism." *Journal of Educational Policy* 20(3): 313–45.

Peck, Jaime. 2013. *Constructions of Neoliberal Reason.* New York: Oxford University Press.

Powers, Joshua B. 2003. "Commercializing Academic Research: Resource Effects of Performance of University Technology Transfer." *The Journal of Higher Education* 74 (1): 26–50.

Rachleff, Peter J. 2006. "Neoliberalism: Context for a New Workers' Struggle." *Working USA* 9 (4): 457–65.

Rhoades, Gary. 2006. "The Higher Education We Choose: A Question of Balance." *The Review of Higher Education* 29 (3): 381–404.

Rosenbaum, James E. 2001. *Beyond College for All: Career Paths for the Forgotten Half.* New York: Russell Sage Foundation.

Saunders, Daniel B. 2010. "Neoliberal Ideology and Public Higher Education in the United States." *Journal for Critical Education Policy Studies* 8 (1): 41–77.

Slaughter, Sheila. 1998. "Federal Policy and Supply-Side Institutional Resource Allocation at Public Research Universities." *The Review of Higher Education* 21 (3): 209–44.

Slaughter, Sheila, and Gary Rhoades. 2004. *Academic Capitalism and the New Economy: Markets, State, and Higher Education.* Baltimore: Johns Hopkins University Press.

Titus, Jordan J. 2008. "Student Ratings in a Consumerist Academy: Leveraging Pedagogical Control and Authority." *Sociological Perspectives* 51 (2): 397–422.

Vander Kloet, Marie, and Erin Aspenlieder. 2013. "Educational Development for Responsible Graduate Students in the Neoliberal University." *Critical Studies in Education* 54 (3): 286–298.

Wellen, Richard. 2005. "The University Student in a Reflexive Society: Consequences of Consumerism and Competition." *Higher Education Perspectives* 2 (1): 24–36.

Wills, Jane. 1996. "Laboring for Love? A Comment on Academics and Their Work Hours." *Antipode* 28 (3): 292–303.

Winston, Gordon C. 1999. "Subsidies, Hierarchy, and Peers: The Awkward Economics of Higher Education." *Journal of Economic Perspectives* 13 (1): 13–36.

9

The Leaky Pipeline and the Lost Youth

Why Low-Income Students Don't Make It to Graduate School

JanRose Ottaway Martin

Plato said in *The Republic*, "the direction in which education starts a man, will determine his future in life" (Plato 1901, 112). His words have particular relevance for the modern-day United States, where education has ceased to be one of many tools for social mobility and become the primary requirement for gaining and maintaining higher social class through more advanced and more secure job opportunities. Throughout this era of exponentially increasing educational costs, low-income students have been at a significant disadvantage, struggling to keep up at every level. This has created a loss of low-income students from kindergarten through graduate school, as they bleed out of all levels of the system.

Experts and public opinion have long held higher education to be a requirement for economic opportunity in the form of higher salaries and career options (Mishel 2007; Grubb, and Lazerson 2007). The general public is aware that increased education leads to higher-paying jobs, even early in young people's careers. In 2012, the median income for young adults (ages 25–34) with a high-school education was $30,000, compared to those with a bachelor's degree at $46,900, or a master's or higher at $59,600 (NCES 2014). It seems clear that the higher an individual's education, the greater the likelihood that they will have financial success. As it is estimated that 70% of the fastest-growing jobs in the United States require some postsecondary education, these entry-level jobs are sure to become more reliant on educational credentials (Choitz and Widom 2003).

If education is a requirement for higher-paying jobs, it is also one of the only tools of social mobility for low-income students—important not only for them individually, but for the overall social and economic equality of the United States. Without some postsecondary schooling, there are few opportunities for increased wages or socio-economic mobility (Strawn and Martinson 2000). If low-income students are denied higher education for any reason, the majority will, at best, maintain their current class and income bracket, while the middle class will continue to erode.

While there has been a great deal of research regarding low-income students' access to higher education, it has largely focused on initial programs (e.g., associate's and bachelor's); access to graduate school has been largely left untouched. Perhaps this results from an assumption that admission to graduate school is an indicator of academic success, exemplifying each student's individual drive and academic rigor. However, if every level of education continues to fail low-income youth, leading them to drop out of school earlier than their higher-income counterparts, it seems likely that the relative absence of low-income students in graduate programs results not from any difference in drive or rigor, but from additional challenges associated with income disparity. Large gaps exist in graduate enrollment even between those low-income students and their higher-income counterparts who have achieved their baccalaureate degrees. According to Engle and Tinto (2008), though low-income students were as likely to desire to continue their education, only 21% of low-income, first-generation students earned a graduate degree, compared to 36% of their peers. Their study found that low-income students were both less likely to enroll in graduate school and less likely to finish once enrolled.

It is essential to acknowledge within this discussion the intersectionality of race/ethnicity and low-income status in terms of access to education at all levels. Studies have long shown minority students have many barriers throughout all levels of school, outside of economic factors, which preclude them from advancing. Among these barriers are structural racism in the educational system (Powell 2007), educator bias (Farkas et al. 1990), lack of educational options for language-minority students (Thomas and Collier 2002), overrepresentation of minority students in special education programs (Artiles and Trent 1994), and lack of peers who are educationally driven (Caldas and Bankston 1997). These factors and more affect a minority student's ability to succeed at every level of education, which is only compounded if they are also of lower socio-economic status. As racial and ethnic minorities, in general, are disproportionately represented among the poor, a disproportionate number of lower-income students are also minorities (House and Williams 2000). While it is outside the scope of this chapter to underline each instance in which race/ethnicity compounds known barriers to the low-income community, please note that each obstacle described below is likely to be even more challenging if the low-income students affected also belong to a racial or ethnic minority group.

This chapter will examine sequential levels of schooling and how current factors influence low-income students' successes and failures and their eventual educational outcomes. If we view the education system as a pipeline extending from kindergarten all the way through graduate school, we can see how attrition at each level of schooling lessens the likelihood of low-income students' attending graduate school. They leak out of the system until they are largely unrepresented in the highest levels of education. This chapter will evaluate the progress of low-income students through the education system in its entirety, starting with cultural and financial constraints in K–12 school systems, through the jump to universities and colleges, and on to the eventual arrival (or lack thereof) in graduate school. Recently, there have been some successful attempts to level the playing field, such as greater attention to college preparation during high school, specialized support mechanisms for first-generation students—often in the form of cohort-based models, technology-based learning, and expansion of the Pay As You Earn loan repayment options, which may make lower-income students more willing to finance education through loans—and stronger connections between two-year and four-year universities, which can allow low-income students to begin their education at less expensive institutions and transfer to more expensive four-year institution when their general education requirements are met (Executive Office of the President 2014). However, these solutions are not widespread across all states and all universities, and the leaky pipeline has not been fixed. The topic merits further research as well as further societal efforts to effect significant change.

Grade School and Middle School: The Foundation Years

Elementary school and middle school form a base for all students in terms of their knowledge, skills, and attitudes moving forward—raising questions about the preparedness of lower-income students. Will they learn what they need to succeed in high school and beyond? Will they learn societal norms and interactional skills that will help them navigate workplaces and community functions? Will they engage in lifelong learning and view it with pleasure, or will they try to quit school early as they don't see the point or haven't felt successful? These are competencies and confidences learned at a relatively early age. A student without a solid base will be less likely to do well in future educational endeavors, as they do not possess the skill set (Havighurst 1953). Low-income students do not receive the same base as their higher-income counterparts, and as a result they often experience more difficulty at higher levels of education and in future careers (McLoyd 1998). Due to external pressures and stresses, they are not able to gain the knowledge, skills, and attitudes that would help them navigate into higher education. Here we see the initial weakening of the educational pipeline.

There are approximately 41 million children in the United States between the ages of five and fourteen, the average ages for kindergarten through middle school (U.S. Census Bureau 2011). Per the federal definition of poverty, approximately 20% of all children live in poverty (Kaiser Family Foundation 2017). An additional 23% belong to low-income families that are also struggling to make ends meet, and face similar issues (Addy, Engelhardt, and Skinner 2013). This makes for a total of 43%—almost half of all children in the United States—who live in low-income or impoverished households. Altogether, that is almost 18.5 million children between the ages of five and fourteen living in financially stressed households.

For many, elementary school often evokes fond memories: the classic classroom settings, time with parents, and making friends. However, for these 18.5 million low-income children, there are unseen complexities. Every activity and every small purchase that has to be made—school clothes, school supplies, joining clubs, participating in sports—comes with a disproportionate price tag. Family budget concerns not only affect what these students are able to do and achieve in school, but also add strain to the home environment, negatively affecting children for many years to come. Until recently, there was little insight into how poverty affected children's outcomes in the early years. Then came the ACE studies.

ACE is the acronym created by Vincent Felitti in his groundbreaking research on Adverse Childhood Experiences (Tough 2012). The ACE studies began as health questionnaires asking respondents about their personal histories and examining the relationship between childhood trauma and long-term medical outcomes. Initially surprised by the sheer number of patients who had experienced some kind of household dysfunction in their childhoods, Felitti and his fellow researchers were also surprised by the apparent direct correlation between adverse childhood experiences and negative adult outcomes. The greater the childhood adversity in the participants' histories, the more likely they were to experience long-term health issues like heart disease, addictions, depression, obesity, and cancer. They were also far more likely to take health risks in the form of poor long-term decisions such as smoking, early first sexual experience, etc. (Felitti et al. 1998).

The ACE studies explored participants' experiences of psychological, physical, or sexual abuse. These included witnessing domestic violence and living with household members who were substance abusers, mentally ill or suicidal, or imprisoned (Felitti et al. 1998). However, no studies have directly explored the connection between poverty and the likelihood of experiencing adverse childhood events. Participants in the original ACE studies were overwhelmingly adults with health insurance—meaning, primarily, those who were successful enough to find jobs that subsidize their insurance. If low-income students are less likely to get a higher education, and thus less likely to get a good job with benefits such as insurance, then the study may have been biased towards those from higher socio-economic backgrounds. Finkelhor et al. (2013) sought to improve the original assessment tool in the ACE studies, and did find that socio-economic status served as an additional measure of ACEs, along with other experiences of trauma and adverse events. It all comes down to stress—specifically, stress on the child's developing mind.

Stress is bound to be high if a family is under constant pressure to pay bills and meet their most essential needs. Protecting children may become more difficult as stress mounts, tempers begin to fray, and emotions come closer to the surface. In these moments of increased and continuous stress, parents might lash out, and the potential for abuse or violence in the household increases. Studies have shown that even after adjusting for differences in reporting (lower-income families are more likely to be reported to Child Protective Services), child abuse is more prevalent in lower-income families (Trickett et al. 1991). Rates of domestic violence are significantly increased in households with lower incomes (Field and Caetano 2004), and research has shown a direct correlation between children living in houses with domestic violence and significantly decreased phonological and reading awareness (Blackburn 2008).

Low-income/working-class jobs are not easy. They often involve physically draining, repetitive movements and long days—often at multiple jobs—as parents try to meet resource deficits in the family. As such, parents often come home exhausted and then have to prioritize home activities, both in terms of need and their mental and physical ability to do the tasks in question. The time left to talk to children, help them with their homework, engage with school systems, and so forth, can be limited. Lower-income parents tend to have shorter, abbreviated conversations with and are less responsive to their children, so that those children have smaller vocabularies compared to their higher-income counterparts (Bornstein and Bradley 2014). Financially struggling parents are also less likely to have time to read to their children, go over homework, or teach their children outside of the classroom, with the result that children of lower socio-economic status have disproportionally weakened language and executive abilities (Noble, Norman, and Farah 2005).

Compounding the already difficult situations low-income families battle daily, a combination of neighborhood poverty (Williams and Latkin 2007) and individual socio-economic status (Jones-Webb, Hsiao, and Hanna 1995) has been tied to increased potential for alcohol and drug addictions. Such addictions in turn increase the possibility of violence in the household (Field and Caetano 2004), and can impede parenting and the provision of a nurturing environment for children (Barnard and McKeganey 2004). In households where drugs and alcohol are a factor, children are more likely to be taken out of the home and placed in foster care. These children may be shifted between multiple schools, experience breaks in learning, and face further complications. Children who enter the foster care system are more likely to experience the juvenile criminal system, have behavioral issues, and have overall lower scholastic competency than their peers who have not been in the foster care system—effects that can actually be compounded if they are then returned to their families of origin (Taussig, Clyman, and Landsverk 2001).

All this means that a huge proportion of the almost 18.5 million children living in poverty grow up and develop into adulthood without a strong foundation to move up in the academic system. There are avenues that can help—making connections with strong support networks, having a family that prioritizes academics, being able to participate in school activities—but few of these students receive any of the resources they need to succeed. Our public school system is not well financed or equipped to deal with this population and the greater support needed not only for the child, but for the parents who are struggling. Many will either get lost in the system and just "pass through," or will be placed into special education classes. As noted earlier, racial/ethnic minority status often conspires with poverty to place positive outcomes even further from reach. We are just beginning to understand how to assist these families—and we must continue on that path.

High School

As low-income students progress to high school, often with a weaker and less developed core of skills to help them continue in their education, they encounter new issues. Now surrounded by more intense social pressures, oncoming adulthood, and the challenges of making long-term life decisions—while often still living in potentially stressed homes—they are expected to start navigating their education more independently. So what happens to these students at this point? Since grade- and middle-school students are less likely to have the opportunity to leave school, high school is often the time that we see the first actual "leak" in the educational pipeline, with low-income students choosing to drop out of school altogether. On average, 7.4% of low-income students drop out of school before they complete the twelfth grade, compared to 3.4% of their middle-income peers and 1.4% of their high-income peers (Chapman and Kewel-Ramani 2011).

While politicians and the media often critique the poorer academic performance of low-income students and their early focus on the job market, we have already established that low-income students do not make a "choice" to do poorly in school. As discussed above, by the time they enter high school, they are already at a deficit in regards to language, math, and cognitive abilities. These individual variables are compounded by additional factors that increase the likelihood that low-income students will be either less academically successful than their higher income peers in high school and/or more likely to drop out of school entirely (Sikhan 2013).

As in elementary school, additional stresses at home continue to affect students' overall success. Parental involvement has been established as a tool to motivate students to *want* to do better in school and master their scholastic subjects (Gonzalez, Holbein, and Quilter 2002). In many cases, the style of parenting most effective with high-school-aged child is an authoritative approach, with clearly defined rules and boundaries, direct oversight on homework and other scholastic activities, imposed curfews, and so forth; this involves a fair amount of time and supervision (Steinberg, et al. 1992). Parents who are working low-paying, hour-intensive jobs (perhaps more than one), do not always have the time to supervise their children to the extent the child needs in order to be motivated in their studies. Unsurprisingly, continued lack of parental time and access correlates with low-income students struggling academically in high school (Sikhan 2013).

The overall socio-economic status of students' neighborhoods can also contribute to students' opportunities and outcomes. As peers become more important to students' sense of self and external motivations, their peer networks' origins, beliefs, and socio-economic status also come into play. Expectations and scholastic motivations can become shared within a peer group, so that they too influence individual low-income students' success in high school (Caldas and Bankston 1997). Additionally, research in some African American communities has revealed students' perception of a connection between success in school and "acting white" (Fordham and Ogbu 1986; Cook and Ludwig 1998). It is unknown if low-income students in general feel the need to put on an affect of "acting rich" in order to be successful, and we may benefit from additional research on this subject.

Beyond this sense of shared expectations and motivations in peer groups, low-income neighborhoods also tend to have lower-funded school systems (Renchler 1993). These school districts have fewer resources to allocate to extracurricular programs and teacher salaries, or to keep class size down; they also have overall lower test scores and poorer scholastic outcomes (Feldman 1992). Of all students, low-income youth, with their pre-existing deficits compared to higher-income peers, would benefit from additional funding for programs designed to help them catch up—but that funding doesn't exist in financially strapped schools.

While low-income students often come into the classroom with behavioral issues, lower core knowledge, and a lower sense of self (Rist 1970)—due in part to educational failure or a lack of buy-in—educators and their expectations of the child also play an important role (Cotton 1989). This issue is exacerbated if the youth is both of minority and low-income status (Rist 1970). Imagine a youth who consistently scores poorly on tests, doesn't seem to pay attention in the classroom, and has a history of spending his time with a peer group known for similar presentation and potential behavioral issues. It can be difficult for a teacher to see the potential in this student, let alone positively reinforce the youth in question. Yet teachers are in a unique position to help these students, by offering more time (in and outside the classroom), by conveying a sense of the students' value and potential, and crucially, by communicating higher expectations. Higher expectations can provide some hope to low-income students. In classrooms where students can tell the teacher has expectations, the students try to meet those expectations more consistently (Cotton 1989), which can lead to better overall outcomes.

Extracurricular activities can act as a protective factor in helping students feel more involved and invested in their schools and academic futures (Mahoney and Cairns 1997). Many low-income students start working while they are still in high school to make extra money, conflicting with school sports and clubs that often meet after school. Furthermore, school sports and clubs are typically not free. Thus, low-income families and students are faced with having to prioritize extracurricular activities over other family needs, assuming that there is any flexibility in their family budget. Even though some schools may offer options for low-income students to participate in clubs and activities for free or pay a reduced price, even the act of filling out applications and providing financial proof of income status may be too much of a hurdle for families that are not only income-deficient, but time-deficient. Such families are unlikely to use their limited time on efforts that are not strictly necessary. Moreover, low-income students may not be given those options in the first place, since underfunded schools are less likely to offer extracurricular activities.

As they experience failure or lack of buy-in academically, and as home demands remain constant or increase, low-income students begin to feel the pressure to "adultify" earlier in life than their higher-income counterparts—not only to meet their own needs but to contribute to their family's well-being (Dodson et al. 2012). These students may no longer see the point of high school or higher education when they are able to start earning money. It becomes difficult to think of the long-term money-earning potential associated with additional education in the face of immediate everyday bills and basic needs.

Low-income students who are able to surmount all of these obstacles and graduate from high school then face the choice of continuing their education or finding employment. The Scholastic Aptitude Test (SAT) required by most bachelor's-granting universities currently costs $46 ($60 with essay), not including any preparation classes (College Board 2017).

The average cost of a college application is approximately $41, with at least one school charging as much as $90 (Snider 2015). These applications and up-front fees, which do not offer any immediate guarantee of success, make them difficult to prioritize within tight budgets.

As many low-income students who decide to go to college are first-generation college students, they also lack an inherent tool that their higher-income peers take for granted: the informational resources and social capital inherent in having family members or family friends who have gone to college. Higher-income students are likely to have people in their lives who have imparted knowledge about higher education informally for years and can offer guidance. Lower-income students navigating the process for the first time in high school often do not even know what questions they should be asking. Family and friends who have experience with higher education may be able to offer advice on everything from choices between schools, to putting the cost of attendance within a larger social-cultural-economic context, to advice on financial aid choices, touring campuses, and so on.

The largest leak in the pipeline happens at this point, with only 50.9% of all low-income high-school graduates enrolling in a two- or four-year college in 2012. By comparison, 64.7% of middle-income and 80.7% of high-income graduates enrolled in two- or four-year college programs (Desilver 2014). Meanwhile, for the half of all low-income students who do continue on to higher education, challenges do not cease.

Undergraduate Studies: A History of Low-Income Student Exclusion

In analyzing the reasons that low-income students do not go on to attend, or do not finish, undergraduate education, it is enlightening to examine the history of higher education in America and further understand why low-income students have not traditionally had access to this system. According to Ronald Story (1975), higher education was originally created for the benefit of an elite of wealthy, land-owning white men, with little to no focus on the lower classes. Either intentionally or unintentionally, this served to reinforce and maintain strength among the wealthy, by creating another symbol of their status and social class that others of lesser means could not access. It is also important to understand the history of the college system, as it is upon this framework that our current system has been built.

At Harvard and many other universities during the 1800s, admission requirements were minimal, but tuition was high and selective requirements disproportionately benefited the children of alumni (Story 1975). Universities and colleges primarily accepted only those who could pay tuition. As Bowen, Kurtzweil, and Tobin point out, "their most transparent … role in 19th-century America [was] as a differentiating force separating the learned from the laboring classes" (2005, 19), thereby establishing a culture that values the segregating power of education—a culture that exists to this day. Education worked to reinforce the socioeconomic stratification of the United States: if only the rich could afford tuition, and schools worked diligently to market education as a requirement to be and become elite, how could the poor ever achieve social mobility? Restricted by their inability to pay tuition, they were not permitted to walk through the hallowed doors of higher education.

Unlike those who have been excluded based on race, gender, and religion, children of poor families have not explicitly been barred from higher education (Bowen, Kurtzweil, and Tobin 2005). Historically, institutions of higher learning have sought out "disadvantaged students," but have specifically aimed for the "right kind." These students were seen as "promising," primarily for their ability to broaden and enhance the education of middle- and upper-class students (Bowen, Kurtzweil, and Tobin 2005).

In 1862, the Morrill Land Grant Act created some of the first universities aimed specifically at the children of farmers and other lower-income groups. However, as in modern times, a high-school diploma was a requirement for higher education, and though many had advocated tax-supported high schools as far back as the 1820s, these schools would not come into existence for many more decades (Bowen, Kurtzweil, and Tobin 2005). Thus, students who could not afford private high schools had no access even to the state-funded universities of the time. Eventually, universities and colleges would begin to offer financial aid in order to make higher education more accessible to a small population of lower-class (but still white and male) students. Often, however, these students were limited in what they could study (Bowen, Kurzweil, and Tobin 2005).

In 1946, President Truman created a Commission on Higher Education in the shadow of the Cold War. The commission's task was to determine what role higher education should play in American life and seek answers regarding accessibility and barriers imposed on the basis of race, class, culture, ethnicity, and religion (Bowen, Kurzweil, and Tobin 2005). The Truman Commission observed, "one of the gravest charges to which American society is subject is that of failing to provide a reasonable equality of educational opportunity for its youth" (Zook 1947, 1:27). Seven years before *Brown v. Board of Education*, the Truman Commission recommended an end to segregation in order to make the school system stronger and more equal for all (Zook 1947). Between 1880 and 1920 some diversification occurred; however, studies at the time (which did not usually identify participants by family income) showed that those who went to college usually came from older, established families who were more likely to be "professional" (Bowen, Kurzweil, and Tobin 2005).

This history of continued stratification did not really alter until military men from World War II were offered the G.I. Bill (Bowen, Kurzweil, and Tobin 2005). Many veterans of lower-class origin took the opportunity offered and sought out higher education. This change was only seen within the military, male population, but it is notable as the first instance of a large population of lower-class people advancing to higher education, giving them an opportunity for social mobility. While the G.I. Bill did not address racial barriers, it still represents a significant curtailment of socio-economic prejudice.

Undergraduate Education: Modern Barriers and Inequalities

As only 50% of low-income students make it to college, it becomes essential to retain as many of these students as possible. Half of all people from high-income families have a bachelor's degree by the age of 25, while only one in ten people from low-income families attain the same (Executive Office of the President 2014; Bailey and Dynarski 2011).

When lower-class students do move on to some sort of postsecondary education, it often takes the form of two-year community college degree programs or technical training (Gladieux 2004). While community colleges represent reduced educational cost, there are obstacles to low-income students completing their associate's degrees and transferring to baccalaureate-granting programs at other universities (Cabrera, La Nasa, and Burkum 2001). Gladieux reports that "only one in five students from the bottom socioeconomic quartile enroll in a four-year institution … while two of three from the top quartile [do]"; additionally, those from the top quartile are significantly more likely to complete a bachelor's degree than those from the lowest quartile—42% versus 6% (2004, 21). Obstacles to finishing school include extra stress, the cost of tuition, universities' propensity to allocate the majority of their federal aid to the freshman class (to the disadvantage of lower-income students transferring in from community colleges), and academic preparation. While any amount of college education can increase social mobility, the greatest gains are reserved for those achieving a bachelor's degree (NCES 2014).

Low-income students often choose community colleges and lower-ranked schools for their location and perceived affordability (Gladieux 2004). However, schools that are more challenging or more highly ranked often have higher budgets for the very programs shown to be effective in retaining students from low-income families through to degree completion—including student services, advising, financial aid, cultural and academic groups, and campus inclusion initiatives (Smith, Pender, and Howell 2013). Paradoxically, low-income students are less likely to enroll at the institutions best equipped to serve them.

Low-income students are often also first-generation students, and may need additional assistance to complete their degree programs (Thayer 2000). Additional courses or college preparation programs can help ease the transition to higher education (Engle and Tinto 2008). For example, structured first-year and learning community programs—which group students together from the beginning of their education—allow low-income, first-generation students to meet and make connections with peers from higher-income backgrounds. This approach may help retain low-income students by creating a sense of social capital on campus (Thayer 2000).

Not having family members or close friends who attended college poses a different set of problems in regard to pre-existing social capital. Low-income students are less likely to have connections who can advise them on their choices regarding classes or degree programs, involvement in campus opportunities, or ongoing financial aid decisions, or who can provide a knowledgeable and sympathetic ear for their experiences at college, both socially and academically. Furthermore, first-generation students may encounter growing cultural separation from family members who do not understand the experience of going to college. Anecdotally, first-generation students have more issues with their family in terms of confusion and frustration from both sides regarding the meaning of and reasons for higher education (Adair and Dahlberg 2003). Families may see the student as trying to escape a life that everyone else in the family shares, while students may not feel that their families understand what they are going through. This can create schisms in the student's support network, causing additional stress.

Of course, the most obvious barrier to higher education for low-income students is cost. The affordability of college has severely decreased in recent years, with 49 states failing affordability tests designed to assess the gap between financial aid and other resources offered and the overall cost of tuition/attendance, including room and board (Kirwan 2010). Financial aid generally comes in the form of grants, tuition reduction, loans, scholarships, and work-study awards. In general, financial aid has been shown to make school possible for many low-income students, but this possibility is still constrained by determinations regarding who is eligible and how much aid they can receive. Choitz and Widom give an example: "For a single mother of two, if the family's earnings are less than $13,000—about 90% of the federal poverty line—there is an automatic Expected Family Contribution of zero" (2003, 6). However, that means that a single mother of two who makes slightly more—say, $22,530 (which is 50% above the poverty line)—would be expected to contribute some amount, even though her financial resources are still extremely low (Choitz and Widom 2003). More than two in five students drop out of college, and the majority cite financial stress, rather than academic failure, as the primary cause (Kirwan 2010). Students often leave four-year institutions almost $21,000 in debt upon graduation, while low-income students often have an even higher debt load (Kirwan 2010). Facing increasing college costs and soaring debt load, students increasingly limit their options by choosing community colleges or relatively inexpensive state institutions rather than top-tier universities (Burdman 2005).

Financial aid has steadily increased access to some form of post-secondary education or training for low-income students over the past half-century (Gladieux 2004). However, financial aid is not a solution unto itself. As programs have expanded and diversified, the increasing complexity has created greater confusion among parents and students (Dynarski and Scott-Clayton 2013). Financial literacy, the time needed to complete long applications, and the difficulty of understanding the financial aid process may all contribute to low-income students' failure to fully embrace and utilize financial aid programs. Moreover, financial aid processes must be completed annually, posing an ongoing barrier. De La Rosa (2006) found that low-income students also interpret information on financial aid differently depending on their school culture, perceptions of college affordability, and family backgrounds; as a result, financial aid has not had the amount of impact it should for low-income students. For example, they may not fully understand payback options post-graduation, which may include Pay As You Earn or forgiveness programs that make loans more affordable in the long term. Low-income students may not fully understand the differences in the types of financial aid they are offered (loans, grants, scholarships, work-study, etc.). Also, many financial aid departments do not offer the maximum amount of loans that a student may be eligible for. Often this is done for good reason, so as to prevent students from overburdening themselves with loans. However, low-income students may not know they can request additional loans as needed—for example, if their schoolwork burden increases and they are unable to work as many hours as in previous terms.

There has been some recent political attention focused on making college more affordable and accessible for lower- and middle-income students through educational tax credits. Unfortunately, initial research has shown that these tax credits may actually widen income gaps in U.S. college enrollment (Dynarski 2000), largely because they do not assist low-income families who already have lower tax liability (Long 2004). This is partially because many education credits take the form of deductions to overall tax burdens, so that families that do not make enough money to owe taxes are unable to reap any savings. Families with higher earnings, on the other hand, may well benefit from this tax credit, creating a wider income gap between the groups. The American Opportunity Tax Credit (AOTC), implemented in 2009 as an updated version of the original Hope credit, attempted a partial remedy to this problem. The AOTC broadened the scope of families that can claim the credit to incorporate both higher-earning families and ones with no tax burden (IRS 2013). But this can be problematic, for two reasons. First, the credit is only given once a year, corresponding with the annual tax-filing cycle, which does not necessarily align with school-year expenses. Families already struggling to pay their bills are likely to spend the money on basic needs, before tuition bills arrive. While this can be beneficial to the overall family unit, it does not always achieve the intended goal of making education more widely accessible. Second, families with no tax burden do not necessarily file taxes, and may not know about the availability of this credit.

Finally, low-income students often face challenges in accessing the full range of opportunities that college enrollment makes available to their more affluent peers. For instance, students from low-income backgrounds tend to engage in fewer extracurricular activities on their college campuses (McCarron and Inkelas 2006). Given that many low-income students are on tight budgets and rely on financial aid, prioritizing costly extracurricular activities over basic needs is a difficult decision. For such students, engaging in extracurriculars may increase the likelihood that they will struggle academically or drop out of school (Lotkowski, Robbins, and Noeth 2004).

As noted earlier, we are left with only 10% of low-income students attaining a bachelor's degree, compared to 50% of those from higher-income backgrounds (Executive Office of the President 2014; Bailey and Dynarski 2011). Of the 50% of low-income students who went to college in the first place, an additional 40% have leaked out of the academic system due to barriers such as those examined above. This is not surprising, given that higher education was originally designed to maintain the status quo of the class system. While efforts have been made to bring more diversity in all forms to the college campus, it is difficult to fix a system with such varied and long-established disparities. At this point in our analysis, what began as a large flow of 18.5 million low-income students through the pipeline has slowed to a trickle of 1.8 million bachelor's degree holders eligible to move on to graduate school.

Lower-Class Students in Graduate School and Academia: Included but Still Excluded

It is difficult to determine how many low-income students go to graduate school, as this has not been an area of research to date. Compounding the problem, many people go to graduate school after they have entered the workplace, sometimes much later in life. Longitudinal research is needed to establish how many of the 10% of low-income students who completed their bachelor's degrees go on to enroll in, much less complete, a graduate program. Graduate school is important in the United States, largely as a way to make voices heard: the opinions of those lacking "appropriate" credentials are often dismissed. A graduate degree in a subject is often interpreted as a token of authority. In many contexts, a master's degree is also a relevant teaching credential, affording the power to share opinions and ideas with other generations of students. To exclude low-income voices from this discussion leaves a large portion of American society silenced.

Most of the information we have about low-income students in graduate school is anecdotal, but in their voices and stories we can understand more about this portion of the pipeline. Alienation seems to be a pervasive theme within the stories of low-income students in graduate school (Sullivan 2003; Adair and Dahlberg 2003; Dews and Law 1995).

Initially, this can be felt as alienation from the family. Many low-income students who attend graduate school are among the first in their family to do so (Ambert 1998). For students in graduate school who come from families with members that have attended university, this issue may seem minute, but it can be debilitating for the low-income student. Families that provided support throughout an undergraduate degree may be confused as to why an even higher degree is needed, and may interpret the student's aspiration as a further judgment on their lack of higher education. Students in this situation may be left to find their own ways through financial aid, educational, housing, and social systems to which they are not accustomed, despite undergraduate experiences—and this time with even less familial support. Graduate students from higher income brackets can rely on advice from people they care about and trust; lower-class students do not have that option.

Beyond a lack of family support, many low-income graduate students may sense a lack of cultural support—a feeling that their culture, story, experiences, and problems are not recognized or respected in universities (Adair and Dahlberg 2003; Dews and Law 1995). In fact, there are few universities that offer any sustained programs promoting the study of the working and poverty classes, and even fewer of these programs are complex enough to convey the diversity within lower classes and respect the differences that exist, without oversimplification. The only one Sandra Dahlberg discovered throughout her years of research on the subject was the Center for Working-Class Studies at Youngstown State University in Ohio (Dahlberg 2003). While classes celebrating and affirming the diverse cultures of other minority and disadvantaged groups are offered at virtually all institutions of any size, "poverty culture" is not represented. Such lack of recognition sends a message to low-income students that they have somehow *earned* discrimination, or that class- or income-driven discrimination is not as serious as discrimination based on some other status. As their class roots are often "invisible" by the time they reach graduate school, others may not even recognize their membership in a group that has experienced struggle and class-based discrimination.

Often students are taught that a university education is their tool to "better" themselves. This line of thought assumes that what they (and their families) were before they attended university somehow amounts to "less than" the societal norms of the middle class. In her article, "Academic Constructions of 'White Trash,'" Nell Sullivan describes her personal experiences of classism in higher education: "Lessons of shame were … abundant in college and graduate school…. Everyone assumed that I was at least middle class or, if not, that I would pretend to be. In such settings, economic need supposedly becomes a moot (or perhaps mute) point" (2003, 56). Sullivan goes on to explain that she felt silenced when other students (and professors) talked about buying specific clothing as a necessity for a job, translating the comments as "if you do not have the right clothes, you cannot get the job." She consistently heard "white trash" used as a term of derision, and was repeatedly reminded by the school system that those who were poor were considered to have a diminished mental capacity (2003).

Sandra Dahlberg (2003) refers to the process of revealing her class origins to people in academia (graduate school) as "coming out of the broom closet." She maintains that the process can be extremely damaging and fill the person making the revelation with a sense of shame. Dahlberg, now a professor, states, "I have been … on the periphery of higher education, allowed measured access and systematically reminded that only provisional acceptance has been granted until I abandon my culture of origin and refashion myself in middle-class customs" (67). Dahlberg maintains that universities that serve a large body of lower- and working-class students would benefit from hiring professors from similar backgrounds to serve as positive role models and advisors, although she is aware of the pitfalls with this proposal:

> I work at a public university with an open admission policy. The vast majority of my students are of the poverty class and the working class. Most are first-generation college students…. Even in this environment, I have to be careful when I reveal my poverty-class roots so as not to undermine my authority as a 'middle-class' professor. My students … want to see me as middle-class because they are attending college so that they can "become middle class." The privileging of middle-class cultural norms in academe—that is, models of oral exchange, intellectual engagement, and subject matter—works to transfer these students from their cultures of origin to a white, middle class norm, a process that will always mark them as Other…. I am concerned with the psychic contradictions that this poverty-class–middle-class duality poses for my students…. (70)

In this scenario, there is not only the shame of having a history of poverty, there is also a powerful impetus for low-income students to see their education as a way to break with this "shameful" past, to better themselves for a different future in which they separate themselves from their class of origin.

Without further study, it is difficult to know how much of the leaky pipeline to graduate school is explained by the barriers discussed throughout this chapter, and how much can be attributed to a cultural schism. In some cases, these students have continuously conformed to the overall culture of academia, potentially at the cost of their own cultural background. Given that the low-income student is already a minority in academia, it would stand to reason that the culture of academia originates from the middle and upper classes. As students progress through undergraduate studies, are they told that they have value—not only to the school, not only to society, not because or in spite of achieving a different social class—but simply because of who they are, because of the barriers they have overcome, and because they bring a different voice to the table? If the low-income students who make it through graduate school succeed only because they have conformed to a different culture and class, then we have not diversified the voices on campus or in the discourse of higher education. We have merely espoused conformity.

Conclusion

In an increasingly global society and knowledge-based economy, it is in America's best interest to have increasing numbers of students who not only attend college, but complete their degrees. As the importance of education has risen in the United States, graduate school has become increasingly important as proof of mastery in a subject, potential ability to teach, and "expertise" in a field. If we do not offer the same opportunities to everyone in our society—if not all experiences and thought processes can be brought to the table—we weaken the potential for creative solutions to pressing problems. We also silence, to some extent, a very large portion of our society—and a very diverse one, as race, ethnicity, gender, and sexual minority status cut across social class, with many lower- and working-class students belonging to multiple groups.

Only one in ten low-income students completes a bachelor's degree. That means 90% of low-income students encounter barriers that expel them from the educational pipeline. Weakened school systems, adverse childhood events, lack of purchasing power, the overwhelming cost of higher education, financial aid and financial literacy issues, lack of familial support, absence of cultural awareness, lack of social capital, and many other factors all contribute to this outcome. It seems clear that lack of academic vigor or ability cannot be used to explain the dearth of low-income students in graduate school. More specific research is needed, not only to assess the actual representation of low-income students in graduate school, but to determine what is lost by their absence—lost by the students, and lost by society at large. Beyond research, greater efforts need to be made at all educational levels to stop the leak of low-income students throughout the system.

Works Cited

Adair, Vivyan C., and Sandra L. Dahlberg, eds. 2009. *Reclaiming Class: Women, Poverty, and the Promise of Higher Education in America.* Philadelphia: Temple University Press.

Addy, Sophia, Will Engelhardt, and Curtis Skinner. 2013. "Basic Facts about Low-Income Children: Children under 18 Years, 2011." National Center for Children in Poverty. http://www.nccp.org/publications/pub_1074.html

Ambert, Anne-Marie. 1998. *The Web of Poverty: Psychosocial Perspectives.* Vol. 1. Binghamton, NY: Psychology Press.

Artiles, Alfredo J., and Stanley C. Trent. 1994. "Overrepresentation of Minority Students in Special Education: A Continuing Debate." *Journal of Special Education* 27 (4): 410–37.

Bailey, Martha J., and Susan M. Dynarski. 2011. "Inequality in Post-Secondary Education." In *Whither Opportunity? Rising Inequality, Schools, and Children's Life Chances*, edited by Greg Duncan and Richard Murnane, 117–32. New York: Russell Sage.

Barnard, Marina, and Neil McKeganey. 2004. "The Impact of Parental Problem Drug Use on Children: What Is the Problem and What Can Be Done to Help?" *Addiction* 99 (5): 552–59.

Barton, Paul E. 2008. "How Many College Graduates Does the U.S. Labor Force Really Need?" *Change: The Magazine of Higher Learning* 40 (1): 16–21.

Blackburn, Judith F. 2008. "Reading and Phonological Awareness Skills in Children Exposed to Domestic Violence." *Journal of Aggression, Maltreatment, and Trauma* 17 (4): 415–38.

Bornstein, Marc H., and Robert H. Bradley, eds. 2014. *Socioeconomic Status, Parenting, and Child Development.* New York: Routledge.

Bowen, William, Martin Kurzweil, and Eugene Tobin, eds. 2006. *Equity and Excellence in American Higher Education*. Charlottesville: University of Virginia Press.

Burdman, Pamela. 2005. "The Student Debt Dilemma: Debt Aversion as a Barrier to College Access." Center for Studies in Higher Education Research and Occasional Papers Series. Berkeley: University of California.

Cabrera, Alberto F., Steven M. La Nasa, and Kurt R. Burkum. 2001. "Pathways to a Four-year Degree: The Higher Education Story of One Generation." New York: Century Foundation. http://www.education.umd.edu/Academics/Faculty/Bios/facData/CHSE/cabrera/PathwaytoaFour-YearDegree.pdf

Caldas, Stephen J., and Carl Bankston. 1997. "Effect of School Population Socioeconomic Status on Individual Academic Achievement." *Journal of Educational Research* 90 (5): 269–77.

Chapman, Chris, Jennifer Laird, Nicole Ifill, and Angelina KewalRamani. 2011. *Trends in High School Dropout and Completion Rates in the United States, 1972–2009* (NCES 2012-006). U.S. Department of Education. Washington, DC: National Center for Education Statistics.

Choitz, Victoria, and Rebecca Widom. 2003. *Money Matters: How Financial Aid Affects Nontraditional Students in Community Colleges*. New York: MDRC.

College Board. 2017. "SAT Suite of Assessments: Fees." http://sat.collegeboard.org/register/us-services-fees

Cook, Philip J., and Jens Ludwig. 1998. "The Burden of 'Acting White': Do Black Adolescents Disparage Academic Achievement?" In *The Black-White Test Score Gap*, edited by Christopher Jencks and Meredith Phillips, 375–400. Washington, DC: Brookings Institution Press.

Cotton, Kathleen. 1989. *Expectations and Student Outcomes*. Portland, OR: Northwest Regional Educational Laboratory.

Dahlberg, Sandra L. 2003. "Survival in a Not So Brave New World." In *Reclaiming Class: Women, Poverty, and the Promise of Higher Education in America*, edited by Vivyan C. Adair and Sandra L. Dahlberg, 67–84. Philadelphia: Temple University Press.

De La Rosa, Mari Luna. 2006. "Is Opportunity Knocking? Low-Income Students' Perceptions of College and Financial Aid." *American Behavioral Scientist* 49 (12): 1670–86.

Desilver, Drew. 2014. "College Enrollment among Low-Income Students

Still Trails Richer Groups." Pew Research Center Fact Tank. January 15. http://www.pewresearch.org/fact-tank/2014/01/15/college-enrollment-among-low-income-students-still-trails-richer-groups

Dews, C. L. Barney, and Carolyn Leste Law, eds. 1995. *This Fine Place So Far from Home: Voices of Academics from the Working Class*. Philadelphia: Temple University Press.

Dodson, Lisa, Randy Albeda, Diana Salas Coronado, and Marya Mtshali. 2012. "How Youth Are Put at Risk by Parents' Low-Wage Jobs." Center for Social Policy Publications 68. Boston: University of Massachusetts.

Dynarski, Susan. 2000. "Hope for Whom? Financial Aid for the Middle Class and Its Impact on College Attendance." NBER Working Paper 7756. Cambridge, MA: National Bureau of Economic Research.

Engle, Jennifer, and Vincent Tinto. 2008. "Moving Beyond Access: College Success for Low-Income, First-Generation Students." Pell Institute for the Study of Opportunity in Higher Education. Washington, DC: Pell Institute.

Executive Office of the President. 2014. "Increasing College Opportunity for Low-Income Students." January 16. Washington, DC: author. https://obamawhitehouse.archives.gov/sites/default/files/docs/increasing_college_opportunity_for_low-income_students_report.pdf

Farkas, George, Robert P. Grobe, Daniel Sheehan, and Yuan Shuan. 1990. "Cultural Resources and School Success: Gender, Ethnicity, and Poverty Groups within an Urban School District." *American Sociological Review* 55 (1): 127–42.

Feldman, Sandra. 1992. "Children in Crisis: The Tragedy of Underfunded Schools and the Students They Serve." *American Educator* 16 (1): 8–17.

Felitti, Vincent J., Robert F. Anda, Dale Nordenberg, David F. Williamson, Alison M. Spitz, Valerie Edwards, Mary P. Koss, and James S. Marks. 1998. "Relationship of Childhood Abuse and Household Dysfunction to Many of the Leading Causes of Death in Adults: The Adverse Childhood Experiences (ACE) Study." *American Journal of Preventive Medicine* 14 (4): 245–58.

Field, Craig A., and Raul Caetano. 2004. "Ethnic Differences in Intimate Partner Violence in the U.S. General Population: The Role of Alcohol Use and Socioeconomic Status." *Trauma, Violence, and Abuse* 5 (4): 303–17.

Finkelhor, David, Anne Shattuck, Heather Turner, and Sherry Hamby.

2013. "Improving the Adverse Childhood Experiences Study Scale." *JAMA Pediatrics* 167 (1): 70–75.

Fordham, Signithia, and John U. Ogbu. 1986. "Black Students' School Success: Coping with the 'Burden of "Acting White"'." *Urban Review* 18 (3): 176–206.

Gerardi, Steven. 2006. "Positive College Attitudes among Minority and Low-Income Students as an Indicator of Academic Success." *Social Science Journal* 43 (1): 185–90.

Gladieux, Lawrence E. 2004. "Low-Income Students and the Affordability of Higher Education." In *America's Untapped Resource: Low-Income Students in Higher Education,* edited by R. Kahlenberg, 17–53. New York: Century Foundation Press.

Gonzalez, Alyssa R., Marie F. Doan Holbein, and Shawn Quilter. 2002. "High School Students' Goal Orientations and Their Relationship to Perceived Parenting Styles." *Contemporary Educational Psychology* 27 (3): 450–70.

Grubb, W. Norton, and Marvin Lazerson. 2007. *The Education Gospel: The Economic Power of Schooling.* Cambridge, MA: Harvard University Press.

Havighurst, Robert J. 1953. *Human Development and Education.* New York: Longmans, Green.

House, James S., and David R. Williams. 2000. "Understanding and Reducing Socioeconomic and Racial/Ethnic Disparities in Health." In *Promoting Health: Intervention Strategies from Social and Behavioral Research,* edited by Brian D. Smedley and S. Leonard Syme, 81–124. Washington, DC: National Academy Press.

Internal Revenue Service [IRS]. 2013. "American Opportunity Tax Credit." Last modified May 31. https://www.irs.gov/uac/american-opportunity-tax-credit

Jones-Webb, Rhonda J., Charng-Yi Hsiao, and Peter Hannan. 1995. "Relationships between Socioeconomic Status and Drinking Problems among Black and White Men." *Alcoholism: Clinical and Experimental Research* 19 (3): 623–27.

Johnson, Kirk A. 2000. "The Peer Effect on Academic Achievement among Public Elementary School Students." Heritage Center for Data Analysis CDA00-06. Washington, DC: Heritage Foundation. http://www.heritage.org/research/reports/2000/05/peer-effect-on-achievement-among-elementary-school-students

Kaiser Family Foundation. 2017. "Poverty Rate by Age, 2015." State Health Facts. http://kff.org/other/state-indicator/poverty-rate-by-age

Kirwan, William E. 2010. "Investing in Student Success." *Change: The Magazine of Higher Learning* 42 (3): 14–16.

Long, Bridget T. 2004. "The Impact of Federal Tax Credits for Higher Education Expenses." In *College Choices: The Economics of Where to Go, When to Go, and How to Pay for It*, edited by Carloine M. Hoxby, 101–68. Chicago: University of Chicago Press.

Lotkowski, Veronica A., Steven B. Robbins, and Richard J. Noeth. 2004. "The Role of Academic and Non-Academic Factors in Improving College Retention." ACT Policy Report. Iowa City, IA: ACT.

Mahoney, Joseph L., and Robert B. Cairns. 1997. "Do Extracurricular Activities Protect against Early School Dropout?" *Developmental Psychology* 33 (2): 241–53.

McCarron, Graziella Pagliarulo, and Karen Kurotsuchi Inkelas. 2006. "The Gap between Educational Aspirations and Attainment for First-Generation College Students and the Role of Parental Involvement." *Journal of College Student Development* 47 (5): 534–49.

McLoyd, Vonnie C. 1998. "Socioeconomic Disadvantage and Child Development." *American Psychologist* 53 (2): 185–204.

Mishel, Lawrence. 2007. "Future Jobs Much Like Current Jobs." Economic Policy Institute. December 19. http://www.epi.org/economic_snapshots/entry/webfeatures_snapshots_20071219

National Center for Education Statistics [NCES]. 2014. "Income of Young Adults." Fast Facts. http://nces.ed.gov/fastfacts/display.aspid=77

Noble, Kimberly G., M. Frank Norman, and Martha J. Farah. 2005. "Neurocognitive Correlates of Socioeconomic Status in Kindergarten Children." *Developmental Science* 8 (1): 74–87.

Plato. 1901. *The Republic of Plato: An Ideal Commonwealth*. Revised edition. Translated by Benjamin Jowett. New York: Colonial Press.

Powell, John A. 2007. "Structural Racism: Building upon the Insights of John Calmore." *North Carolina Law Review* 86:791–816.

Renchler, Ron. 1993. "Poverty and Learning." ERIC Digest 83. ED357433. http://files.eric.ed.gov/fulltext/ED357433.pdf

Rist, Ray. 1970. "Student Social Class and Teacher Expectations: The Self-Fulfilling Prophecy in Ghetto Education." *Harvard Educational Review*

40 (3): 411–51.

Sikhan, Kara. 2013. "Low-Income Students Six Times More Likely to Drop Out of High School." World Socialist Web Site. April 10. https://www.wsws.org/en/articles/2013/04/10/hsdo-a10.html

Smith, Jonathan, Matea Pender, and Jessica Howell. 2013. "The Full Extent of Student–College Academic Undermatch." *Economics of Education Review* 32:247–61.

Snider, Susannah. 2014. "Colleges that Charge the Most for Applying." *U.S. News and World Report.* December 1. https://www.usnews.com/education/best-colleges/the-short-list-college/articles/2015/12/01/colleges-that-charge-students-the-most-to-apply

Steinberg, Laurence, Susie D. Lamborn, Sanford M. Dornbusch, and Nancy Darling. 1992. "Impact of Parenting Practices on Adolescent Achievement: Authoritative Parenting, School Involvement, and Encouragement to Succeed." *Child Development* 63 (5): 1266–81.

Story, Ronald. 1975. "Harvard Students, the Boston Elite, and the New England Preparatory System, 1800–1876." *History of Education Quarterly* 15 (3): 281–98.

Strawn, Julie, and Karin Martinson. 2000. *Steady Work and Better Jobs: How to Help Low-Income Parents Sustain Employment and Advance in the Workforce.* New York: MDRC.

Sullivan, Nell. 2003. "Academic Constructions of 'White Trash,' or How to Insult Poor People without Really Trying." In *Reclaiming Class: Women, Poverty, and the Promise of Higher Education in America*, edited by Vivyan C. Adair and Sandra L. Dahlberg, 53–66. Philadelphia: Temple University Press.

Taussig, Heather N., Robert B. Clyman, and John Landsverk. 2001. "Children Who Return Home from Foster Care: A 6-year Prospective Study of Behavioral Health Outcomes in Adolescence." *Pediatrics* 108 (1): e10. doi:10.1542/peds.108.1.e10

Thayer, Paul B. 2000. "Retention of Students from First Generation and Low Income Backgrounds." U.S. Department of Education. Washington, DC: National TRIO Clearinghouse.

Thomas, Wayne P., and Virginia P. Collier. 2002. "A National Study of School Effectiveness for Language Minority Students' Long-Term Academic Achievement." Center for Research on Education, Diversity, and Excellence. Santa Cruz: University of California.

Tough, Paul. 2012. *How Children Succeed: Grit, Curiosity, and the Hidden Power of Character*. Boston: Houghton Mifflin Harcourt.

Trickett, Penelope K., J. Lawrence Aber, Vicki Carlson, and Dante Cicchetti. 1991. "Relationship of Socioeconomic Status to the Etiology and Developmental Sequelae of Physical Child Abuse." *Developmental Psychology* 27 (1): 148–58.

U.S. Census Bureau. 2011. "Back to School 2011–2012." Facts for Features. June 27. http://www.census.gov/newsroom/releases/archives/facts_for_features_special_editions/cb11-ff15.html

Williams, Chyvette T., and Carl A. Latkin. 2007. "Neighborhood Socioeconomic Status, Personal Network Attributes, and Use of Heroin and Cocaine." *American Journal of Preventive Medicine* 32 (6): S203–S210.

Zook, George F. 1947. *Higher Education for American Democracy*. Report of the Commission on Higher Education. 6 vols. Washington, DC: U.S. Government Printing Office.

10

First-Generation Graduates
Challenges in Transitioning into Employment

Malar Hirudayaraj

The socio-economic and cultural challenges that first-generation students face during their undergraduate years do not disappear upon graduation and continue to impact their educational outcomes in graduate school (Kniffin 2007; Gardner 2013; Holley and Gardner 2012) and their employment outcomes beyond (Hirudayaraj 2014). Researchers have documented the issues faced by first-generation students in postsecondary education, including access, academic preparedness, education outcomes, academic and social integration, lack of information, and awareness.[1] However, the existing research on first-generation students rarely forays beyond their undergraduate years. Researchers who attempt to examine the experiences of first-generation college graduates in workplaces mostly focus on those of first-generation faculty in post-secondary education. Very few studies explore the challenges faced by first-generation master's degree holders who are seeking employment that is commensurate with their qualifications or the difficulties they encounter in workplaces outside of academia. In this chapter, I present what we know about the experiences of first-generation college graduates (first-generation students who have graduated with bachelor's, master's, or doctoral degrees) as they prepare to transition into the labor market, identify areas for further research, and argue for the need to investigate the impact of first-generation status on transitioning into professional employment.

Background

College education is considered the great leveler (Pascarella et al. 2004; Brown and Hesketh 2004; Brown, Hesketh, and Williams 2003), the "X factor" that enables students who did not enter college on equal terms with their more privileged peers to exit on equal terms with them. Policy-makers believe that college education negates the impact of structural barriers such as lack of education in the family, that higher education levels out the playing field, and that creating equal access to higher education will lead to equal opportunities or outcomes after college (Lynch 2000). These beliefs feed into the assumption that exposure to college education compensates for the cultural and social capital their families could not offer, and therefore that graduates, regardless of their backgrounds, leave college enriched in knowledge and awareness about the world of the educated (Pascarella et al. 2004). Such an assumption ignores decades of research providing evidence of the unique challenges faced by students due to their educational biographies or parental level of education (Thomas and Quinn 2007). Among all structural barriers, first-generation status is most determining of students' educational access or attainment, and of their social and economic status attainment after college (Pascarella et al. 2004; Thomas and Quinn 2007), yet little work has been done on how first-generation status impacts employment outcomes after graduation (Hirudayaraj 2014).

The Graduate Labor Market

To understand the challenges first-generation graduates face in their attempts to gain access to professional employment that matches their qualifications, we must begin with a discussion of the graduate employment context. Contrary to the popular belief that advanced degrees are driven by market needs, the job market for advanced degree holders is not always very discrete or segmented from the market for bachelor's degree holders, and the recruitment processes are not clearly defined (Tomilson 2012). Even though there is a growing emphasis on producing more highly skilled employees for the knowledge economy, not many industries recruit and nurture fresh advanced degree holders. For instance, the most recent National Association of Colleges and Employers report shows that while 98.2% of the U.S. employers who participated in the study planned to hire new bachelor's degree holders, only 75.4% had plans to hire master's degree holders (NACE 2016). In fact, the Bureau of Labor Statistics reports that only 33 fields specifically require a master's degree for entry and that the wage premium for a master's degree varies across industries (Torpey and Terrell 2015). Graduates in disciplines such as business, engineering, and computer and information sciences have greater opportunity, followed by math and science graduates. Employers seek master's degree holders primarily because of their superior and updated subject knowledge. Most employers also expect master's degree holders to demonstrate higher levels of maturity, problem-solving ability, leadership, and commercial or industry awareness (Tomilson 2012; Wender et al. 2010; Wender et al. 2012). Among master's degree holders in the United States, 30% are employed in the private sector, 22% in education, and the rest in the nonprofit and public sectors (Wender et al. 2010). However, very little is known about the career pathways of master's degree holders outside academia, beyond which industries prefer master's degree holders and what the median salaries of these employees are (Wender et al. 2012). What we know is that graduates who complete master's degrees in programs such as business and education, which are closely related to labor market needs, face lower unemployment rates than master's degree holders in the arts and humanities (Torpey and Terrell 2015). We are still in the process of exploring the set of specific challenges that first-generation master's degree holders face as they navigate the recruitment processes into appropriate professional employment.

First-Generation Master's Degree Holders

Professional work environments are predominantly populated and controlled by groups that enjoy inherited privilege because of their race, class, gender, and/or educational background (Brown and Hesketh 2004). In his book on first-generation graduates, *Limbo: Blue-Collar Roots, White-Collar Aspirations,* Alfred Lubrano (2004) captures the lived experiences of first-generation individuals with advanced degrees, some from the most elite universities in the country. Lubrano describes these first-generation graduates who try to have a foot in two worlds—the one of their origin and the one that they aspire to enter—as "straddlers." These individuals struggle to navigate toward and work in environments that are not culturally familiar, and force them to learn new norms of being and behaving. What we understand from the experiences of Lubrano's straddlers is that their socio-cultural struggles persist after their years in college and into the world of work.[2]

My interactions with first-generation master's degree holders and doctoral students during my doctoral studies and my dissertation research show that first-generation master's degree holders trying to use their educational credentials to break into environments of privilege report challenges that are similar to those expressed by first-generation bachelor's degree holders (Hirudayaraj 2014). My doctoral dissertation focused on understanding the challenges first-generation graduates faced in obtaining professional employment within the corporate sector. For this dissertation research I interviewed 14 first-generation graduates (bachelor's and master's degree holders) working in a multinational financial corporation in the United States. Of these 14 interviewees, ten were female and four were male; seven were African American and seven were Caucasian; six were master's degree holders and eight had bachelor's degrees. All of 14 of them worked in a midwestern metropolitan city in the United States. While the examples that illustrate the transition challenges of first-generation master's degree holders in this chapter are primarily drawn from my dissertation research, some are drawn from my interactions with first-generation graduates as a doctoral student interested in the subject of employability of first-generation graduates. My interactions with first-generation master's degree holders indicated that graduate school did not create an overall familiarity with the professional world that these individuals aspired to enter. As they sought to transition into careers outside academia, these first-generation master's degree holders were distinctly disadvantaged on four grounds: career decision-making, career preparation, access to professionals in one's chosen field, and familiarity with expectations of the professional world.

Career Decision-Making

First-generation students are often the pride of their families. They may receive emotional support from their families when they struggle in school or college, but rarely any guidance regarding academic or career choices or preparation for a career. These families lack the knowledge required to give informed advice about college majors or career pathways. The environments first-generation graduates grow up in do not foster future-oriented conversations that help them explore their interests and strengths as individuals or consider professional career options. Rarely do families of first-generation students inquire about the students' career aspirations or goals, or help them connect their strengths and talents to career pathways. Without reflective conversations, opportunities for self-appraisal, or future-oriented discussions within the family, even academically gifted first-generation students enter college with very basic ideas about careers. If their families do not speak about careers much, neither do most of their professors. During their undergraduate years, first-generation students often go from course to course, year to year without actual opportunities to identify a field of interest or connect their interests to academic pathways or a career. Consequently, most first-generation students pursue a major without considering the career pathways to which it could lead, in contrast to the career-based academic choices that non-first-generation graduates seem to make.

Much the same applies at the graduate level. Even though first-generation master's students choose their program based on some interest sparked during their undergraduate years, they often embark on the graduate journey uninformed about the career options associated with those programs. For instance, I had occasion to interact with a part-time shuttle bus driver at a midwestern university, who earned a master's degree in a humanities field from a land-grant university near his hometown. He had applied and been admitted into the program because he liked working with people and had a 3.6 undergraduate GPA, but he did not know what kind of jobs he could obtain with a master's degree in his field. This first-generation master's degree holder could not find a job that required a master's degree in the small midwestern college town where he found himself and was forced to work as a shuttle bus driver for five years until he found a better job in the closest city. First-generation graduates like this bus driver often fail to thoroughly consider the option of acquiring a master's degree. First, they do not consider why a master's degree might benefit them (Lunceford 2011; Lopez 2014; Carlton 2015). Second, they do not deliberate as to whether an advanced degree in a particular field would suit their particular circumstances, or whether it would be better for them to pursue a master's degree immediately after their bachelor's degree or after a few years of work experience in a relevant field (Wender et al. 2012). Third, they do not research where they should pursue a master's degree. Not thinking through these decisions often results in first-generation students like the bus driver starting an advanced degree program with vaguely defined career goals and without being fully aware of the challenges in realizing those goals.

This shuttle bus driver did not have anyone in his close family circle to advise him about appropriate career pathways or to model a successful transition to a professional career. Many graduates in a similar situation have started advanced degree programs at smaller institutions close to their homes, or that were otherwise familiar to them, without understanding the implications of their choices. They do not understand that employers who recruit master's degree holders prefer recruiting graduates from elite universities and renowned programs over those from smaller colleges or lesser-known programs (Brown and Hesketh 2004; Tomilson 2012). Moreover, first-generation graduate students in smaller institutions or rural locations are denied the opportunity to participate in the robust career fairs organized by top-tier institutions. When employers do not go out of their way to recruit advanced degree holders from lesser-known or smaller universities, the onus is on the graduate to seek out the employers, which greatly reduces their chances. When the supply of graduates exceeds the demand in any given field, or when the pool of graduates available to choose from is large, recruiting processes tend to favor graduates from privileged backgrounds and elite universities.

Career Preparation

If not thinking through their graduate education options hurts first-generation graduates in terms of getting hired, their preparation for the world of work—or the lack of it—adds an additional challenge to their employment prospects. In her influential book on child-rearing practices across different classes, Annette Lareau (2003) captured the differences between the preparatory practices of parents with a college education and professional employment as compared with parents with no college education and blue-collar jobs. Lareau showed that college-educated parents with professional careers understood the need to prepare their children from the elementary-school years for college and beyond, and made deliberate efforts to provide their children with the experiences and confidence required to maximize their privilege. On the contrary, parents with no college education did not see the need to provide preparatory experiences to their children and did not know how to nurture the children's talents. This lack of understanding continues to influence first-generation students in their preparation for employment, even if they possess a master's degree.

Parents of first-generation students often believe that earning a degree is sufficient to enter professional employment (Hirudayaraj 2014). They may not appreciate the role of extracurricular activities and experiences in developing and demonstrating a well-rounded personality and may underrate the importance of creating opportunities to nurture the talents or gifts of their children. Most lower-income parents cannot afford such experiences in any case, yet even those parents who could afford them do not see the need. First-generation students, therefore, may grow up without understanding the need to prepare to demonstrate a persona that would appeal to employers. The primary goal, even of highly motivated and determined first-generation undergraduate and graduate students, is to graduate; the "what next" question most often arises only upon graduation.

If they do not understand the need to prepare to enter the professional world, first-generation students will not seek out experiences that would attract the attention of employers. Employers clearly state their preference for applicants with some relevant work experience over young master's degree holders who lack it (Tomilson 2012). Yet most first-generation students in my study did not take up an internship (especially if it was unpaid) or co-op opportunities in their undergraduate years, and their work experience was mostly in blue-collar jobs not related to the fields they aspired to enter. Unaware that employers expected them to show work experience in environments similar to the ones they aspired to join, first-generation graduate students predominantly pursued blue-collar jobs during their student years. Without relevant work experience and the opportunities to hone their leadership skills, teamwork, and professional communication, first-generation master's students graduated very much like their undergraduate counterparts: unprepared to satisfy the expectations of employers.

For instance, one participant in my research had a master's degree in finance, but he worked for a large multinational financial institution in an entry-level position that did not require anything more than a high-school diploma. He was a first-generation graduate who had worked in a bar during his undergraduate and graduate years. He shared that he was twice rejected for a job he was qualified for because his résumé did not demonstrate leadership skills, the ability to work in a team in a professional setting, or the capacity to convert his academic knowledge into practical solutions in work situations. Therefore, despite his master's degree, he was forced to start in a data-entry position, gain experience in a relevant environment, cultivate familiarity with the professional world, and then work his way up toward a position commensurate with his academic credentials. The graduates who were successful in gaining a position that matched their educational qualifications were those that sought experiences that could catch the attention of employers. In the group of 14 that I interviewed, there was one who utilized a practicum opportunity as part of his M.B.A. program and joined the same organization upon graduation in a middle-managerial-level position. None of the others took advantage of such options.

On one level, first-generation graduates can fail to understand the need for white-collar work experiences; on another, their part-time, blue-collar jobs deprive them of the opportunity to spend more time on campus or acquire what Mary Kosut (2006) has called *temporal capital.* Since they spend less time on campus, their interaction with faculty is limited to the classroom, providing fewer opportunities for the faculty to get to know them. Restricted access to temporal capital can also prevent first-generation graduate students from developing vital academic networks that could ease their pathways into positions suitable to their qualifications. Most of the first-generation graduates I interviewed completed their master's programs without a robust relationship with their faculty; worse still, they graduated without being aware that a lack of such connections could impact their job prospects. For instance, strong and positive recommendation letters detailing the strengths, academic ability, and people and leadership skills of a graduate are an essential aspect of the entry process into many managerial or professional jobs. However, if first-generation graduate students fail to cultivate effective relationships with faculty, they cannot expect personalized letters that project them as suitable candidates for higher-level positions suited to their qualifications. More importantly, restricted networking with faculty also prevents first-generation graduates from capitalizing on the contacts of their faculty within the job market. Rather than the more effective process of gaining entry into the professional world through referrals (Crispin and Mehler 2013), first-generation graduates often resort to applying for openings posted in job or company websites—a route that lessens the possibility of being called for an interview.

In the absence of guidance from within their families and personal circles, first-generation students may nonetheless rely on campus resources such as academic advisors, faculty, career counselors, or informal mentors for support in making career decisions and seeking employment. Yet these very students hesitate to use such campus resources (Hirudayaraj 2014). The academic advisors who helped them navigate their coursework and proceed toward graduation are often not equipped to indicate how these academic pathways could connect to a career after college (Kniffin 2007; Wender et al. 2010; Wender et al. 2012). Just as first-generation students rarely muster the courage to talk to faculty outside class or seek their guidance, very few first-generation graduates I interviewed had visited the career services office on campus or sought the support of professional career counselors to prepare for their transition into employment (Hirudayaraj 2014). Career counselors are equipped to help students comb their academic, extracurricular, and work-related experiences and identify situations where they demonstrated the much-needed soft skills or attributes that employers look for, such as leadership, collaboration, conflict resolution, or the ability to communicate with and relate to diverse groups. Nevertheless, none of the first-generation graduate participants in the study I conducted ever visited career services during their college years. Without purposeful conversations with career counselors, the résumé of a first-generation graduate often consists of a string of part-time work experiences listing job titles and organizations. One first-generation M.B.A. graduate I interviewed confessed that she did not know what a typical résumé for a corporate position looked like or what skills and experiences needed to be included and highlighted until she started attending the career development sessions on her first entry-level job within a multinational corporation. Like her fellow first-generation graduates in the study, she felt that she was not adequately prepared to meet the expectations of the employers even after graduating with a master's degree, and therefore was forced to start at an entry-level position in a large organization. First-generation graduates like these most often knock on professional doors without adequate awareness of the need to prepare for employment that matches their qualifications. As another participant explained, only after getting a glimpse into the industry did she realize that her educational credentials unfortunately were just the entry ticket, and that years of deliberate preparation need to precede access to graduate-level employment.

Access to Professionals

An important factor that challenges first-generation graduates' preparation for and progression into employment commensurate with their education is a lack of networks or personal contacts within the professional world. Parents of first-generation students are predominantly in blue-collar or technical jobs with limited access to the professional world. This lack of proximity results in first-generation graduates not having access to individuals within their circle or sponsors from within the profession who could create access to graduate-level jobs. Influential people within large organizations have access to inside information about positions that may open or managers who might lead the hiring process for any such position, while first-generation graduates often find themselves on the outside, with no patron from within. It is common for the children of senior managers to attain managerial positions directly after their bachelor's degree. The first-generation graduates that I interviewed believed that a master's degree would automatically open doors for them and did not realize that 24% of jobs for managerial positions are filled by referrals (Crispin and Mehler 2013). As a result, first-generation graduates without any patron on the inside often spend years working towards jobs that they have been qualified for from day one.

Familiarity with the Professional World

Lack of access to individuals employed in professional fields also deprives first-generation graduates of familiarity with the world they aspire to enter—a familiarity that is a given for graduates with parents and other adults in the family working in such fields. Not having college-educated adults in their immediate circle means that first-generation graduates have to make sense of the professional world all by themselves, without a cognitive map to guide them. Most of their career-related decisions, including initial choice of career path, are consequently based more on trial and error than on observation or research into options. First-generation graduate students grew up without role models in professional fields to observe and on which to model their career aspirations. Therefore, they often have to wait until they have entered a professional field to explore and refine their career aspirations, thus delaying the realization of their potential.

Lack of familiarity with the professional world is a grave liability for first-generation graduates when it comes to gaining access to higher-level positions within organizations. Very often the only professional world they have familiarity with is academia. Most first-generation graduate students in my study stated that their familiarity with the professional world came primarily through television soap operas. One first-generation M.B.A. graduate I interviewed said she did not know how managers thought, how they negotiated their way through their roles, what decisions they made on a daily basis, or how they communicated with their peers, supervisors, or subordinates. Her communication courses in business school taught her to write reports and memos but did not introduce her to the everyday communication of the professional world. All she had been exposed to while growing up and in academia was the "I say, you do" culture of command and expected obedience, which rarely involved any negotiation or conflict resolution. Like many of her counterparts, this first-generation graduate had to start at the lowest rung of the ladder and grow from within as she observed her managers closely and cultivated a mode of communication that had been alien to her but was essential for her professional survival and growth.

Furthermore, first-generation graduates are often clueless about the basic expectations of the recruitment process, even in such matters as appropriate dress and decorum—common knowledge for a graduate from a professional background. Participants in my research struggled to identify or demonstrate the knowledge, skills, attributes, or experiences specific to the jobs they desired. On the one hand, they did not have work experiences that enabled them to extrapolate the attributes that employers wanted in them; on the other, they did not know how to demonstrate specific skills such as leadership, working in a team, or conflict management during the recruitment process.

If making their résumés stand out was a challenge, navigating the multiple rounds of the interview process was another major impediment for first-generation graduates in my study, who were often totally unprepared for the grueling behavioral interview processes used by corporations to select the most suitable candidate from among a multitude of applicants. Knowledge about the need to acquire and demonstrate experiences and soft skills expected in the professional world was very minimal among these graduates. Therefore, they tended to navigate the recruitment processes through trial and error, learning from their repeated attempts to gain access to graduate-level positions. One first-generation graduate in the study said that like many of her counterparts she did not know what to wear for an interview with a big corporation. She recalled how one of the interviewers was kind enough to explain to her after the interview that she should have worn a jacket. This participant was grateful for that piece of advice, but felt embarrassed that she did not know something as simple as that. She could not remember having seen her mother, a nursing assistant, wear a jacket to work.

Another first-generation graduate waited for almost a year to gain an interview with a large corporation. On the interview, she expected to be asked about her accomplishments in college and what she could do for the company. In total contrast to her expectations, the interview was based on situations in which she had demonstrated leadership, how she had resolved conflicts, how she would communicate in crisis situations, and so on. One graduate with a master's degree in sociology equated the interview process to being in a psychiatrist's office—a harrowing experience in which the interviewers tried to understand her thinking process. Another graduate equated the interview processes in big corporations to a first date, where embellishment was the norm rather than the exception. He explained how first-generation graduates with a blue-collar upbringing like his had a tough time bragging about their accomplishments during interview processes, as the culture in their families constantly had discouraged them from doing so. One first-generation graduate explained why cracking the interview was difficult for first-generation graduates like her in contrast to her second- or later generation peers. Graduates with parents who were college-educated and employed in professional fields had always been exposed to the workings of the professional world through their conversations and interactions with their parents and other adults in their families. First-generation graduates, on the other hand, had no access to professionals who could guide them on how to prepare to clear the entry processes.

First-generation graduates often approach the interview as an interrogation in which the interviewers ask questions and the candidate responds to them, rather than as a conversation in which the hiring team assesses how the candidate would fit into their organization. The interview can become a smoothly flowing conversation when the candidate shares the interests or passions of the interviewers and can demonstrate similarity in tastes and preferences. However, first-generation graduates often do not feel comfortable conversing casually with a group of professionals who look and sound privileged, and have had the luxury of indulging in leisure activities such as travel or golf. In contrast, second- or later generation graduates may be able to exude a natural comfort and confidence in the company of such professionals, thus easily establishing a rapport with the hiring team with ease. Lacking the confidence to articulate—and embellish—their accomplishments, and not being able to demonstrate a sense of similarity with the hiring team, first-generation graduates are left at a disadvantage with respect to their peers from professional backgrounds.

The first-generation graduates I interviewed needed to deliberately cultivate a sense of familiarity with professionals in their fields, and create a network that would enable them to move upward professionally from their entry-level positions. They had to indulge in leisure activities such as golf just to gain access to senior officials within their organizations. They also learned with time that they had to make themselves visible to managers in order to be offered opportunities that matched their qualifications. Some sought out mentors from within their organizations who could speak for them and endorse them for internal opportunities. All these efforts took years to bear fruit and meant that first-generation graduates with advanced degrees needed to wait a minimum of three years to access positions that matched their qualifications.

The challenges first-generation graduates encounter on their way to graduate-level positions may vary across disciplines and fields, but are very similar whether the individuals are white or African American, low income or middle income, male or female. The family environments in which the graduates I interviewed grew up, and the nurturing experiences they were exposed to or deprived of, were analogous regardless of their race or economic background. For instance, a white male first-generation graduate, with at least one parent with technical certifications and employed in a middle- or high-income blue-collar job, struggled with a lack of familiarity with the professional world just as much as an African American first-generation female graduate who grew up in a low-income family. This is not to say that the social or economic background of the graduate did not play a role in their transition from education into employment, or to deny the intersectionality of multiple structural factors. Rather, first-generation status or lack of college education within the family cuts across all other disadvantages and is a primary driver behind the challenges faced by first-generation graduates in their attempts to seek employment requiring a graduate education. African American female participants did acknowledge that they faced challenges because of their gender and race, but their situation was compounded by their first-generation status. They felt that as regards employment, their educational background had more direct impact on their awareness and opportunities than did their race or gender. These experiences of first-generation graduates with advanced degrees in different fields remind us that the impact of level of parental education extends beyond the undergraduate years into graduate school—and even beyond, into doctoral education.

First-Generation Doctorate Recipients in Higher Education

Regardless of their disciplines, doctoral recipients who are first-generation graduates are more likely than others to be employed within the education sector—within the school system and in postsecondary education (NCSES 2015). Even first-generation students entering doctoral programs are often unclear about their career path or what they want to do after earning their doctorate (Kniffin 2007; Lunceford 2011; Lopez 2014). Changing or refining career paths while in a doctoral program is not uncommon among students of all backgrounds. However, first-generation doctoral students are more likely to do so without being armed with the knowledge or understanding required to make informed career decisions.

The influence of parental educational level extends far beyond the undergraduate years and determines the institutions where students enroll for doctoral programs. While students with college-educated parents sought Research-1 (R1) and Research-2 (R2) institutions, the majority of first-generation students do not understand the difference in classification of doctoral degree granting universities and tend to enroll in regional public universities or smaller private universities with moderate research activity, but that are cheaper, closer to their homes, or otherwise more familiar (Holley and Gardner 2010; Kniffin 2007; NCES 1994; Lipset and Ladd 1979). The institutions where students pursue doctoral education are a significant factor in determining the type and level of academic institutions in which doctorate recipients find employment. Consequently, faculty in R1 and R2 universities, liberal arts colleges, and Ivy League institutions are predominantly from middle-class families with a history of higher education; in contrast, first-generation doctorate recipients are more commonly employed in public four-year teaching institutions and community colleges, and rarely in R2 and R2 universities (Kniffin, 2007; Kosut 2006; NCES 1994; Lipset and Ladd 1979).

Even though they have been enrolled in doctoral programs and surrounded by faculty, first-generation doctoral students often lack awareness of the recruitment process and requirements for faculty positions in higher education, such as a strong faculty application package with a convincing cover letter, a portfolio of teaching, research experience, publications, writing samples, and highly positive letters of recommendation from research and teaching faculty (Lunceford 2011). Thus, they often go through their programs without preparing to meet these requirements. Susan Gardner (2013) has argued that first-generation graduates do not possess the cognitive maps or mental models that help them make sense of their experience in graduate school or make informed choices. In the absence of productive interactions within family circles that could provide these mental maps, first-generation doctoral students need to seek out faculty, academic mentors, or career counselors who can help them navigate through and beyond their doctoral programs. Yet not all first-generation graduates access these resources.

First, financial commitments that force them to work full-time or part-time while pursuing graduate school can prevent them from actively engaging in research with faculty beyond what is required for their dissertations. Doctoral students who look at assistantships only as a means of income and a possible tuition waiver may be content with the role of graduate assistant (GA) in their departments or other administrative units. They often do not understand that being a GA rather than a teaching or research assistant (TA or RA) denies them possibilities for gaining teaching and research experience, which are essential components of the faculty application package.

Second, first-generation doctoral students are more likely to possess a low academic self-concept (Ostrove, Stewart, and Curtin 2011), consistently undermining their sense of belonging within academia. This means that, although they are ostensibly working towards a career in academia, they cannot actually see themselves in their faculty's shoes (Gardner 2013; Holley and Gardner 2012). Consequently, they rarely seek research experiences or opportunities to interact with communities of researchers in spaces such as academic conferences. With limited engagement with research and the community of scholars and researchers who could be their future peers, first-generation doctoral students often miss out on publication and academic networking opportunities. Lack of publications can also lead to missing yet another essential component of the faculty application package: writing samples reviewed and refined by scholars in the field.

Most importantly, and very much like master's students of similar backgrounds, first-generation doctoral students tend to demonstrate less institutional engagement (Holley and Gardner 2012), including fewer interactions with faculty outside of class and diminished opportunities for or confidence in seeking out academic mentors or mentoring relationships. When interactions with doctoral students are limited to the classroom, it is impossible for faculty to get to know them personally, to appreciate their research interests, and to engage them in research activities. All of these factors impact the quality of the letters of recommendation faculty write for their students as part of the recruitment process. Additionally, limited interactions with faculty prevent doctoral students from creating and nurturing professional networks that could help ease their way into faculty roles upon graduation.

Those first-generation doctorate recipients who do manage to enter tenure-track positions within teaching or research universities continue to face challenges in the tenure process, especially regarding factors unrelated to job performance, such as accent, attire, food, and socializing practices. First-generation faculty often report a sense of *cultural dissonance* in academia (Kniffin 2007), which, coupled with their frequent awkwardness in social interactions with their non-first-generation peers, impacts their growth within the field. Even everyday practices such as style of dress and manner of articulating their ideas in informal and formal gatherings often attract subtle or overt criticism in academic settings where faculty hail predominantly from privileged groups (Kosut 2006). However, there is still not enough evidence to show that first-generation status is a deterrent to gaining tenure or promotion within academia.

While the challenges facing faculty from underrepresented groups, including first-generation college students, are consistently documented in academic research, in-depth research on first-generation doctorate recipients outside academia, and their process of transition into nonacademic employment, is completely absent. According to the National Science Foundation's report *Doctorate Recipients from U.S. Universities 2014* (NCSES 2015), nearly 50% of first-generation doctorate recipients in 2014 were employed outside academia. Unfortunately, information available on the career transition experiences of this group is largely anecdotal. What we know is that the challenges first-generation graduates face after their master's and bachelor's degrees continue into the doctoral program and beyond. Very rarely are first-generation doctoral students aware of employer expectations for research-based positions such as "discipline-specific conceptual knowledge, research skill development, communication skills, professionalism, leadership and management skills, and responsible conduct of research" (Wender et al. 2012, 9). Employers expect doctoral degree holders to bring "scientific and technological leadership to drive scientific discovery, inspire innovation, and solve tough challenges" (Wender et al. 2012, 10). However, academic institutions may not be aware of specific employer expectations and so unable to clearly convey these to doctoral students (Wender et al. 2010; Lunceford 2011). In these cases, first-generation students applying for nonacademic positions likely do so without awareness of employer expectations.

First-generation students remain haunted by a lack of understanding of career pathways outside of academia and a concomitant lack of opportunities to prepare for these while still in their doctoral programs. They often make career choices and revise them based on faculty input or the experiences of fellow graduate students or alums. Nevertheless, guiding doctoral graduates on opportunities outside academia is often challenging for faculty and research advisors who have limited or no contact with nonacademic industries or fields (Wendy et al. 2010). Faculty themselves may lack knowledge and awareness about opportunities in the government, not-for-profit, or private sectors.

Employers expect more than theoretical research capability; they anticipate that prospective employees will demonstrate an ability to lead a team of employees on a research project; to collaborate with researchers and employees across disciplines to design, create, test, and market a product; and to solve problems (Tomilson 2012; Wendy et al. 2010). The tasks and expectations may vary based on the nature and size of the organization, yet being a researcher in any organization demands a wide array of people skills and soft skills that are grounded in culture. First-generation doctoral recipients frequently enter the job search at a distinct disadvantage, due to limited firsthand exposure to the field they wish to enter, a lack of understanding of the opportunities available, and restricted access to the networks that could create opportunities within the field. The situation is worse for young doctorate recipients with no work experience in their fields prior to their doctoral programs, and for those seeking employment in fields not directly related to their area of specialization. These young first-generation doctoral recipients have spent most of their adult lives within academia and therefore are not familiar with professional norms and everyday practices in other sectors of employment. Their knowledge of how a researcher conducts herself within a given sector can be very rudimentary. They may also struggle to demonstrate leadership and higher-level collaboration and problem-solving abilities during their interviews, or to articulate how they think through research problems or processes. However, what we know about how first-generation doctorate recipients seek access to a business environment, how they navigate the transition process or take charge of their professional growth, or the trials they face in the process is very limited, and this is an area that certainly needs further exploration.

Conclusion

The experiences of first-generation graduates with advanced degrees clearly indicate that years of exposure to college education do not level the playing field; these graduates do not exit higher education on equal footing with graduates from college-educated families. With limited access to the cultural capital of the educated and professional worlds, first-generation graduates operate with a restricted, outsider's knowledge and understanding of the preferences, expectations, and norms of the professional class. Lack of access to the educated and professional world outside of academia inhibits the possibilities for first-generation graduates to develop and demonstrate the knowledge, skills, attributes, and experiences expected by employers in a knowledge-based economy. These challenges postpone their access to master's- or doctorate-level positions and middle-class wages, resulting in delayed and staggered social mobility.

More research on the early employment outcomes of first-generation graduates and the challenges they face in gaining entry into appropriate positions across different sectors or industries is required to bring the issue to the attention of policymakers. Only with more broad-based, evidence-backed research can governments be impelled to focus on job creation and to initiate policies that support the transition of first-generation students into employment suitable to their credentials. Research in this area is also required to demand socially just recruitment policies and practices in work environments. The transition challenges of first-generation graduates across sectors need to be identified and reported for organizations to consider first-generation status as a dimension of diversity that could impact their recruitment and promotion procedures. Research on recruitment practices in different sectors can establish the potential for disparate impacts for graduates from disadvantaged backgrounds. Cultural audits of recruitment processes are necessary to ensure that the practices are not just objective or neutral but also fair to first-generation graduates (Hirudayaraj 2014).

Documenting the structural challenges first-generation graduates face in gaining access to employment they are qualified for is imperative in attracting attention to the need for policies or programs to support their transition from student to professional. At this juncture, federally funded programs such as the TRIO or McNair Scholars programs are not mandated to provide career transition support. Without policy initiatives and funding, programs specifically focused on enabling the transition of first-generation graduates into suitable professional positions will continue to be a distant dream.

With regard to what institutions of higher education can do, first and foremost it is important for institutions to recognize that first-generation students need support to prepare for and enter the professional world. Nevertheless, since most first-generation students are not aware of the necessity to think about the world of work beyond college, and to prepare for it when they are still in college, they may not seek out faculty or other campus resources for support. Therefore, any programs intended to provide such support must focus on outreach. In addition to offering specific career transition support programs on campus, institutions need to actively involve faculty in creating career-oriented thinking among their students. The faculty themselves need to recognize the role they can play in initiating career self-efficacy among their students. Their role could involve engaging in deliberate, career-focused conversations with students, mentoring, and/or providing career-focused inputs such as information on companies or organizations in a given field or trends in the industry. Faculty could also actively encourage students to engage in experiential learning opportunities such as internships and co-ops, placing them in contexts where they can develop a personal network with alumni and other professionals—one that goes beyond the ad hoc and often superficial connections they may establish in networking forums. Exposure to professionals and the professional world can greatly benefit first-generation students who otherwise would not have such access. These opportunities can increase the students' chances of finding suitable employment within their preferred fields.

Career centers on campuses need to focus on graduate students and the needs of special populations such as the first-generation graduate student who might struggle to connect his educational and work experiences to career pathways. They also could adopt proactive measures to reach out to graduate students and demonstrate how they can support them in preparing for a career in the professional world. Most importantly, career services offices need to collect and make available employer expectations, industry reports, and realities of the professional workplace; this information needs to be displayed prominently to catch the attention of students who might not seek it out on their own. Finally, institutions need to take into account the anxieties and struggles of these students as they get ready to transition out of academia into the world of work, and to create programs that address the transition issues. Programs targeting first-generation students as they arrive on campus could be expanded to include support for career preparation.

Since socio-cultural challenges faced by first-generation graduates continue to persist even after years of higher education, it becomes imperative to explore in greater detail how these challenges manifest in their transition into professional employment. More research in this area is required to bring about any policy or programmatic changes that could enable first-generation graduates to transition smoothly into professional employment within higher education, government, or the private sector.

Notes

1. See Choy 2001; Hendrix 2009; Housel and Harvey 2011; Ishitani 2003; Jæger 2009; Jehangir 2009; Knighton and Mirza 2002; Pascarella et al. 2004; Stieha 2010; and Thomas and Quinn 2007.

2. On this phenomenon see also Kniffin 2007; Gardner 2013; Holley and Gardner 2012; Lunceford 2011; Lopez 2014; and Carlton 2015.

Works Cited

Brown, Phillip, and Anthony Hesketh. 2004. *The Mismanagement of Talent: Employability and Jobs in the Knowledge Economy.* New York: Oxford University Press.

Brown, Phillip, Anthony Hesketh, and Sara Williams. 2003. "Employability in a Knowledge-Driven Economy." *Journal of Education and Work* 16 (2): 108–26.

Carlton, Morgan T. 2015. "First-Generation Students and Post-Undergraduate Aspirations." *SAGE Open* 5 (4): 1-8. doi: 10.1177/2158244015618433

Choy, Susan. 2001. *Students Whose Parents Did Not Go to College: Postsecondary Access, Persistence, and Attainment* (NCES2001-126). U.S. Department of Education. Washington, DC: National Center for Education Statistics. http://nces.ed.gov/pubs2001/2001126.pdf

Crispin, Gerry, and Mark Mehler. 2013. "Sources of Hire 2013: Perception Is Reality." CareerXRoads Source of Hire Report. http://www.careerxroads.com/news/SourcesOfHire2013.pdf

Gardner, Susan K. 2013. "The Challenges of First-Generation Doctoral Students." *New Directions for Higher Education* 163:43–54. doi: 10.1002/he.20064

Hendrix, Ellen H. 2009. "A Long Row to Hoe: Life and Learning for First-Generation College Students in the 21st-Century Rural South." Ph.D. diss., Indiana University, Pennsylvania.

Hirudayaraj, Malar. 2014. "First-Generation Graduates and Issues of Employability." Ph.D. diss., Southern Illinois University.

Holley, Karri A., and Susan Gardner. 2012. "Navigating the Pipeline: How Socio-cultural Influences Impact First-Generation Doctoral Students." *Journal of Diversity in Higher Education* 5 (2): 112–21.

Housel, Teresa H., and Vicki Harvey. 2011. "Introduction: Shall We Gather in the Classroom?" *New Directions for Teaching and Learning* 127:5–10. doi:10.1002/tl.461

Ishitani, Terry T. 2003. "A Longitudinal Approach to Assessing Attrition Behavior among First-Generation Students: Time-Varying Effects of Pre-college Characteristics." *Research in Higher Education* 44 (4): 433–49. https://www.iwu.edu/first-generation/Ishitani.pdf

Jæger, Mads M. 2009. "Equal Access but Unequal Outcomes: Cultural Capital and Educational Choice in a Meritocratic Society." *Social Forces* 87 (4): 1943–71. doi: 10.1353/sof.0.0192

Jehangir, Rashne R. 2009. "Cultivating Voice: First-Generation Students Seek Full Academic Citizenship in Multicultural Learning Communities." *Innovative Higher Education* 34 (1): 33–49. doi: 10.1007/s10755-008-9089-5

Kniffin, Kevin M. 2007. "Accessibility to the Ph.D. and Professoriate for First-Generation College Graduates: Review and Implications for Students, Faculty, and Campus Policies." *American Academic* 3:49–79.

Knighton, Tamara, and Sheba Mirza. 2002. "Postsecondary Participation: The Effects of Parents' Education and Household Income." *Education Quarterly Review* 8 (3): 25–32.

Kosut, Mary. 2006. "Professorial Capital: Blue-Collar Reflections on Class, Culture, and the Academy." *Critical Studies ↔ Critical Methodologies* 6 (2): 245–62. doi: 10.1177/1532708604268222

Lareau, Annette. 2003. *Unequal Childhoods: Class, Race, and Family Life.* Berkeley and Los Angeles: University of California Press.

Lipset, Seymour M., and Everett Ladd, Jr. 1979. "The Changing Social Origins of American Academics." In *Qualitative and Quantitative Social Research: Papers in Honor of Paul L. Lazarsfeld*, edited by Robert K. Merton, James Coleman, and Peter Rossi, 319–38. New York: Free Press.

Lopez, Marissa. 2014. "On Mentoring First Generation and Graduate Students of Color." *Race and Ethnicity*, April 25. https://clpc.mla.hcommons.org/on-mentoring-first-generation-and-graduate-students-of-color

Lubrano, Alfred. 2004. *Limbo: Blue-Collar Roots, White-Collar Dreams.* Hoboken, NJ: Wiley.

Lunceford, Brett. 2011. "When First-Generation Students Go to Graduate School." *New Directions for Teaching and Learning* 127:13–20. doi: 10.1002/tl.453

Lynch, Kathleen. 2000. "Research and Theory on Equality and Education." In *Handbook of the Sociology of Education*, edited by Maureen T. Hallinan, 85–106. New York: Kluwer Academic/Plenum Publishers.

National Association of Colleges and Employers [NACE]. 2016. "Job Outlook 2017." November. https://www.csuci.edu/careerdevelopment/documents/2017-nace-job-outlook-full-report.pdf

National Center for Education Statistics [NCES]. 1994. *National Study of Postsecondary Faculty*. Washington, DC: U.S. Department of Education. http://nces.ed.gov/surveys/npsas/das.asp

National Center for Science and Engineering Statistics [NCSES]. 2015. *Doctorate Recipients from U.S. Universities: 2014* (NSF 16-300). December. National Science Foundation. https://www.nsf.gov/statistics/2016/nsf16300/digest/nsf16300.pdf

Ostrove, Joan M., Abigail Stewart, and Nicola Curtin. 2011. "Social Class and Belonging: Implications for Graduate Students' Career Aspirations." *Journal of Higher Education* 82 (6): 748–74. https://muse.jhu.edu/article/456569

Pascarella, Ernest T., Christopher Pierson, Gregory Wolniak, and Patrick Terenzini. 2004. "First-Generation College Students: Additional Evidence on College Experiences and Outcomes." *Journal of Higher Education* 75 (3): 249–84. http://muse.jhu.edu/article/55195

Stieha, Vicki. 2010. "Expectations and Experiences: The Voice of a First-Generation First-Year College Student and the Question of Student Persistence." *International Journal of Qualitative Studies in Education* 23 (2): 237–49.

Thomas, Liz, and Jocey Quinn. 2007. *First Generation Entry into Higher Education: An International Study*. Maidenhead, UK: Society for Research into Higher Education and Open University Press.

Tomlinson, Michael. 2012. "Graduate Employment: A Review of Conceptual and Empirical Themes." *Higher Education Policy* 25:407–31. http://link.springer.com/article/10.1057/hep.2011.26

Torpey, Elka, and Dalton Terrell. 2015. "Should I Get a Master's Degree?" *Career Outlook*. September. U.S. Department of Labor,

Bureau of Labor Statistics. http://www.bls.gov/careeroutlook/2015/article/should-i-get-a-masters-degree.htm

Wender, Cathy, Brent Bridgeman, Fred Cline, Catherine Millett, JoAnn Rock, Nathan Bell, and Patricia MacAllister. 2010. *The Path Forward: The Future of Graduate Education in the United States.* Report from the Commission on the Future of Graduate Education in the United States. Council of Graduate Schools and Educational Testing Service. Princeton, NJ: ETS.

Wender, Cathy, Brent Bridgeman, Ross Markel, Fred Cline, Nathan Bell, Patricia MacAllister, and Julia Kent. 2012. *Pathways through Graduate School and into Careers.* Report from the Commission on Pathways through Graduate School and into Careers. Council of Graduate Schools and Educational Testing Service. Princeton, NJ: ETS.

PART THREE

Sharing Our Stories

Advice and Narratives on Surviving and Thriving

11

From Trailer Park to Ivory Tower

Preserving, Protecting, and Promoting the Academic Potential of Disadvantaged Students

Sarah Smith

I had everything to gain and everything to lose when I decided to go to college. As a first-generation student from a low-income background, I didn't know what I was getting myself into; I just knew that I was passionately curious about the world. An additional driver to pursue college was that I knew the endless series of mind-numbing dead-end jobs and instability that awaited me if I didn't go. This pressure to succeed and take my life on a new path beyond my parents' guidance, compounded by being catapulted into the professional middle class, makes it difficult to describe the weight and isolation of being the first in your family to go to college and later graduate school. Immersed in this new world that I was not prepared for, most of my undergraduate time was spent white-knuckling life, just trying to make sense of the new norms and manage ever-mounting expectations. I received good grades but struggled with the unknowns of this new path. I desperately needed help and pursued every avenue I could find, but was turned away from established support programs and left to flounder on my own at both the undergraduate and graduate levels.

As a white woman who grew up low-income in a suburban setting, I found no support for the complex needs I had as a first-generation college student. Though I am a motivated and driven scholar, I know I have not reached my full potential because of the lack of support mechanisms to remove the barriers I faced or to provide opportunities where they wouldn't normally exist for a student in my shoes. In fact, as I will describe below, it seems I was bureaucratically disentitled from any existing support for first-generation and low-income students at the undergraduate level that would have dramatically improved my academic and professional trajectory. I was only able to graduate due to my extraordinary determination, stubbornness, and luck. But luck should not be a determining factor in student success, no matter one's background. Furthermore, I have a rare perspective since I was in roughly the bottom 20% of families by income growing up but have exposure to people in the upper 20%—including a relationship with one such person—so that I have a foot in each of these two culturally different worlds where opportunities are not equally shared. Before offering recommendations for universities to better support graduate students with identities similar to mine, I will share more about my background growing up poor in a rich area, followed by a description of my undergraduate and graduate school experiences.

From Trailer Trash to Valedictorian

In the early 1980s, my parents moved from an apartment in an inner-city slum of a large metropolis to a developing suburb known for having good schools. The only place they could afford was a single-wide mobile home built in 1970. This was before there were solid regulations regarding mobile home construction, so it was poorly built and rotting from the inside out. The ceiling leaked when it rained and was caving in at some parts. There were holes in the floor. The mold on the walls made us ill. My parents didn't intend to stay there long, but something always came up that drained their savings—a car breakdown, water pipes bursting, a job layoff—they could never save enough to afford to move out, and we were stuck.

We managed to live as comfortably as possible, given the circumstances, but the social stigma and isolation of living in the trailer park of an otherwise affluent area was more debilitating than the substandard living conditions. Our neighborhood was kept as separate as possible from the more affluent community, to the point that we were bused past an elementary school blocks away to one three miles away. I learned from one of my former teachers who attended the school boundary meetings that there was a vocal minority of parents who didn't want the trailer park kids to go to school with their kids. Ironically, I would find out later, at a family dinner where she recalled those contentious boundary meetings, that my fiancé's mother was a member of this vocal minority. Not wanting her kids to have any disruptions in their lives, she rationalized my neighborhood taking the brunt of the impacts by arguing that we were "transients" anyway. I was dumbfounded by the detached manner in which she described her perspective, with me sitting right in front of her—the hypocrisy of introducing more instability into the lives of children who likely face a lot of instability at home escaped her. I am now seeing more attention to the dynamic whereby the upper 20% of the middle class wields a disproportionate amount of power to protect their interests at the expense of the poor (e.g., Reeves 2017). It is hidden though, and it has taken me quite a while to identify it because the people are so polite and speak in coded language to your face—for example, making use of evasions and false justifications to mask their true intentions. Only with extensive education and exposure have I been able to see how power and status accumulate within a small group by staying separate and hidden. This translates into barriers for higher education and the professional world. By design, these disjointed school boundaries made it difficult for myself and my brothers to build relationships outside the families who stayed in our neighborhood as long as we did. Every few years we had to make completely new friends, even though we never moved.

Despite the stereotype that people are impoverished because they are lazy, both of my parents worked full time—just in low-paying, physically demanding, dead-end jobs. They were part of what I have learned is a class called "the Working Poor." Work was practically the only thing they did. They were perpetually stressed trying to make ends meet, they worked until they were exhausted, dealt with abusive supervisors and volatile co-workers, and made significant sacrifices for my brothers and me. For instance, since day care was too expensive, they worked different shifts so one parent was at home sleeping while the other was at work. My parents always did the best they could, and I never doubted that I was deeply loved, but we didn't always have enough food, and much of the food we did have was unhealthy and highly processed. With my parents' disjointed work schedules, we often had FFY ("Fend For Yourself") nights instead of family dinners. In another instance of sacrifice, my father had to cash out his modest retirement savings to retain the little stability we had during a tough time—to keep from foreclosing on the trailer. My professional middle-class peers have no idea how badly people are treated in unskilled professions and how the conditions have eroded over the past 30 years, with the dismantling of unions, increased competition due to globalization, and technology–knowledge gaps. These richer peers grew up in a separate world where their parents had pensions and retirement accounts, owned multiple homes, and advanced in their careers. In this world, hard work is rewarded, they have a direct path for advancement in their careers, and their voices are heard. What they don't see is the power dimension: in a low-skilled profession, even if you work hard you are not rewarded appropriately because you are continually reminded how you are replaceable if you don't do whatever you are asked to do. I was dumbfounded when, on my first professional job, I saw a co-worker online with Facebook during working hours; I had been socialized by my parents to work as hard as humanly possible all the time—which is unrealistic and not expected of my professional middle-class peers.

School was one of the stabilizing forces in my life, and I absolutely loved learning (I received the President's Education Award in elementary and middle school). My education surpassed my parents' by the time I was in middle school, and I was often looked to for support. When I was 15 and learning how to write my first résumé in school, my dad had recently been laid off from his job. We sat down together and wrote his first résumé, which helped him land a job he held for 10 years. Yet going to college was never a part of my life plan—and my parents never pressured me—so I didn't seriously think about going until my junior year, after getting straight A's for the previous two years. Since my parents didn't go to college, and I didn't really understand what Advanced Placement courses were, I didn't take any that were offered except for one during my senior year. I thought, "Why would I take college classes if I'm not completely sure I'm going to be able to go to college?" It seemed that the students in those classes were placed on that track a long time before, were all friends, and were rich by my standards. To use standardized tests as an (admittedly flawed) indicator of where I ranked in the early 2000s: my ACT score was 27 and my SAT score was 1230. Not genius-level, but above average, especially considering my background. However, I have since learned how much emphasis is placed on those tests—tests to which richer students devote thousands of dollars in prep courses, leading to perfect scores and full-ride scholarships. Had I known how much weight those scores would have in college admissions decisions, I would have spent more time preparing and less on receiving good grades in my classes. Nevertheless, thanks to many sleepless nights and relentless work, I became valedictorian of my high school class of over 500 students (full disclosure: there were nine valedictorians), was selected as the Social Studies Student of the Year by my teachers, and was an All-State musician. One of my teachers wrote me a note that I keep in a binder to remind me of how far I've come; it reads, "of the 300+ students I had this year, *no one* outworked you."

Continuing my education in college was something I deeply wanted, but I had no one to guide me through the process. The dead ends I encountered were not due to a lack of trying to find assistance. I distinctly remember going to my high-school guidance counselor and asking if I should indicate that I was a "nontraditional" student on my college application because my parents didn't go to college and I lived in the trailer park. "No," he chuckled, "that is just reserved for students who are refugees from other countries." I left confused, knowing that I wasn't like the majority of my affluent peers but unable to articulate that difference in a way my guidance counselor could understand.

I initially decided the nearby state university would be too big and overwhelming for me, given the tens of thousands of students enrolled. I wanted to stay in the Midwest and go to a prestigious school, but I was rejected from a selective university. I wasn't a star athlete, and I wasn't aware of the influence of legacy status in admissions, so in hindsight I really had little to no chance of getting in. Again, there was a power dimension that had little to do with my merit but a lot to do with the affiliations and status of my parents. Luckily, I applied to a couple of liberal arts colleges and chose the one that gave me the most funding: a small (two thousand students total), moderately selective, rural one that was about 90 minutes away from my parent's home.

The week before I started school, my mom was laid off from her job, which left her deeply depressed and our family without health insurance. Not knowing what to do, I lied on my registration, using my old health insurance information and hoping I wouldn't need it. Luckily, I didn't get sick, but the fear that I might added to the stress of adjusting to college life. Fortunately, with the Affordable Care Act (ACA), many families no longer have to go without health insurance the way mine did about ten years ago. For instance, my younger brother is able to stay on my parent's health insurance until he is 26 and won't have to take a dead-end job just for the health insurance benefit. Also, my older brother was diagnosed with a rare and chronic illness in 2011, one year after the ACA was enacted. For the time being, he is protected from being dropped by his insurance carrier for having a pre-existing condition and doesn't have a lifetime limit on reimbursable expenses for his care. Granted, in the current political context those provisions of the ACA may be repealed.

My college orientation was inspiring, and I was excited to move in and start this new chapter of my life. But that didn't last long. Simply by moving into my dorm room, I was propelled upward socially, without being aware of it. I wasn't prepared for the culture shock. I remember being astonished at the lack of racial and ethnic diversity. Almost everyone looked like me: blonde hair and light eyes. Although I looked like I fit in, I felt completely out of place. Everyone seemed so happy and carefree while I felt the weight of the world crushing down on me. The diversity of my background was largely invisible, and in many ways I was embarrassed and ashamed of where I came from, having been called "trailer trash," "white trash," and "cesspool" growing up. One thing that stood out to me was having a meal plan, since I had never had access to so much food—and quality food at that. I don't understand why people complain about college food, because I loved eating fresh fruits and Belgian waffles all the time. Furthermore, my dorm room was larger than my childhood room, in addition to being mold-free and really warm in the winter. It was a huge upgrade, and I often felt deeply guilty that I lived a much more comfortable life than did my family.

I felt alone and isolated from the college community; I didn't know the language and kept bumping into obstacles related to classism that I didn't even know were there. Everyone seemed so at ease while I was overwhelmed. I think a major component was that, given my upbringing of being socially isolated from my richer peers, I was unaware of the importance of the social aspects of college. I didn't understand the culture around college sports or how people had so much free time and money for recreation. I didn't have that luxury. I know now that my peers only did because they had strong support systems. Little did I know at that time how involved the parents of my peers were in all their college decisions and in providing continued support. College was just a part of their life plan, and they had many people in their families and peer networks to support them on that journey. If they had a question, they knew where to turn. Many of their problems were taken care of before they even became problems. Their path was paved, and all they had to do was enjoy the walk.

However, I didn't enjoy many of the activities I was involved in because most of my energy was spent processing this new world. Why did these people have so much, when my family had so little? What were all these new terms and expectations? I frequently experienced a veiled form of classism, as when I noticed that many people were fixated on their parents' college affiliations and professions. There was a competitive banter as to which colleges had better programs or teams, but when it came to sharing our parents' working lives, there was a silent judgment I am now accustomed to but didn't understand at the time. The people I was around were deeply competitive, and keeping score on how they and organizations they were affiliated with ranked on an unofficial scale that had "us" on one end and "them" on the other.

On top of not understanding the social aspects of college, I didn't even know what most majors were, or how everything from college would translate into the "real world." I only had a paradigm for what I had been exposed to, like teaching or the dead-end jobs my parents had. I had no exposure to careers in engineering or business. I didn't know what an internship was or that many were unpaid. I didn't know what job titles meant. Even if I was told a technical definition of these things, I would have had no conceptual anchor to solidify my understanding. I needed someone to help translate this new world into something grounded in my reality. My peers had room to fail, room to explore with people that would catch them if they fell, while I was in the middle of the ocean trying to keep my head above the surface.

Feeling that failure was not an option—since I knew what my life would look like without a college degree—anxiety started to consume me. I thought I needed to focus all of my energy on school or I would fail. My life felt out of control and I didn't know how to get it back on course. I ran track and cross-country in high school, so I used running as an outlet for my anxiety. However, as my anxiety intensified, so did the length of my runs—to the point where I would run for hours a day, until I was too exhausted to feel anything. Within months, I would wake up with my knees aching and I knew that I had to reduce my runs or risk permanently damaging my body. My body couldn't take the physical exertion, but life still felt out of control. I felt that I needed to be perfect in everything I did to prove that I deserved to be there. The one thing I still felt I could control was my weight, so I picked a goal weight 20 pounds below my natural weight. This developed into an eating disorder, further isolating me and heightening my anxiety.

Pressures from my family also intensified, since I was away at college and they couldn't rely on me for support. It hurt having my brothers tell me that I abandoned them when all I was doing was trying to make a better life for myself. It wasn't until after college that I learned I had anxiety and depression from the instability of my upbringing, and that this lack of stability triggered the eating disorder. However, when you grow up poor, you don't go to the doctor often, especially for mental health issues. Unhealthy environments were normalized, and instability was all my family and I knew.

I didn't know where to turn, but eventually decided to transfer to the state university, which was closer to home, less expensive, and could provide treatment for my eating disorder. As a transfer student at a large state university, I only had a four-hour orientation, and then I was on my own to start my new journey. Despite the lack of individual attention, I liked walking within the crowds on campus, seeing people from all around the world, being anonymous.

With even more options in terms of a major, I still couldn't decide on one. Floundering, I changed it three times, bouncing around to new advisors whose names and faces I don't remember. One of my advisors found out I was a first-generation student and gave me the email of the university's TRIO program, which explicitly identified first-generation and low-income students as a target population. I reached out to them, only to be told that the program wasn't for me, with no reason given. It was the email equivalent of a door slammed in my face with no other options or direction that I could pursue as an alternative. To judge from the publicly available requirements, I qualified both as a first-generation student and as a low-income student, since I received a Pell Grant every semester of college. Maybe there were more students than they could help, and the fact that I was, on paper, a high achiever worked against me. However, I suspect that since, as a transfer student, I was not included in the four-year graduation rate metric, the university did not want to expend resources on me.

Doing All the Right Things in All the Wrong Ways

I thought I did everything right. I earned a bachelor's degree from a respectable state university; I received good grades on top of working part-time. Undergrad was rough for cultural reasons that I didn't completely understand at the time and due to lack of support for the challenges I faced. But when I graduated in 2008, my world would collapse around me.

Despite the good grades I earned, the activities I participated in, and the jobs I held throughout college, I could not land a professional job. "We're on a hiring freeze" was something I began expecting to hear from potential employers, and my morale continued to shrink. I didn't know what I had done wrong that meant I couldn't get any sort of offer. In one year I went to nine job fairs—which I have since learned is one of the worst ways to get a job, and among the most unpleasant.

Part of it was bad timing with the economy, but more of it stemmed from the fact that I was never taught the rules of the professional world. In addition to the social glass ceiling from my lack of cultural capital, there were invisible glass walls—in the language I used and the instability in my home life—separating me from my more affluent peers. Both of these kept me from taking advantage of several opportunities. I was fully qualified, but still blocked from opportunities because of what I didn't know. I didn't have a mentor or close friend who understood my unique blind spots and could help me prepare. I went to a number of workshops hosted by the college career services office, but the information did not address the nuances of professional culture that my peers took for granted. Some of my roommates' parents, who were already covering the entire cost of a college education, found their children paid internships that seemed to open the door for additional opportunities. I might have been able to find something if the economy were better, but the devastation of repeated rejection and not knowing what I was doing wrong forced me to take a new approach to my career. Hard work was not enough. Being a good person was not enough. With my student loan repayments looming, I took three part-time jobs: one though a temp agency, one at an amusement park, and one at a deli. I remember thinking to myself on my first day at the deli, as a concealed tear fell: "I shouldn't be here. I didn't go to college for this." Although I was thankful I was working—and determined that if this were my best opportunity, I would be the best deli worker I could be and try to work my way up—I was incredibly unhappy being there and continued my professional job search in the rare moments when I was not at work.

I began to realize that I was raised following a different set of rules for life than my professional middle-class peers—rules that are meant to keep working-class people in their place without being conscious of it: work hard to the point of exhaustion, do as you're told, do not question authority, people are the most important, if something goes wrong it is your fault, never break the rules, never complain, and on and on. To make sense of why I was socialized in such a completely different manner than my affluent peers, I have been trying to understand social class better as a function within a capitalist society. Specifically, I have been reading Andrew Carnegie's *The Gospel of Wealth* (2006) and other economics books with ideas that I was never exposed to. Everything, in my current understanding, comes down to competition. Capitalists compete with other capitalists, but also with labor to keep wages and benefits down. People like me were socialized to be cooperative and thus disadvantaged when it came to demanding higher wages, better benefits, and improved working conditions. Clearly, I had to learn a new set of norms to be able to compete in the new playing field I had unknowingly entered. Similarly, the competition for students in higher education is becoming more and more intense, placing more and more pressure on those from disadvantaged backgrounds. Many of the screening devices that universities use may inadvertently disadvantage low-income students. On my undergrad application to the state university, I remember there being a field to write an essay explaining any special circumstances. However, since my high-school guidance counselor said I was considered a normal student, I left it blank. I had no idea that any mental health or family issues would be a factor in acceptance or support. A different screening tool on my graduate application was a field to list other colleges where I had applied and been accepted. I didn't know why they asked that and I hadn't applied anywhere else. I now know that colleges will negotiate with students who were accepted to other programs and give them more financial aid or perks to choose their college. I was completely oblivious to this mechanism to ensure I received the best offer. To tout the prestige of the incoming class, a list of schools that students turned down was read at the orientation. A student with a network of people with experience in college acceptance would have a tremendous competitive advantage over a low-income and first-generation student, totally apart from academic merit. I don't know how I would have learned that, what kind of questions I might have asked, or how I would have had enough time to make such inquiries, between full-time work, family obligations, and taking part-time classes.

It's Not What You Know, It's Who You Know

Job interviewers in 2008 frequently informed me that I didn't have enough research experience and that I hadn't taken enough math classes even for temp jobs that didn't use any math. I have a suspicion that the generic "math skills" requirement is a hidden way to screen for social class due to the high level of conceptual and executive thinking that math requires; when you live in a poor and unstable environment, executive functioning is a luxury distant to survival. I focused on environmental consulting positions but soon realized that such jobs were better suited to people with civil engineering backgrounds. Since I had a work-study position as an undergrad in a research lab at the university, I contacted my old supervisor and asked if I could volunteer in order to gain research experience. I had washed the test tubes and made petri dishes full of growth medium, but I was never involved in research as an undergraduate major in biology. However, I was ready to work hard and, as luck would have it, an entry-level research position opened up and the principal professor said I was welcome to interview for it.

The interview went well and I was offered a temporary position, with the professor noting that my previous supervisor spoke highly of me. I would not have had that opportunity if my supervisor didn't advocate for me. That job changed my life; I was able to work with postdocs from Harvard, Stanford, and Duke, and with scientists around the world, from Germany to Iran, from Taiwan to Israel. It was surreal, and I often had to pinch myself. However, I started to learn more of the cultural norms of academia and middle-class life, even though I still struggled with the cultural disconnect to my background.

I know I would not have made it to graduate school without the training and support I received in that lab. I am immensely grateful to my supervisor and lead professor for giving me the opportunity to learn alongside remarkable world-class scientists. I worked there for three years and learned as many techniques as I could, taking numerous classes and enrolling in professional development activities outside of work. I even convinced my mom to take a career planning class at the university with me, since she was stuck at a low-paying factory job making barely above minimum wage. Since this was considered an upper-division class at the university, my mom—who had never been to college—felt intimidated being surrounded by 21- and 22-year-olds. Though overwhelmed at times, she stuck with it and improved her computer skills, gave a presentation, and participated in many discussions. She created a cover letter and résumé and was able to get a job that paid thousands of dollars more a year, with substantially better health and retirement benefits. It has proved the best $1,000 investment I've ever made, with a return of over $50,000 in five years along with her being much happier at her current job.

Learning Everything the Hard Way

I loved working in the lab, but I knew I wanted to devote my career to the social aspect of environmental science. Another college at the same state university offered a graduate program in public affairs that focused on implementing environmental policy, and since it seemed to balance the social justice and technical aspects of environmental policy, I applied and was accepted with a full-tuition scholarship for the first year.

My first semester of graduate school was devastating. In the first month, my advisor told me I had made a mistake coming there and suggested I leave. Not only were most faculty members unsupportive, I was also broadsided by how privileged the majority of my peers were and how blind they were to it. I had the expectation that a public policy school at a state institution would have more people like me, or at least that my colleagues would be aware of their power and privilege, wanting to give voice to the less fortunate. But many came from elite liberal arts schools with annual tuitions in excess of what my parents make in a year combined. They seemed to still be in this social bubble. Even if they ventured out to do a service project in a poor area, the empathy that comes with deep understanding did not seem to take root with many of my peers. Instead of being motivated by a drive for social equity, they seemed to regard the school as another step in their life plan. I was surprised at the role of parental connections in the stories some students shared about how they came to enroll in the school. One mentioned her father was a friend of a professor there and another said her advisor connected her with a professor. Connections almost seemed more important than anything else for funding, research, and having faculty invest in you. It was similar to my experience as a freshman at the small, private liberal arts college. I felt I had earned my place, but the series of blatantly classist and ignorant comments I heard in many of my classes—even if not directed at me—made me feel like I was still an unwelcome outsider. I was still oblivious to the importance of these social networks and markers of status that would open doors for me. I never experienced any reality behind the rhetoric of an inclusive campus, and felt that I needed to change in order to be valued.

Below is a series of observations or statements I heard as a graduate student, the stories behind them, and my reflections. This is in no way complete list, nor are the incidents equivalent in severity, but they are offered to show the complexity of messages I was sorting out in addition to completing my coursework.

"This is normal."

As an undergrad, I received treatment for my eating disorder, but there was not much support in terms of mental health care. It was too much for my family to support me so I had to figure it out as I went. I didn't know what I needed or what questions to ask, so after speaking with a couple of doctors, I decided if all they were going to do was prescribe medication, I would just wing it, and stopped seeing a psychiatrist. Growing up, I had been taught that only crazy people took medication. Also, I was never informed of any disability accommodations that could help me be successful and manage my anxiety and depression.

I had seen a doctor outside of the university during my last year in the lab, and was placed on medication for these problems. At first the drugs seemed to help, but the side effects started to negatively impact my life, so I decided to wean myself off all medication. The few months of tapering were a blur of withdrawal symptoms, and I started graduate school without any medication.

In the first two weeks of the semester, I was completely overwhelmed by everything being thrown at me. I had a few panic attacks but had to wait for weeks to get an appointment with a mental health practitioner at the university, where there were too many students in need of mental health services and not enough doctors. I spoke with a crisis nurse during a panic attack and was told my options were to do nothing or check myself into a mental health hospital.

Since I was falling behind in my classes, I went to my advisor and tried to explain how overwhelmed I was. However, she brushed it off, saying my experience "was normal" and that I needed to find my "locus of control." Both pieces of advice were completely unhelpful, and with a series of other considerations I eventually decided to sever ties with that advisor and change my research focus.

"At least you didn't grow up walking barefoot in Africa like one of my other clients."

When I was finally able to get treatment through the university clinic, I met with a social worker who would act as a therapist to help me work through some of the issues I faced. She had worked with low-income families in the past, so would be sensitive to some of these challenges—or so I thought. I distinctly remember her dismissive and invalidating response, quoted above, to my explanation of some of the trauma of my past. I grew up in poverty right here in the United States, about a 30-minute drive from that campus. I understand it is not the same as poverty in a developing country, but how was that helpful? Needless to say, I stopped seeing her when it was clear our sessions were not productive.

"I don't understand your upbringing when you say you grew up poor. Why didn't your parents just work? ... You're white!"

A fellow graduate student, who is a person of color and was born in a different country, said this to me after I shared a little of my background.

Her family is what I would consider affluent, given that both of her parents are college professors. She just could not wrap her head around the idea of a poor white family that actually worked. In the series of statements she sputtered at me, she didn't even give me a chance to respond or leave room to build bridges between our identities. Confused and bewildered, I later discussed this with my boss, the Director of Diversity Student Services, who understood right away the dynamic I experienced. He told me that she didn't understand the dimensions of her privilege as an educated and affluent Hispanic woman of European descent, and that people with different forms of social disadvantage often try to one-up each other in what he called the "Oppression Olympics." It was outside her worldview to picture a hardworking white person experiencing poverty. She was not open to seeing the world in this way. After that conversation, I became hyper-aware of my whiteness and how the perception that "white equals rich" impacted how people treated me, regardless of the reality of poverty. Although I was lumped in with them, I was nothing like my rich, white counterparts. Perhaps I enjoyed certain protections of white privilege, but in the professional middle-class world of the university I was marked as "other"—and lesser—by my white peers, some of whom thought nothing of using terms like "white trash" when they never would have imagined using a racial, ethnic, or religious slur. All this was lost on my fellow graduate student, with her unshakeable belief that, as a white person, I had nothing to complain about compared to the injustices experienced by people of color.

My Saving Grace

I don't know if I would have made it through graduate school without the job I had as a teaching assistant working with underrepresented students—students of color, immigrants, LGBT, first-generation, and low-income students. Roughly 4% of the incoming freshman class was placed in that program, based on criteria established by the admissions committee. When I initially saw the posting for the job, I was surprised that a college access program existed, since as an undergraduate I had experienced such a hard time finding help (I later found out the program began after I graduated). Although first-generation/low-income students represented only a small fraction of the students served through this program, I knew that sharing my experience of learning things "the hard way" could make college easier and more enjoyable for them. Not wanting them to experience the confusion and isolation I had felt, I would share as much as

I could about my journey, in hopes of steering them toward resources, letting them know they are not alone, and enabling them to focus their efforts on academics or building other professional skills. Also, my academic interests include promoting environmental and educational justice for vulnerable populations—especially those in poverty—so I felt this program aligned with my personal beliefs.

For the first time in my ten years as a student and working at the university, I met others with similar backgrounds to mine—and I couldn't have been happier. The curriculum of the program opened up my own understanding of my world alongside the students'. It was surreal and validating, learning about and leading discussions on classism. For the first time in my life, I was exposed to other scholars who had similar backgrounds to mine, including Linda Stout, Dorothy Allison, and Alfred Lubrano. In addition, I was learning and discussing other social justice issues like racism, environmental justice, food justice, homelessness—things I never talked about when I was an undergrad but that are integral to understanding our society.

One of the most influential people in my life was my boss, the Director of Diversity Student Services, who was also a first-generation student from a low-income background. He was the first person I met who knew what my life looked like growing up, without me having to explain it. Whenever I tried to better understand various issues that came up related to my background, he was the one person I could turn to for support. I am forever indebted to him for allowing me to be a part of that amazing program and changing the way I see the world.

Juggling Family Obligations

Toward the end of my first year in graduate school, my dad was laid off from his job. He didn't know where to turn or what to do. I wanted to help him right away, but as a graduate student, I was working two jobs with a full course load, and about to speak at a national conference before going to out of the country to study renewable energy. I was stretched too thin. After the summer passed, I decided to take the fall semester off from graduate school to help my dad in a meaningful way. We applied to the state Dislocated Worker Program, which offers career planning and support services for laid-off workers, and he was accepted. We attended a number of workforce career classes together, and I was able to "translate" the topics (mostly targeted towards college-educated professionals) to his situation. "Networking" and "branding" are not familiar concepts to working-class people, as I made clear on the surveys that followed each workshop. I was also able to advocate for him when he met with a career counselor—securing funding for him to attend truck-driving school, even though the counselor was trying to talk him out of it. I cited statistics showing it would be a great investment for the state and would help him be gainfully employed instead of chronically laid off from low-level jobs. He is now a commercial truck driver with more job security and opportunities for advancement than he has ever had, and I have never seen him so happy in my life. None of this was easy or straightforward, and it would not have happened without my advocacy.

More recently, my grandfather, who was living in his home, was rushed to the emergency room in such a poor condition that the nurse said it would be reported to the state as neglect. I later found out that his caregiver, my uncle, is a drug addict and had been extorting money from him. When I visited my grandfather in a nursing home, he asked me to assume power of attorney and get his finances in order. I couldn't say no to my grandfather, even though it is an immense responsibility. These compounding family obligations were major obstacles in completing my degree. What helped me juggle these important aspects of my life while I finished my thesis was the ability to take a grade of Incomplete and maintain my active student status without paying any more in tuition for an extra year. First-generation students with low-income backgrounds would be better served if colleges described such opportunities for flexibility *before* a crisis occurs, to minimize any disruption to the students' coursework and lives. This is especially important given the instability that many of these students have in their families and the disproportionate responsibility they bear.

Summary of Major Problems and Recommendations for Graduate Schools

There are a number of problems that first-generation graduate students from low-income backgrounds face that inhibit their ability to reach their potential; many are invisible to the untrained eye. Here I summarize a few major problems I encountered and suggest some resources that I found helpful, or that would have been helpful in allowing me to focus more on my studies.

One problem I experienced was prolonged and toxic stress, well beyond the pressures an average student would face. The instability of my family life, the misconceptions and inadequate coping skills I was taught, the disproportionate family responsibilities I had (also called "parentification"), and the lack of mental health care access all intensified this stress. This was in stark contrast to what I learned about the family dynamics of my peers, many of whom had a stay-at-home parent take care of any and every worry the student might have outside the classroom.

To address the issues related to toxic stress that first-generation graduate students are likely to face, I suggest flexibility in terms of leaves of absence or reduced course loads. It was invaluable for me to take a semester off in graduate school so I could help my father with his job training; without that flexibility, I likely would have dropped out entirely. I didn't even know about these options until I was in crisis and it would have been infinitely more helpful to have an advisor or counselor who could check in and proactively inform me of my options. Having teaching or research assistantships available on a semester-to-semester basis helped as well, so I didn't have to forfeit my funding by taking a semester leave. Another valuable resource at the university was a graduate student support group that met biweekly with a psychologist to facilitate discussion and suggest healthy coping skills. Although I was often the only first-generation student in the group, it helped normalize some of the challenges and gave me an extra brick to steady my foundation so I could continue my degree.

An additional recommendation is to make mental health care a priority, and to train staff to assist students dealing with the multiple traumas of chronic poverty. When I got to college, I didn't know how to go about getting help, and had many negative perceptions that further prevented me from getting effective treatment—like the beliefs that only crazy people needed help or that therapy was for rich people. Specifically, I have found the techniques of Cognitive Behavioral Therapy (CBT) to be helpful for recognizing unhealthy coping skills and moving towards healthier ones.

Another major issue I had was the lack of cultural knowledge and social capital necessary to enter the professional middle-class world of academia. My middle-class peers had family or other connections to help them get their feet in the door for internships or jobs, but after years of being a social pariah in a trailer park, those connections were not a part of my world. Throughout graduate school, I tried to seek out mentors who had a similar background but was unable to find one who had experienced the same challenges of chronic instability. My first graduate mentor, despite having a parent who was a first-generation college student, had not intimately experienced poverty and its associated punishments for herself (only at arm's length through the Peace Corps), and I could tell she had little sympathy for or understanding of the challenges I faced, and was more passionate about issues for immigrants. My second mentor grew up in an apartment with a single mother, but he said she went to college around the same time he did and the hardship he experienced was temporary. What I needed more than anything was to be seen and understood, and to find where I belonged in my professional community. I needed someone who was still going through challenges similar to those I faced.

To address the gap in cultural knowledge and social capital, I found resources in unexpected places. One place was the university writing center. By the time I was in graduate school, I knew how to screen for the consultants with the most experience, usually those with or pursuing Ph.D.'s. It was a godsend to receive instant feedback on my thesis work and be able to discuss and develop my ideas. I strongly recommend that all first-generation graduate students utilize their writing center—especially if their faculty advisors are too busy to provide constructive and timely feedback. I found an additional unexpected cultural resource in the form of workshops designed for international students. The topics seemed applicable to me, and I had nothing to lose, so I decided to go. One particular workshop described, through an outsider's lens, how to effectively communicate in American professional culture. This would have been even more helpful a decade earlier, but still allowed me to better understand the rules of the professional game. As part of that workshop I was introduced to a book that gives a framework for understanding and adapting to cultural differences, and that I highly recommend for first-generation students—*Global Dexterity: How to Adapt Your Behavior across Cultures without Losing Yourself in the Process,* by Andy Molinsky (2013).

Colleges and universities can also address the gap in social capital by providing incentives for professors to work with disadvantaged students. Especially at institutions with graduate programs, professors compete with each other for funding and publications, and so tend to avoid and deflect students with time-consuming special needs. However, if faculty can get service credit or additional compensation to provide guidance and mentorship to disadvantaged students, I think many would take on that extra potential burden.

The last major issue involves the invisible disadvantage and prevalent misconceptions surrounding social class. The pervasive attitude I encountered from peers, faculty, and the institutions I attended was that socioeconomic class background wasn't a valid measure of social disadvantage compared to racial, ethnic, or gender/sexuality categories. My identity and experiences were invalidated so many times that, without the support of being a teaching assistant in the college access program, I would have started to internalize those misconceptions and believe that I or my parents simply weren't working hard enough, even when I did everything I possibly could do to be successful—instead of examining the structural barriers that prevented me from reaching my potential.

Creating a more inclusive campus by enhancing the understanding of the functions of social class and oppression is not easy. One tool we used in the college access program to make the invisible visible was "the privilege walk." The class held hands in a row while I read a series of statements that conferred social advantage or disadvantage. Those to whom statements of advantage applied took one or more steps forward (depending on the degree of advantage conferred), while those to whom statements of disadvantage applied took one or more steps backward. As the students' hands separated, a divide split those at the front and back of the classroom, and I saw the truly disadvantaged students' eyes open to what they were experiencing, even if they couldn't articulate it in that moment. This exercise would have saved me a lot of confusion and heartache in understanding my own place in the larger college community if I had been exposed to it at age 18 instead of 28. On the other hand, I distinctly remember two students, white women from relatively privileged backgrounds, reacting strongly and negatively towards this particular exercise. They complained about me to the professor, uncomfortable with having someone who looked like them highlight their advantages and, seemingly, imply their life was easy. This sense of entitlement to avoid discomfort at all times was strongest with my most privileged students; the campus climate would greatly improve if those students had a better understanding of their place in the university's power structure. I am not sure how to reconcile the tension between rugged American individualism, with its competitive ethos and constant status anxiety, and the goal of a more interdependent and inclusive community. Even at the graduate level, my peers in a public policy class cracked jokes about how giving cash grants to the poor instead of food stamps would allow them to "feed their children potato chips, buy beer, and visit prostitutes." I was mortified that my peers in public policy felt emboldened to make light of a situation as horrible as American poverty in front of everyone. To combat this and other comments I heard, I tried to get funding to invite to campus a nonprofit that aims to reduce classism for a workshop on the realities of socioeconomic class. Every diversity office I contacted university-wide said they didn't have funds for what they considered a short-term initiative. On paper, socio-economic class was a valued dimension of campus diversity—but if you follow where money is spent, you will see where a university's true values lie, and my university couldn't have cared less about socio-economic diversity. In fact, the general college that was an access point for many low-income and disadvantaged students closed, and an administrator justified the closure by saying the state had excellent community colleges for those students to attend. The message this sent to me was: Those students don't belong here and don't deserve the opportunities and privileges of being a part of a large university.

Conclusion

My identity as a first-generation graduate student from a low-income background has profoundly shaped my experiences in graduate school. Only by chance was I involved as a teaching assistant in a program that helped me develop a better sense of myself and enrich my studies. Higher education is becoming less and less accessible to the populations who would benefit most from a bachelors or advanced degree. Although my university claims to include socio-economic and first-generation status as markers of diversity, only a handful of the students who qualified for the college access program I participated in as a teaching assistant are first-generation or low-income. But such programs have tremendous potential to increase cultural competence for all students, empower other marginalized groups, and create a more inclusive campus. It is shocking to me that I didn't even learn about white privilege and other manifestations of oppression until graduate school. I consider myself incredibly lucky to have made it through both undergraduate and graduate programs. But success should come from merit, ability, and motivation, not from luck.

Work Cited

Carnegie, Andrew. 2006. *The "Gospel of Wealth" Essays and Other Writings.* New York: Penguin.

Molinsky, Andy. 2013. *Global Dexterity: How to Adapt Your Behavior across Cultures without Losing Yourself in the Process.* Boston: Harvard Business Review Press.

Reeves, Richard V. 2017. *Dream Hoarders: How the American Upper Middle Class Is Leaving Everyone Else in the Dust, Why That Is a Problem, and What to Do about It.* Washington, DC: Brookings Institution Press.

12

Surviving in the Land of Oz

Harvesting Academic Capital for Graduate School Success

Saran Donahoo

In L. Frank Baum's classic American fairy tale, an exceptionally strong tornado transports Dorothy and her dog Toto from their rural home in Kansas to the magical Land of Oz. Upon her arrival, Dorothy quickly learns that her previous knowledge and skills are not enough to help her navigate through Oz, avoid its dangers, or ensure that she will reach her goal of returning home. As the story unfolds, Dorothy must build new relationships, gain different knowledge, and reshape her perspective to attain her goal. Essentially, Dorothy must accumulate and expend capital that is specifically useful in the Land of Oz.

Much like Dorothy, students who enter graduate school often find that the capital that helped them to arrive at this point is not enough to get the degrees and jobs that they desire. Once they arrive, first-generation graduate students need to amass fresh capital that will allow them to succeed in their new academic environments. Seeking to assist with this process, this chapter discusses academic capital, identifies ways that students can earn this form of capital, and offers suggestions regarding how to use this capital to complete their degrees, improve their skills, and obtain related employment.

Academic Capital: The Currency of Graduate Education

Every society operates with its own rules and currency. Transported to the

Land of Oz, Dorothy quickly learns that the rules that govern life in agrarian Kansas do not apply to her new temporary home. Similarly, the guidelines and expectations of graduate school also necessitate that students acquire new skills and credits that they can use to complete an additional degree.

To successfully complete a graduate degree, students must both attain and expend academic capital. A specialized form of human capital, academic capital refers to the competencies and abilities that students use and hope to expand upon while enrolled in an educational experience such as graduate school. Much like human capital, academic capital creates opportunities for those who possess it to access better employment for higher compensation (Donahoo 2011, 207–208).

Students must demonstrate ownership of some academic capital in order to gain admission to graduate programs. First, students must earn a bachelor's or other prerequisite degree, which illustrates eligibility for additional education, provides evidence of the ability to navigate post-secondary education, and suggests the possibility of future academic success. Second, prospective students must also exhibit academic competency as measured by grade point average (GPA), standardized exam scores, and writing or other samples related to their selected academic program (Dodge and Derwin 2008, 2-4). While researchers challenge the accuracy of standardized exams in predicting graduate school success (Curry 2001, A23; Feeley, Williams, and Wise, 2005, 239–240; Gardner 2009, 384–385; Jacobson 2003, A27; Lovitts 2008, 301; Sacks 2001), the fact that many programs use these scores to frame the selectivity of their admissions mandates that interested student amass this form of academic capital (Curry 2001, A23; Dodge and Derwin 2008, 2-4; Donahoo 2011, 207–208). Lastly, students must dispense some of their academic social capital to gain access to graduate school by gathering positive letters of recommendation from faculty members, professionals, and other individuals who support their desires to pursue another degree (Donahoo 2011, 209–210; Halberstam and Redstone 2005, 268; Petress 1999, 485–487). Although not always honest about the academic limitations that students possess (Grote, Robiner, and Haut 2001, 656), these letters can help to personalize applications by showing that students are more than just their GPAs and test scores.

Despite the range of requirements, the academic capital that students dispense in order to gain admission to graduate school is not enough to complete this next phase of their educational journey. Just as Dorothy has to learn how to travel through Oz and return home from the (Good)

Witch of the North, the Wizard, and her other companions, graduate students must also form new associations, expand their knowledge, and face unexpected challenges as they navigate their new educational environments.

New Friends and Relationships for the Journey

In working with new graduate students, I often find that one difference between those who transition well and those who encounter difficulties is their approach to establishing relationships with others. Even after successfully completing undergraduate degrees, first-generation graduate students do not always readily acclimate to a more political academic environment where simply completing assignments or following directions do not guarantee goal attainment. Once they enter graduate school, first-generation students have do things differently in order to succeed. As Dorothy progresses down the Yellow Brick Road, her approach and response to others also evolves. When she encounters the Scarecrow, Dorothy is initially too fearful and apprehensive to recognize the potential benefits that association with such a creature may offer. Similarly, graduate students sometimes believe that the most effective way to complete their journey toward an advanced degree is to deal with things on their own. However, this often proves to be a self-defeating approach to graduate school life, since students need connections with and assistance from others to gain funding, research opportunities, guidance regarding publications and presentations, and direction and support in obtaining post-degree employment (Curtin, Stewart, and Ostrove 2013, 111–113; Davis 2007, 218–219; Donahoo 2011, 213; Fountaine 2012, 142; Noy and Ray 2012, 878–881; Schlemper 2011, 70–71; Strayhorn and Terrell 2007, 77–78).

As part of their study of the graduate students' advising experiences, Noy and Ray (2012, 878–881) identify six types of advisors that students may encounter:

- *The affective advisor* offers emotional, personal, and professional support, often utilizing a therapeutic approach;
- *The instrumental advisor* functions as a professional training an apprentice and seeks to establish a mutually beneficial professional relationship;
- *The intellectual advisor* provides assessments of the students' work and directions on improving outcomes. S/he is more of a grader

than the instrumental advisor, and not very interested in having students contribute to his/her work;

- *The available advisor* serves as a sounding board by helping students to work through their issues and provide direction on how to proceed through their programs, concentrating on academic issues;
- *The respectful advisor* appreciates both who students are and the intellectual contributions that they make, often recommending or introducing these students to others;
- *The exploitative advisor* uses students for their own academic and professional benefit. S/he often abuses students with excessive demands and does not consider or address the needs that students may have.

Although she did not journey to Oz to obtain an education, Dorothy also encountered individuals who illustrated some elements of these advisor types. Considering Dorothy's responses to the advice offered to her can provide some valuable lessons for graduate students.

Using Your Head

Although the Scarecrow constantly complains about his lack of a brain, he proves to be very helpful to Dorothy while in Oz. Throughout their journey, the Scarecrow serves as an *instrumental advisor* by educating her on the people and landscapes of Oz. Likewise, he encourages her to persevere to the end even as he learns to do so for himself. The Scarecrow thereby reminds graduate students that they can succeed in their academic and professional pursuits. Even if things seem bleak, the information provided by individuals on their campuses can help graduate students to expand their academic capital by gaining the knowledge they need to complete the journey. Within the context of campus life, likely sources of instrumental advising may include junior faculty members who bear a strong and recent affinity to graduate student life, individuals in different disciplines who share their academic and professional interests, and other graduate students both in and outside of their academic units.

Following Your Heart

For his part, the Tin Man functions as an *affective advisor*. Like the Scarecrow, the Tin Man seeks to guide Dorothy during their journey, yet does so in a more emotional manner. Indeed, it is because the Tin Man comes to care for Dorothy that he wants to help her attain her goal. Likewise, graduate students will also find that they too can benefit from relationships that they establish with individuals who develop a vested interest in their emotional, academic, and personal well-being. However, students cannot obtain these relationships if they live in a cocoon of isolation. Instead, they need to build connections with others. Connections that can help first-generation students succeed in graduate school include:

- reading groups where they can learn about the curriculum and culture of their programs from other graduate students;
- formal and informal research groups where students can collaborate and practice applying the knowledge that they acquire outside of class;
- student organizations in and outside of their academic units that will allow them to document their leadership skills as they participate in various levels of institutional operations, while also positively interacting with faculty, staff, and administrators;
- professional organizations off-campus where students can establish broader networks across their academic fields and desired career areas.

Using their academics as a foundation will help to strengthen and increase both the academic and the social (interpersonal) capital that students can attain in graduate school.

Knowledge Is Power

Despite the key roles that they occupy in the plot, Dorothy and her traveling companions are not the most powerful or knowledgeable characters in the story. After the unexpected storm transports Dorothy to Oz, the (Good) Witch of the North gives Dorothy initial directions to find the Wizard and advises her to avoid the (Wicked) Witch of the West. Armed with more knowledge than Dorothy, the Good Witch serves as her *intellectual advisor*, identifying Dorothy's problem areas and directing her on how to fix them—while expressing little interest in examining or validating Dorothy's personal perspective on her situation. Though these individuals do not provide the emotional support generated by the affective advisor or the mutual commitment expressed by the instrumental advisor, graduate students should capitalize on the strengths of their intellectual advisors. Use these individuals to obtain concrete academic knowledge, honest feedback and assessments, and detailed information about the politics and climate of their program and department, as well as the campus units that may help students to succeed in graduate school. In turn, these individuals will appreciate having graduate students who value their expertise, which can serve as the foundation for more personal and committed advising relationships.

Making the Best of It

Like the Witch of the North, the Wizard and the (Wicked) Witch of the West also possess extensive knowledge about the Land of Oz. However, they are not as forthcoming when the occasion arises for them to share information with Dorothy. The Wizard and the Witch of the West only provide Dorothy with enough information to manipulate her into doing what they want. Clearly, these two characters function as *exploitative advisers* by using Dorothy to reach their goals. In spite of their selfish motives, even *exploitative advisers* can provide some benefits to graduate students. Just as learning about the weaknesses of the Wizard and the Witch of the West benefited Dorothy, assisting others with their research serves as a practical opportunity for students to develop these scholarly skills (crafting a research question, conducting a study, collecting and analyzing data, and formally presenting research to others) for themselves. While many graduate students express a desire to learn more about research, faculty members may be reluctant to include students in these processes until they are certain that they possess the requisite skills, such as a basic understanding of the field, some familiarity with the relevant methodology and procedures, strong written and oral communication skills, and a willingness to follow directions and contribute as needed (Austin 2002, 106–111; Lechuga 2011, 762–769). Rather than reject or recoil when faced with exploitative advising situations, students should find ways to gain some academic capital from these experiences, given that establishing research relationships with faculty members can lead to further presentation and publication opportunities.

Relationships as Resources

During their time in school, graduate students do not always have the ability to control who they associate with or how they do so. Nevertheless, it is important to realize that all relationships can serve as practical opportunities for students to develop their social and academic capital. Instead of functioning in isolation, new graduate students should accept the information and advising offered to them and then apply this knowledge critically as they journey towards their degrees.

Following the Brick Road

In addition to the need to establish new and profitable relationships, graduate students also encounter other difficulties in the successful completion of a post-baccalaureate degree. In some cases, students enter graduate school with the goal of earning a degree but possess limited understanding of what they need to do to arrive at their destination. In other cases, students have such a definitive idea of what they want to study and focus on that they have a hard time completing tasks and processes that they feel lack a direct connection to their areas of emphasis. For example, first-generation students may concentrate on earning good grades in their graduate programs; however, they underestimate areas that do not appear on their transcripts such as the value of out-of-class work, getting to know faculty members, or professional organizations, which are crucial to both degree completion and career trajectory. Furthermore, financial issues, family responsibilities, and other life events can distract students inhibiting or even preventing them from reaching their personal goals. First-generation students who must devote their out-of-class time to earning tuition money, maintaining full-time employment, or caring for children or other family members do not receive the same attention from faculty members or opportunities to participate in research and present at conferences because faculty assume that these students are not interested or available for these activities. Unable to meet faculty members on their terms, many first-generation graduate students only access a portion of the educational opportunities that graduate education provides.

From the moment that she arrived in Oz, Dorothy established a clear goal of returning to Kansas. Despite this clarity of purpose, Dorothy still had to learn about Oz and devise a plan for reaching the Emerald City so that she could elicit help from the Wizard to get home. Much like Dorothy, new graduate students need to develop a plan that will allow them to reach their goal of degree completion. Upon gaining admission, graduate students would do well to start accumulating new academic capital by learning about all of the requirements for their degrees and devising a plan to satisfy each of them. This plan should include a preliminary schedule for taking required classes that provides some sequencing based on course offerings and prerequisites, considers possible research projects, identifies relevant and beneficial internships or other practical opportunities, and embraces obtaining the experiences and skills needed to be ready for the student's chosen career. Far too often, students enter graduate programs believing that an advanced degree will provide greater employment and economic opportunities, yet do not take the time to develop the skills that employers in their chosen fields desire of new hires. Leaving graduate school with a degree is a reasonable goal, but it is only part of the process. Rather than rush to complete course and degree requirements, graduate students should focus their efforts on becoming career ready. For many students, this will mean devoting time to tasks outside of class, including conducting empirical research, participating in academic publishing, shadowing and networking with experienced professionals, and gathering specific information about the job-search process for their selected fields.

Encountering and Overcoming the Unexpected

At the outset, following the Yellow Brick Road to the Emerald City appears an easy path that will lead Dorothy to the Wizard, who will help her return home. Yet, throughout their journey, Dorothy and her cohort encounter many sidetracks and setbacks that divert them from their path. Comparably, the journey through graduate school also involves disruptions and diversions. To be sure, life does not stop just because individuals decide to return to college. Rather, the stress and responsibilities of graduate education challenge perspectives, test relationships, and expend academic capital and other resources in ways that students are not always prepared to endure. Graduate students should be prepared to persevere through unexpected circumstances. Following the example of Dorothy, graduate students should bravely face new issues as they arise, address them as needed, learn from them what they can, and continue on their academic journeys in spite of the obstacles that they encounter. These new issues and experiences may include meeting faculty members outside of class to learn more about what they do and what suggestions they have for career success, establishing connections with program alumni to learn more about life after graduation, conducting empirical research, attending and asking questions at hiring events and other public events where others discuss their research, presenting at professional conferences, and contributing to academic publications. While not everything will go as anticipated, facing these new experiences will help first-generation graduate students obtain the capital that they will need to complete their degrees and prosper throughout their careers.

Likewise, success in graduate school will require sacrifices. Expending the academic capital of undergraduate grades, standardized test scores, and letters of recommendation help students gain admission to graduate programs. Once admitted, graduate students must make additional investments and sacrifices by covering the costs of attendance, books, and supplies; foregoing professional opportunities that may interfere with school; and limiting family time and vacations; participating in conferences and other educational activities; and considering a multitude of other life decisions within the context of their academic obligations. Indeed, the need to prioritize school over many other things in life can alter personal relationships, influence childbearing and childrearing, and significantly affect how individuals define themselves (Pifer and Baker 2014, 23–26). In this way, the identity changes and challenges that students face while in graduate school can isolate them from family members and friends who backed their decisions to pursue an additional degree (Gardner 2008, 334; Pifer and Baker 2014, 23–26). Although loved ones may support the idea of returning to school, they do not always understand, appreciate, or easily accept the shift in priorities that results from this decision. Just as Dorothy and her friends responded differently to the obstacles they faced, each student must negotiate relationships, priorities, and responsibilities on their own. Accepting graduate education as an opportunity for self-authorship (Baxter Magolda 1999, 73; Baxter Magolda 2008, 281–283), students must consider and respond to the challenges they face in their own way.

Constantly Recalculating

Although the journey from initiating a graduate program to completing a graduate degree may seem fairly simple and straightforward at the outset, even the best plans sometimes require recalculation and reconsideration. While unexpected changes and challenges may jeopardize success, graduate students do not have to allow these encounters to ruin the journey toward an additional degree. Changes in the curriculum (the Wizard requiring Dorothy and her crew to deal with the Wicked Witch of the West after they finally reach the Emerald City), departure of an advisor (the Wizard leaving Oz without Dorothy), and loss of funding and support (both the Munchkins and the inhabitants of the Emerald City celebrate sending Dorothy on her journey, but stop short of accompanying her) are just a few of the unexpected challenge that first-generation graduate students may encounter. Rather than abandon their academic goals, students will find that the quest for graduate school completion and success mandates that they continuously renegotiate their priorities, relationships, and identities.

Living Beyond the Curtain

After her harrowing journey, which includes facilitating the deaths of two witches, Dorothy arrives at the Emeral City to attain her coveted prize of a trip back home to Kansas. However, even after she completed both the original voyage and the additional tasks resulting from unexpected challenges, Dorothy still could not leave Oz. After returning to the Emerald City, Dorothy learned that the Wizard lacked magical powers. Even when he attempted to take her back to Kansas in the same hot air balloon that brought him to Oz, the balloon departed without Dorothy and Toto. Despite her best efforts, Dorothy's original goal was still out of reach. Many graduate students have similar experiences as they near the end of their degrees. To their dismay, students often find that life and graduate school are not what they originally seemed. During recruitment, prospective students only hear good things, such as fellowships and assistantships that cover enrollment costs; the national and international reputation of faculty members; lists of interesting course offerings; and opportunities to conduct and publish research while pursuing their degrees. In reality, not every student receives funding and even the best funding still leaves some fees that graduate students have to cover from their stipends, student loans, employment, or other sources. Likewise, assistantships include work obligations that often exceed the 10–20 hours per week specified in job descriptions. Well renowned faculty members are not always available and their courses often fill up quickly. Programs have limited opportunities to offer all of the courses listed and students have even more limited opportunities to take them without increasing the time needed to complete their degrees. Conducting and publishing research requires significant time outside of class and work, making it difficult for many first-generation graduate students who cannot afford to forgo their other obligations in order to participate. While graduate students' understanding of reality may change as they expend more time and capital in their programs, students should not be so hasty in allowing these revelations to dissuade them from pursuing their goals.

Additional Expectations

After a complicated journey to the Emeral City, Dorothy and her friends fully anticipated that simply arriving to see the Wizard and making their wishes known to him would produce the results that they traveled the Yellow Brick Road to obtain. Unfortunately, the Wizard places an additional expectation on the four companions by asking that they first dispose of the Witch of the West for him, before he grants their requests. Some graduate students also face similar disappointment when they realize that completing their degrees will require more time, effort, money, and academic capital than they originally anticipated. To be sure, establishing a detailed plan that accounts for all program requirements can help graduate students avoid many unexpected obligations. However, even the best plan cannot prepare students for everything. While not necessarily appealing, final decisions such as exiting the program or simply giving up are always available. The loss of a trusted faculty advisor, the addition of new curricular requirements, significant increases in tuition and fee costs, changes in career and life plans, and the loss or illness of a family member or significant other may lead first-generation students to depart graduate school before completing their degrees. With that in mind, graduate students would do well to respond cautiously to unexpected occurrences, gathering all relevant information before committing to a course of action. Unanticipated developments may sometimes yield advantages and benefits. Consulting with mentors and fellow students can help to ascertain how others responded when similar events affected their progress. It is best to avoid making major life decisions during times of grief or extreme stress. A temporary leave of absence can buy time to deal with personal difficulties without severing ties to a graduate program. Faculty and staff members who know more about institutional policies and resources can be invaluable sources of support and advice. Final decisions should be made in full awareness of the options, and not in the throes of an immediate calamity.

Dealing with Disillusionment

One of the most devastating setbacks of Dorothy's journey home was the discovery that the Wizard, the Great Oz, was just a regular man. Lacking magical powers, the Wizard could not keep his word to Dorothy and return her to Kansas, even after she and her friends fulfilled their side of the bargain by destroying the Witch of the West. This experience left Dorothy disillusioned with both the man and the Land of Oz. Unfortunately, some graduate students encounter similar experiences of disillusionment and dissatisfaction. Despite the time and effort invested, graduate school does not always bring students the advantages or outcomes that they desire.

In spite of Dorothy's commitment, the Wizard knew all along that he did not have the power to give her what she wanted. The economic climate and simplified admissions processes make it easier for students to transition from an undergraduate degree to a graduate education program than it is for many of them to successfully gain full-time employment related to their career goals. According to the U.S. Department of Education (2014), graduate student enrollment increased by 50% between 1990 and 2012. Fueling this increase was the reality that many graduates, unable to find a job, returned to school for additional education and training in the belief that this would help them to obtain employment in a job-scarce market (Ruiz 2010). Yet, as they travel their brick roads, some students discover a disconnect between their career goals and their academic preparation. In these instances, students have four options: 1) continue as is; 2) continue with new goals that align with realistic prospects for their degree and training; 3) shift to a different degree program; or 4) leave without completing a graduate degree.

In many situations, completing a degree program, even if unlikely to result immediately in desired employment, may prove to be the best option for many students. While the degree may not have a direct connection to the individual's ultimate career goals, this does not mean that it is a complete waste of time or energy. Instead, students must learn to be savvy and use the academic capital that they obtain to gain access to the additional capital they desire. In place of specific degrees and academic requirements, many employers tend to prefer candidates who possess the *skills* that they believe will be most useful and beneficial in their organizations. As such, completing the graduate programs that students initiate can help them take the next step towards their careers of choice, even if the degree is not, strictly speaking, a relevant credential.

Although continuing with certain degree programs may not instantly qualify students for their ideal careers, they may discover new career opportunities that directly relate to their graduate degrees and experiences. This is especially true for jobs in emerging or relatively unfamiliar fields, or ones in which graduate degrees are preferred, regardless of the field. Student affairs and student services positions within postsecondary institutions offer a prime example. Most institutions do not hire individuals to fill these roles unless they have some sort of postbaccalaureate training, although the specific graduate degree may be unrelated to the duties of the position (Donahoo 2010; Kuk and Cuyjet 2009, 89–92; Mertz, Eckman, and Strayhorn 2012, 5–8; Richmond and Sherman 1991, 9–10; Taub and McEwen 2006, 206–208; Tull 2011, 125–127). Indeed, many individuals come to pursue careers in student affairs based on their experiences as students and the professionals that they encounter who work in these areas (Donahoo 2010; Taub and McEwen 2006, 210–211). Interactions with professionals possessing graduate degrees afford interested students opportunities to identify and prepare for careers they may have otherwise overlooked. Graduate students in all disciplines should learn more about the range of professional opportunities available in their fields.

Beyond gaining an additional degree, attending graduate school also provides an opportunity for students to continue to refine their thinking about the careers that suit them best. For various reasons, many students find themselves attracted to graduate programs that do not support their personal interests or long-term goals. While some can make the most of it, others may find it best to explore other academic programs that better match their academic and career interests. For example, students may initially enroll in one graduate program, yet take courses in others that they had little exposure to or information on before entering graduate school. Once admitted as a graduate student, institutions and degree programs permit students to take courses, thus allowing both the students and the programs to get to know each other before either side fully commits. While this can be a positive decision, transferring from one graduate program to another will cost students additional academic capital beyond that expended to gain admission, thus requiring students to work harder to gain ground in their new program. Graduate students considering such a change should find out as much as possible in order to make sure that such a move will truly address their concerns. At the same time, doing some investigative work on other programs may give students the chance to inform themselves on differences in financial support, research opportunities, transfer of credit, and so forth. As an alternative to changing programs, graduate students may find it beneficial to craft creative solutions by working with faculty members to blend program courses and requirements, establish a cognate/specialty area, or even pursue dual degrees. As with undergraduate programs, graduate programs often allow faculty members latitude to help students construct individualized degree requirements, allowing students to build in curricular elements aligned with their personal interests and career goals. Examples include joint degrees, internships, cross-listed courses, specialty areas, and graduate certificate programs that allow students to study law, teaching, finance, human resources, leadership, economics, healthcare, management, budgeting, administration, and other subjects from multiple departments, thus helping students bolster their preparation for careers in specific industries and occupations.

Sadly, some students do not find it possible to continue in graduate school. Whether troubled by family obligations, lack of financial support, academic issues, or a personal change in priorities, some graduate students leave programs without completing a degree. Surveying individuals who successfully completed a doctoral degree, the Council of Graduate Schools (2009) found financial support (80%), effective mentoring and advising (65%), and family (social/emotional) support (57%) to be the primary factors that allowed them to finish. It is reasonable to assume that the same factors often lead students to exit prematurely. It is important for students to address these situations as they arise, but not everyone can do so while maintaining their enrollment or continuing to make progress toward a degree. Just as Dorothy preferred to leave rather than participate in the power struggle affecting the Land of Oz, exiting graduate school without a degree may prove to be the best option for some students.

At the conclusion of her journey, Dorothy awakens to life on the farm in Kansas. While things look familiar, Dorothy's time in the Land of Oz has changed her. Now famous and well regarded in Oz, Dorothy returns to Kansas with new capital gathered during her time in Oz that she can use to better her life.

Functioning as a contemporary Land of Oz, graduate school provides students with multiple opportunities to expend and obtain academic capital. Whether their journeys end with a premature exit or the successful acquisition of a degree, participating in graduate education will have an influence on the capital that students possess, utilize to gain and sustain employment, and define themselves. Like Dorothy with her adventures in Oz, students should maximize their time in graduate school by acquiring new knowledge, developing new skills, and establishing new relationships—all of which will help them to achieve success during and after their enrollment. Although the journey toward earning a graduate degree will not always be easy, the academic and other forms of capital obtained in graduate school can help them to succeed and survive in the real world.

Works Cited

Austin, Ann E. 2002. "Preparing the Next Generation of Faculty: Graduate School as Socialization to the Academic Career." *Journal of Higher Education* 73 (1): 94–122.

Baxter Magolda, Marcia B. 1999. *Creating Contexts for Learning and Self-Authorship: Constructive-Developmental Pedagogy* (Vanderbilt Issues in Higher Education). Nashville, TN: Vanderbilt University Press.

Baxter Magolda, Marcia B. 2008. "Three Elements of Self-Authorship." *Journal of College Student Development* 49 (4): 269–284.

Council of Graduate Schools. 2009. *Ph.D. Completion and Attrition: Findings from Exit Surveys of Ph.D. Completers* [Executive Summary]. Washington, DC: Author. http://www.phdcompletion.org/information/Executive_Summary_Exit_Surveys_Book_III.pdf

Curry, Dan. 2001. "Texas Law Limits Use of Standardized Tests in Graduate Admissions." *The Chronicle of Higher Education*, July 13. http://chronicle.com/article/Texas-Law-Limits-Use-of/4236/

Curtin, Nicola, Abigail J. Stewart, and Joan M. Ostrove. 2013. "Fostering Academic Self-Concept: Advisor Support and Sense of Belonging among International and Domestic Graduate Students." *American Educational Research Journal* 50 (1): 108–137. doi: 10.3102/0002831212446662

Davis, Danielle J. 2007. "Access to Academe: The Importance of Mentoring to Black Students." *Negro Educational Review* 58 (3-4): 217–31.

Dodge, Laurie, and Ellen Baker Derwin. 2008. "Overcoming Barriers of Tradition Through an Effective New Graduate Admission Policy." *Journal of Continuing Higher Education* 56 (2): 2–11.

Donahoo, Saran. 2010. "Revealing the 'Hidden Profession': Student Pathways to Master's Degrees in Higher Education and Student Affairs." Paper presentation at the Thirty-fifth Annual Meeting of the Association for the Study of Higher Education, Indianapolis, IN, November 16–20.

Donahoo, Saran. 2011. "Capitalizing on Learning: Forms of Capital that Affect Graduate School Admissions and Achievement." In *Contemporary Perspectives on Capital in Educational Contexts*, edited by RoSusan Bartee, 203–17. Charlotte, NC: Information Age Publishing.

Feeley, Thomas Hugh, Vivian M. Williams, and Timothy J. Wise. 2005. "Testing the Predictive Validity of the GRE Exam on Communication Graduate Student Success: A Case Study at University of Buffalo." *Communication Quarterly* 53 (2): 229–45.

Fountaine, Tiffany Patrice. 2012. "The Impact of Faculty-Student Interaction on Black Doctoral Students Attending Historically Black Institutions." *The Journal of Negro Education* 81 (2): 136–47.

Gardner, Susan K. 2009. "Conceptualizing Success in Doctoral Education: Perspectives of Faculty in Seven Disciplines." *The Review of Higher Education* 32 (3): 383–406.

Gardner, Susan K. 2008. "'What's Too Much and What's Too Little?': The Process of Becoming an Independent Researcher in Doctoral Education." *The Journal of Higher Education* 79 (3): 326–50. doi: 10.1353/jhe.0.0007

Grote, Christopher L., William N. Robiner, and Allyson Haut. 2001. "Disclosure of Negative Information in Letters of Recommendation: Writers' Intentions and Readers' Experiences." *Professional Psychology: Research and Practice* 32 (6): 655–61.

Halberstam, Benjamin, and Fran Redstone. 2005. "The Predictive Value of Admissions Materials on Objective and Subjective Measures of Graduate School Performance in Speech-Language Pathology." *Journal of Higher Education Policy and Management* 27 (2): 261–72.

Jacobson, Robert L. 2003. "Critics Say Graduate Record Exam Does Not Measure Qualities for Success and Is Often Misused." *The Chronicle of Higher Education* 39 (29): A27-A, March 24.

Kuk, Linda, and Michael J. Cuyjet. 2009. "Graduate Preparation Programs: The First Step in Socialization." In *Becoming Socialized in Student Affairs Administration: A Guide for New Professionals and Their Supervisors*, edited by Ashley Tull, Joan B. Hirt, and Sue A. Saunders, 89–108. Sterling, VA: Stylus Publishing.

Lechuga, Vincente. 2011. "Faculty–Graduate Student Mentoring Relationships: Mentors' Perceived Roles and Responsibilities." *Higher Education* 62 (6): 757–71. doi: 10.1007/s10734-011-9416-0

Lovitts, Barbara E. 2008. "The Transition to Independent Research: Who Makes It, Who Doesn't, and Why." *Journal of Higher Education* 79 (3): 296–325.

Mertz, Norma, Ellen Eckman, and Terrell Strayhorn. 2012. "Entering Student Affairs: A Comparative Study of Graduate School Choice." *College Student Affairs Journal*, 30 (2): 1–14.

Noy, Shiri, and Rashwan Ray. 2012. "Graduate Students' Perceptions of Their Advisors: Is There Systematic Disadvantage in Mentorship?"

Journal of Higher Education 83 (6): 876–914.

Petress, Kenneth C. 1999. "Letters of Recommendation: Their Motive and Content." *College Student Journal* 33 (4): 485–87.

Pifer, Meghan J., and Vicki L. Baker. 2014. "'It Could Be Just Because I'm Different': Otherness and Its Outcomes in Doctoral Education." *Journal of Diversity in Higher Education* 7 (1): 14–30. doi: 10.1037/a0035858

Richmond, Jayne and Karen J. Sherman. 1991. "Student-Development Preparation and Placement: A Longitudinal Study of Graduate Students' and New Professionals' Experiences." *Journal of College Student Development* 32: 8–16.

Ruiz, Rebecca R. 2010. "Recession Spurs Interest in Graduate, Law Schools." *New York Times*, January 9. http://www.nytimes.com/2010/01/10/education/10grad.html?_r=0

Sacks, Peter. 2001. "How Admissions Test Hinder Access to Graduate and Professionals Schools." *Chronicle of Higher Education*, June 8. http://chronicle.com/article/How-Admissions-Tests-Hinder/16775

Schlemper, Mary Beth. 2011. "Challenges and Coping in Graduate School." *Geographical Bulletin* 52 (2): 67–72.

Strayhorn, Terrell L., and Melvin C. Terrell. 2007. "Mentoring and Satisfaction with College for Black Students." *Negro Educational Review* 58: 69–83.

Taub, Deborah J., and Marylu K. McEwen. 2006. "Decision to Enter the Profession of Student Affairs." *Journal of College Student Development* 47 (2): 206–16.

Tull, Ashley. 2011. "Promoting Effective Staffing Practices in Student Affairs: A Review of 10 Years of National Conference Curricula." *College Student Affairs Journal* 29 (2): 125–35.

U. S. Department of Education. 2014. *The Condition of Education.* Washington, DC: Institute of Education Sciences, National Center for Education Statistics. http://nces.ed.gov/programs/coe/indicator_chb.asp

13

Still on the Margins

Programs Aimed at Opening Up a Conversation on the Invisible Issue of Social Class in Doctoral Programs

Rosanne Ecker

In 2005, Syracuse University created a new position within its central career services office, specifically dedicated to helping doctoral students with a wide range of career needs, whether they were headed to an academic position or to work outside of the academy. My job included counseling Ph.D. students on an individual basis, helping them identify their interests and design relevant job application materials. In addition, I was responsible for developing programs that would best prepare them for the challenges of the job market.

I noticed that there was a subset of Ph.D. students who had difficulty, not only in preparing for the job market, but in navigating their doctoral programs as well. These were students who were clearly academically qualified, but felt somewhat lost among the intellectual norms of academia, differing in its social conventions and interpersonal expectations from those than they had experienced prior to graduate school. Many of these students were first-generation (first-gen) Ph.D. students, that is, Ph.D. students who came from families where neither parent had attended college, much less graduate school. Having myself been a first-gen Ph.D. student, I understood that social class issues could have a significant impact on students who came from working-class or nonacademic backgrounds as they crossed over into an academic environment with its attendant middle-class values and norms.

Fortunately for me, I was part of a centralized career services unit that provided me, in this groundbreaking position, with the freedom and flexibility to notice a need and design a program to meet that need without any bureaucratic red tape. I also worked collaboratively with the university's Graduate Student Organization, which acknowledged the need for such programs, approved additional funding, and helped market the career events. It is my hope that this chapter will inspire staff, graduate program administrators, and faculty at other universities to create programs that help first-gen Ph.D. students navigate their doctoral programs with confidence and support.

The impact of social-class issues first came to my attention when I met Mary, a doctoral student who came from the working class and whose parents had not even finished high school. She brought a unique perspective that afforded both special strengths and challenges in navigating the social and interpersonal requirements of a university environment and a Ph.D. program. Although clearly academically accomplished, Mary argued instead of debated, was hesitant to ask for help from professors, and had a hard time getting her family to support her pursuit of a Ph.D. I realized that Mary, myself, and others were members of a group that was largely invisible: people from the working class or poorer who were breaking new ground as first-gen Ph.D.'s.

I suspected that there must be more of us around, and sent out an email inviting first-gen Ph.D. students to join Mary and me for lunch. Coming from a New York City working-class family, I expected to see students from similar families—children of truck drivers and waitresses—show up for the program. The four students who heeded the call did, indeed, include someone who grew up poor in the "projects," but also included students who came from other parts of the world and very different backgrounds. One came from a non-college-educated military family. Another had 13 siblings, with little money for advanced schooling. The third came from China, where her family's education had been disrupted by political events. In these different ways, they all met my definition of first-gen, but for reasons I had never imagined.

We all had to learn to navigate the rules of the academy, engage in scholarly discourse, initiate and negotiate original research with an advisor who may not be supportive, and maintain a research or teaching assistantship in order to keep the stipend and tuition waiver that kept us funded at the university. Some had to learn the rules of the U.S. education system as well, including speaking up in class and even calling professors by their first names. All were new to the informal rules of scholarly discourse.

While the group was growing, I was reading *This Fine Place So Far from Home: Voices of Academics from the Working Class* (Dews and Law 1995). In story after story, this edited work spoke to a disconnect between the world of academia and the world of the old neighborhood, and the huge gap between them. It widened my understanding of the variety of students' life circumstances gave me confidence in my inclusive definition of first-gen.

I thought it would be helpful to their development as Ph.D. students and future academics for these students to hear from and be inspired by role models, and hoped that at Syracuse University there would be a few first-generation faculty who might be interested in passing on how they "made it" as faculty, despite the fact that their own parent(s) had not even understood what a dissertation was. So I sent out an email to all faculty to see if any would identify themselves as first-gen Ph.D.'s. My plan was to invite them to join the first-gen Ph.D. students at a social event.

This is the email I sent:

> *Dear faculty,*
>
> *I have started a peer support group for first-generation Ph.D. students as part of my work at SU in graduate student career services. Most of the parents of these doctoral students are from the working class and never attended college. We have met three times; each time we found common ground and had interesting discussions. The group is small but growing by word of mouth.*
>
> *These students are often the first in their entire extended family to have earned a bachelor's degree and are now in the process of getting their Ph.D.'s, moving farther and farther away from their families and from known territory. Most of these doctoral students aspire to be faculty.*
>
> *The group would benefit from meeting faculty who have made this journey themselves and welcome discussing your experience. If your parents did not attend college and you would be interested in coming to one of our meetings and contri-buting to the conversation, please send me an email. The next meeting will take place in mid- to late January.*
>
> *Thanks for your willingness to consider this opportunity to contribute to the professional development of Syracuse University doctoral students.*

The response was overwhelming—not only in numbers, but also in the enthusiasm of the faculty members who replied. I received over 40 responses from faculty, including the following, which came from assistant and associate professors:

I'd be happy to join in the conversation. Neither of my parents graduated from high school, so I definitely qualify! I'm also originally from [Central America] and came to the U.S. for college.

I would be happy to participate. I am the 6th of 7 children, and one sister went to one year of a junior college. Our parents finished 8th grade.

This is my story, too! I had no idea it was common; I assumed I was a rarity. Both of my parents are [high-school] graduates, with my father learning a trade in the military. I am the first in my family to go to college and went straight through to [the] doctorate. I'd be happy to meet with the group.

I come from a blue-collar farming background, but my father was an agricultural school graduate and my mother was a university graduate. I have for my (long) career as an academic felt an increasing gulf between an academic life and an agricultural life.

I'm a new faculty member at Syracuse University. I was the first in my family to go to college (father was a butcher and mother was a … mom). Everything beyond the bachelor's (M.S./Ph.D./postdoc) was completely alien to my family (same for my circle of friends, who are cops, firefighters, sanitation workers, etc.). I'd be more than happy to share my experience (either at one of your group meetings or if students would like to chat individually). I'm not that far removed from the Ph.D. process, so anything I can do to help.

I was delighted with the broad range of backgrounds that were represented by the responders. I hadn't anticipated faculty who came from farming backgrounds, military families, or very large families. It rapidly became apparent that there were many paths to becoming a first-gen Ph.D.

I explained to the group that I had held several meetings and lunches with doctoral students who were the first in their families to graduate college and then go on for a Ph.D., and that these students came from homes where parents may not have read books, or only the newspaper; may not have held intellectual discussions over dinner; or may have been supportive of academic opportunities but did not have a frame of reference for them. Each doctoral student's family is unique, and at the same time, many of us share common experiences. It became clear that these students, soon to become faculty, would benefit from the experience and advice of faculty who had already made this journey. Thus came about the first of six programs that I'd like to describe in varying detail—programs that opened up the opportunity to discuss social class and academia.

Program #1: Student–Faculty Lunch

The initial first-generation Ph.D. student/faculty event was a lunch program focused on social-class background. There were about 40 people in attendance, 25 students and 15 faculty. I had the students and faculty sit at round tables of eight (two faculty members per table), and in order to be sure that everyone got a chance to talk, I placed quotations at each table to use as discussion guides, appointing one of the faculty members as discussion leader. All quotes were taken from *This Fine Place So Far from Home.* These are some of the quotations I left on the tables:

> *I never spoke about my family at school, and I never spoke about school with my family. — A student*
>
> *Class poses different dilemmas than those posed by either race or gender in the academy. We do not cease being men and women, for instance, when we become doctors of Philosophy…. But, most of us do cease being working class when we become professors. — Carolyn Leste Law*
>
> *There is a nagging feeling of inferiority which intimidates many of us, sometimes to such an extent that fine minds never turn to academe. Some start and don't finish because the environment is so alien and because they can no longer tolerate worrying that they are frauds as they compete with those who are entitled.*
>
> *— Julie Charlip*
>
> *I would be reluctant to disclose that I'm from the working class to my colleagues. — A faculty member*
>
> *I will never be fluent in the language of the academy. It will always be at best a reluctantly learned second language. — C. L. Barney Dews*
>
> *My children are part of a social world that my parents, grandparents, and great-grandparents never experienced and one that does not represent my social origins. I am a link in social time and space. I am both insider and outsider in my new and old worlds. — Dwight Lang*

These table discussions were followed by comments from three faculty panelists whom I had selected on the basis of their particularly compelling emails.

The panel was given the following questions:

- How did you find your academic voice?

- How has your working-class background given you expanded tools, extra strength, or the work ethic necessary to face those challenges?
- What advice do you have for doctoral students here today?

It got quite intense in the room as it became clear that first-generation faculty were as eager to give advice as the Ph.D. students in attendance were to hear it. In fact, the panelists all commented that they wished a program like this one had been available to them when they were doctoral students. The tone in the room was personal and the advice was practical, consistent with the faculty's heartfelt interest in helping students avoid obstacles that they had experienced and overcome.

Faculty comments fell into three main categories. The first dealt with the insecurities they felt entering the strange, talk-focused, non-working-class world of academia. One professor likened it to being on Mars: an unfamiliar world of work where the product was not making an object or fixing something, but the intangible goal of creating new knowledge. Another confessed that he felt like an impostor, that he really didn't belong there and might be found out. Yet a third worried that at any moment it could all be taken away from him, that it was too good to be true. Each noted the challenge of straddling two worlds—the working-class world they came from and the academic career they aspired to.

The second category included broader philosophical thoughts. In responding to the question, "Do you feel you fit into academia?" one panelists replied, "Yes and no," explaining that he felt equal to his colleagues in achievements that were based on merit, like publications, but he was not as comfortable or confident in the social aspects of faculty life. Another panelist suggested that students think about the equality of human beings, noting that no person is better than another simply based on education.

Eager to make useful suggestions, all of the panelists urged students to get a mentor. "Ask and ask some more," they advised, pointing to the need for students to be assertive and find faculty members willing to guide them and their work. They also were in agreement in suggesting that students view academia as just another kind of work where you "leave it all on the field." It was clear that many students had learned a laudable work ethic from observing their parents putting forth their best effort. Faculty strongly advised taking their working-class work ethic with them into the academy. In the words of one panelist, "It is a gift!"

Following the panel was a large-group discussion. It was a very ambitious program with its goal of having both doctoral students and faculty share openly about their experience with the little-discussed issue of social class in academia. Emotionally exhausted but very pleased by the openness of the event, we concluded our first student–faculty program, emerging with a feeling of connection to each other, common ground between first-gen Ph.D. students and faculty, and students feeling that they were not alone. They also knew that their academic dreams were feasible, because present in the room were 15 faculty who had accomplished their dream.

Program #2: Mentors for First-Generation Ph.D. Students: How to Engage with Faculty Mentors

Since *mentoring* had emerged as a crucial theme for first-gen Ph.D. success, the next major program I organized (in addition to ongoing small, student-only lunches) was a discussion-focused program on the why's and how's of engaging mentors. I invited two highly motivated faculty to run a discussion group of ten students each. This mentoring program included "table talks" (with a discussion guide) and then a larger "community conversation" that I moderated, all focused on the nitty-gritty of engaging with and making best use of mentors during students' Ph.D. studies.

These are the questions that guided the table discussions, later to be opened up to the entire group in a more freewheeling conversation:

- Why do I need a mentor?
- How exactly do I find a mentor? How do I ask someone to be my mentor?
- Is it OK to look for more than one mentor?
- What is especially difficult about engaging a mentor for first-generation students?
- Should I find mentors outside of my department as well?
- Why would professors want to help me?
- What is reasonable to expect from a mentor?
- What should I contribute to the relationship to make it successful? That is, what does a mentor value in a mentee?
- What constitutes good manners in being mentored? What are the social expectations?

- How have good mentors actually contributed to the success of first-generation faculty?

The recommendations that emerged from the discussion highlighted the value of attending social events and conferences and making connections at each event. While the students were focused on the kind of academic achievement that had brought them to their doctoral program, faculty affirmed that in addition to attending classes, it is vital that students attend social events in their departments so that both the faculty and fellow students can get to know them as people. Faculty also suggested asking senior graduate students for tips on navigating departmental politics, comprehensive exams, and other challenges of a doctoral program. For more advanced students, service to the department, such as membership on a hiring committee, can help extend networks and enhance a student's professional profile. Despite the general good sense of these suggestions, networking is largely a middle-class endeavor and, for first-gen students, not obviously a valuable use of time, so this message was new to many of them.

Faculty also emphasized the importance of engaging with scholars from other departments, and with the life of the campus generally. Most universities offer professional development opportunities that extend across departments and colleges. Campus-wide events and programs give students the chance to broaden their scope, make connections, and even meet future collaborators. The years spent pursuing a Ph.D. will be richer for students with wide social, cultural, and intellectual networks. An academic career requires many mentors and supports, and first-gen students can put themselves at a disadvantage by habitually "pulling themselves up by their bootstraps" and going it alone.

At the same time, faculty affirmed the importance of reaching beyond the university to find collaborators and professional friends among their peers at other institutions. Ph.D. students need to recognize that they have a cohort not only within their departments, but across all Ph.D.-granting universities. Conference attendance is the main avenue for forging relationships within this larger cohort. Funds for conference travel and registration are often available at the department and college levels, through graduate student associations/organizations, or through professional organizations. Although easily lost on students preoccupied with classes, teaching, and working in their labs, professional relationships cultivated at local, regional, national, and international conferences are important for their careers over the long term. However, those relationships need to be nourished with email and other forms of follow-up contact.

Program #3: Advice from Advanced First-Generation Ph.D. Students

The advice from faculty and the mentoring group, facilitated by faculty, were wonderfully instructive and supportive. However, I felt that we also had a great untapped resource in the resilient and tenacious first-gen students who had stuck with their doctoral programs and were now advanced Ph.D. candidates. I very much wanted them to pass on their hard-earned advice on surviving and thriving in their doctoral program to the newer first-gen Ph.D. students, so I set up a panel/lunch program where the advanced students could give insider tips to incoming first-gen doctoral students. Four advanced first-generation Ph.D. candidates from different fields and different countries served as panelists. Each panelist introduced themselves and described their background, as well as some of the challenges they faced in transitioning to life as a Ph.D. student. After the introductions, I asked each panelist to respond to two questions:

1. What do you wish you had known when you began your doctoral program?
2. Looking back over your experiences in your doctoral program, what advice do you most want to pass on?

As soon as the audience became engaged, I opened the floor for questions and a very lively discussion ensued.

One important area that advanced doctoral students emphasized was choosing as an advisor someone who supports Ph.D. students and whose students have a high rate of completing their degree. In some Ph.D. programs the students have an opportunity to get to know the faculty before being paired with an advisor. In addition, they suggested finding out if an advisor or advisor-to-be is planning a sabbatical, and if so, what communication strategy can be put in place to minimize this difficulty. Lastly, it was strongly suggested to cultivate multiple mentors, so alternatives are at hand if a primary faculty supporter is unavailable. This can be very difficult for students who have been accustomed to pulling themselves up by their own bootstraps, so that the very act of asking for help seems like an admission of inadequacy. Understanding that no one accomplishes a Ph.D. alone is a critical step that advanced students urged on their junior colleagues.

Several other valuable themes emerged from these discussions, including:

- The importance of *being able to explain a dissertation to non-experts* and others who may have no concept of what doctoral work entails. Ideas that can't be communicated succinctly are also less likely to be appreciated in professional arenas like conferences and grant applications, or by potential collaborators. Reversing the poles, friends and family members can serve as "expert" consultants in crafting descriptions and explanations that can reach wider audiences.
- The importance of *making the most of the library's resources*—including subject librarians, research databases, and private study carrels—and learning how to use them effectively.
- The importance of *teaching*. It can be difficult to get teaching opportunities in some departments, but liberal arts colleges and many other institutions often prioritize teaching experience in faculty searches, while presentation and interpersonal skills honed in the classroom are in demand by nonacademic employers. Peer observations are a good way to get feedback—and less threatening than classroom visits by faculty, especially for novice teachers.
- The importance of *addressing parental/family expectations*, especially around the earning power of the Ph.D. Family members are likely to regard graduate school as an economic investment, and may have a hard time understanding the logic of lengthy programs that do not lead to spectacular salaries, especially for academics. Conversations that bridge the expectation gap are crucial to keeping families of first-generation students engaged and supportive.

Though by no means exhaustive, these observations provided first-generation graduate students earlier in their programs with strategies for navigating the complexities of graduate school life.

Program #4: First-Generation Ph.D. Social Gathering with Remarks by an Upper-Tier Academic Administrator

I wanted to gather first-generation Ph.D.'s again, so I reached out to a wonderfully strategic and generous upper-tier administrator within Academic Affairs, who herself had a good mentor and is committed to mentoring Ph.D. students. This former scientist grew up in the working class around her family-owned gas station and understood very well the difference between gas-station language and the language used for negotiating academic politics and a successful career. She was also a competitive person by nature and had great advice on what it takes to succeed as a faculty member. I decided to host an informal social gathering and invite this administrator to make some remarks. Once again, the session was intense and highly instructive.

The administrator provided heartfelt yet practical advice, focusing on three key areas: mentorship, peer relationships, and respect. First and foremost, she underscored the importance of caring and invested mentors who will support and advocate for first-gen doctoral students throughout their programs, making connections and opening doors. She referenced her own mentor and discussed how mentors form a link in the chain of one's academic lineage, serving as an "academic parent" to shepherd a doctoral student through the joys and challenges of completing the Ph.D. and entering professional life. It is very important to nurture mentoring relationships and to build a network of supportive faculty.

Similarly, she stressed the importance of connections with peers, especially those who are also first-generation. Classmates will likely go on to work in universities, funding agencies, academic administration, and other fields. Some may go on to become editors of journals. Actively cultivating a peer network in graduate school can yield enormous dividends at later career stages. Doctoral students have a one-time opportunity to form close relationships with future colleagues who can learn from and support each other as their careers unfold and evolve.

Finally, the administrator underscored the need for a respectful posture—not only toward mentors, faculty, and peers, but toward university administrators, office staff, contract employees, and others who keep the academic environment up and running. Learning this lesson in graduate school is great preparation for any professional path, where success will depend on good working relationships at all levels. Ph.D.-holders are fortunate to be able to organize their working lives around their intellectual interests. Getting a Ph.D. is an opportunity to do fulfilling work, not a reason to adopt a superior attitude—however tempting this may be for those who have spent much of their lives laboring under a cloud of "inferiority."

At the end of each program, I always found it useful to tap the captive audience of student attendees for ideas for future Ph.D. career programs. Some ideas that emerged from this program included:

1. learning how to explain what you do in the academy to non-academics;

2. becoming skilled at negotiating both the world of one's origins and the academic world;
3. gaining confidence in how to dress at an academic conference;
4. "owning" being a Ph.D. student and finding an academic voice;
5. learning dining etiquette, specifically for first-gen students who may not feel sufficiently familiar with the finer points of dining.

Again, these are not exhaustive, but they provide a blueprint for future activities that can be undertaken at a wide variety of institutions.

Program #5: Etiquette Dinner for First-Generation Ph.D. Students

This program was a direct outgrowth of a student's suggestion at the event described above. It made so much sense that dining etiquette could be intimidating with its class overtones. Therefore, first-gen students were the first graduate students invited to the next Etiquette Dinner for Graduate Students, and they came and learned and enjoyed themselves. Sometimes the most intimidating part of academic job candidacy can be mealtimes. Campus interviews, which often have a lunch and/or dinner component, can create a lot of anxiety in the applicant regarding which fork to use for what, and other middle-class behaviors that were not part of their background. Proper etiquette is easily learnable, and since table manners are class-related, it made sense to give first-generation students priority at the event.

Clearly, it could be a challenge for some students from working-class backgrounds to encounter, during an already stressful on-campus academic interview, a place setting that involves two glasses, two or three forks, two knives, two spoons, and many plates. It seemed to make sense that, given the class overtones of dining etiquette, these students would benefit from an education in middle-class dining norms.

Many campuses hold etiquette dinners for undergraduate students to prepare them for the corporate world. Therefore, the Syracuse University Faculty Center was prepared to offer an array of challenges, from how to eat soup, to the protocol for passing salad dressing, to the proper use of bread and butter plates, to the best placement of water and wine glasses, and more. This program was similar to undergraduate etiquette dinners, the main difference being that preference in registration was given to first-generation doctoral students, who consequently made up most of the 70 attendees. The presenter included phrases like, "when you go for lunch during an on-campus interview ..." to make it relevant to aspiring academics. The etiquette educator was also attuned to the fact that many students were both first-generation and international, and that it was important to be clear and basic regarding both middle-class norms as well as American dining practice.

Program #6: Trip to See the Play *Good People*

Near the end of the academic year I saw at our local theater David Lindsay-Abaire's play *Good People*, a social-class drama about two people from South Boston, one of whom becomes a physician and "makes it out" of his poor neighborhood via education, while the other remains stuck and left behind. The play addresses such questions as, Why do some people make it out and others don't? Is it all hard work? What about luck or other circumstances? How much does parental support matter? How about values? How important is willingness to ask for help?

I thought this play had a lot to offer to first-gen students, even those from other countries, rural environments, and diverse backgrounds, because it dealt with the degree of control we have over our circumstances—in particular, becoming educated and making it into the middle class. I sent out an invitation to all Ph.D. students. Eighteen attended (two brought partners) and had a lively discussion about it over a beer (or wine, for those transitioning to the middle class!). Students commented that the play reminded them how lucky they were in having come upon the resources to help them pursue a higher education. It made clear that some people never have the choice of pursuing a Ph.D. and that they did, so it helped put their efforts into context.

The theme of what it is like to live in two different worlds—the one you come from and the one you're going to—resonated with many of the attendees. One specific example of straddling two worlds is becoming adept at explaining what you do to people in your old world who may not have had much formal education. The play caused the students to reflect on the difficulty of explaining their work to their families and friends in a meaningful and understandable way. One character in the play reflected on his experience of shifting back and forth between different speech patterns and mannerisms when he was at home with his friends and family versus when he was at school with his academic colleagues. The play-goers acknowledged that this was an ongoing challenge, and a worthy topic for future programming.

All in all, the students truly enjoyed their experience with this quintessentially middle- and upper-class form of entertainment because they could identify with the theme and characters.

Carrying It Forward

Based on the success of the initial set of programs described above, I sought and received funding from Syracuse University's Graduate Student Organization for a series of lunches that would allow first-gen students to mix informally with first-gen faculty outside the confines of anyone's department or program. The lunch series has been renewed each year and now constitutes a regular offering, with each lunch having an announced theme or topic for discussion.

Going forward, I would like to see "first-gen ally" signs on faculty office doors, similar to the "safe zone" signs announcing LGBT allyship, so that doctoral students from the working class and poorer will know where they can have conversations about their backgrounds with academics who have "been there." But while private, confidential discussions are essential, we also need to create space for wider conversations on the impact of social class on students and professors in today's academic world. These conversations should not only center on the disadvantages and deficits first-gen Ph.D. students face; they should likewise celebrate the fortitude and courage of those who make the journey from a non-academic life (possibly one in which books are not valued) to a life of creating new knowledge and sharing it with the world. Crucially, we must acknowledge the importance of building community within the first-gen population, and the key role that can be played in this by faculty with true empathy and a willingness to provide mentorship and guidance.

There is also a role for formal programming, as I hope to have shown. Whether originating in a career services office, a graduate school, a graduate student organization, an individual school or college, or elsewhere, orchestrated events can help first-gen students identify each other—the first, indispensable step in community building. Such events also signal that the institution recognizes and values first-gen identity in the same way that it honors racial, ethnic, gender/sexuality, and religious difference within the campus community. Without that recognition, first-gen students can easily feel isolated and reluctant to integrate fully. While there is no guarantee that all programs aimed at first-gen doctoral students will succeed on their own terms, something is most definitely better than nothing. Even modest gestures of institutional support can go a long way toward creating the conditions for first-gen doctoral students to thrive on their long and demanding path.

Work Cited

Dews, C. L. Barney, and Carolyn Leste Law, eds. 1995. *This Fine Place So Far from Home: Voices of Academics from the Working Class*. Philadelphia: Temple University Press.

14

The House that Networking Built
Perspectives from a First-Generation Scholar

Taren Swindle

As a first-generation student from a farming family, I knew little about professional networking as I entered higher education. I had heard the phrase, "It's not what you know, it's who you know." I assumed this was a cynical cliché, and that I could get where I wanted to be in life based on merit and hard work. I was wrong. With the passage of time and the benefit of experience, I now realize that my achievements, my research interests, and my ideas can only propel me toward the career I desire if they are known by others. It *is* a little about who you know, but it is a *lot* about who knows you.

First-generation college students, those like me, not only don't believe in the power of networking, they don't really have any clue what it is in a practical sense. As I came to find out, networking is "sharing your ideas and passion, listening to your colleagues and their current research, finding new collaborators, and introducing people to one another to make ideas and projects grow" (Carpenter 2014). Networking requires actively building and maintaining relationships with those in your career field. Research on net-working suggests that networking behaviors (e.g., increasing visibility, engaging in professional activities) are predictive of promotions, compensation, and perceived success (Forret and Dougherty 2004; Wolff and Moser 2009).

These research findings are consistent with social capital theory, which posits that capital, like money, can be leveraged to secure something of value. Capital comes in three forms: economic, social, and cultural (Bourdieu 1989). One type of capital can be exchanged for another type of capital. Cultural capital is defined as "the habitus of cultural practices, knowledge, and demeanors learned through exposure to role models in the family and other environments" (Portes 2000, 5); economic capital refers to financial resources; and social capital has to do with the social structures that allow one to pursue one's interests (Baker 1990). Greater social capital is related to a host of positive outcomes, including career success (Ng et al. 2005), which is explained largely by increased access to information and resources (Seibert, Kraimer, and Liden 2001). Given that first-generation students are likely to come from families of lower socio-economic status and to have fewer examples of successful academic role models in their home environment, first-generation academics begin their professional journeys at a "capital disadvantage." It is better that we are aware of this disadvantage and improve this position through the tools available. Networking is one such crucial tool allowing first-generation scholars to overcome disadvantaged histories, increase available capital, and propel careers forward.

However, many first-generation scholars, including myself, suffer some degree of impostor syndrome, which can be a barrier to networking and success. Impostor syndrome is the feeling that one does not belong in in a particular social or occupational space, such as the academy, because of one's inferiority to others. Valerie Young (2011), building on the earlier work of Clance and Imes (1978), applied this concept to understanding successful women who, despite their success, struggled to discard the idea that they are not as intelligent or capable as their colleagues. A recent review by Parkman and colleagues (2016) finds that impostor syndrome occurs among both men and women, among college students and faculty, and across a range of professions and academic majors. Most relevant to this discussion, their review found that family background was an important predictor of impostor feelings. Specifically, individuals coming from homes where they had to execute a parenting function (i.e., parentification), or from homes where they were first to exceed the family norms regarding education or employment, were more likely to have impostor feelings. Minority status was another key correlate of impostor syndrome. For example, Drew (2012) found that minorities may feel that they have helped an institution "check the box" for diversity rather than viewing their position as earned. It's no wonder that first-generation students have impostor feelings! Notably, however, there were no studies in the Parkman review linking impostor feelings to actual ability; these feelings aren't grounded in reality.

Despite its prevalence, impostor syndrome is accompanied by potentially serious consequences. Impostor feelings may encourage first-generation students to turn inward, contributing to social isolation rather than effective networking and career-building. Impostor syndrome can lead to anxiety, depression, and decreased self-efficacy (Parkman 2016). Given that first-generation scholars are particularly vulnerable to impostor feelings, we must be diligent in opposing it and the negative effects it can convey. Based on current research, I present several recommendations to fight impostor syndrome:

Realize that a range of feelings are normal but not necessarily true. We are not our thoughts (Tolle 2004, 9–18). This was an enormous revelation to me. Before being exposed to this concept, I blindly accepted whatever thoughts crossed my mind as truth. If I thought I was less capable, then it must be true. Over time and with practice, I have begun to question my thoughts. I ask myself, "What evidence do I have to support this feeling? Is this a helpful mindset?" I find that I am better able (but still practicing) to disregard thoughts that have no basis in fact or that are not productive.

Focus on what you do well and become even better. Many first-generation academics (and many people more broadly) focus on fixing weaknesses rather than bolstering strengths, frequently to their detriment (Rath 2007). In fact, I was five years into my professional career before someone introduced me to this idea through Rath's (2007) StrengthsFinder assessment. If you are struggling to know your own strengths and build upon them, this tool provides an accessible and practical way to get started.

Write down successes, large and small (e.g., exam grades, discussion leadership). No one has a success to celebrate each day. However, it can often be those days without successes, or perhaps a stretch of those days, that may trigger a slip into impostor feelings. It is in these stretches that we may need a source of external validation to put these feelings aside. Refer to the list when comparison to others is tempting (Drew 2012, 16).

Pursue logic to its natural end. This is a core component of an evidence-based approach called Rational Emotive Behavior Therapy (Ellis 1999). While it can be helpful to see a therapist to change thought patterns, this strategy can also be applied by an individual herself. This practice is complementary to, yet distinct from, the previously discussed concept of challenging our thoughts. For example, first-generation scholars may think they are the least qualified in the room. Rather than repressing this thought or surrendering to feelings of inferiority, a scholar employing principles of Rational Emotive Behavior Therapy might ask, "If this is true, what follows from it?"—a possible conclusion being that the scholar has a greater opportunity to learn than do non-first-generation colleagues (a wonderful thing!). Ellis states, "When people keep challenging and questioning their self-disturbing core philosophies, after a while they tend to automatically, and even in advance, bring new, rational, self-helping attitudes to their life problems and thereby make themselves significantly less upsettable, sometimes for the rest of their lives" (71).

Whatever we do, first-generation students cannot let false feelings of inferiority keep us from making intentional and powerful connections with others through networking. While I will not provide an exhaustive review of the literature on networking impacts and tactics, I can provide an outline of my personal experiences with and perspectives on networking from the vantage point of a first-generation scholar. I will describe how networks, much like houses, are built in phases that require a specific set of strategies at each stage. Using the metaphor of home construction, I will describe how each career stage may entail different goals, and different strategies to achieve those goals. For each stage, I have provided questions to aid in developing a habit of intentional self-reflection. In doing so, I hope to offer a practical and ongoing method of self-assessment that scholars can use to evaluate their networking strategies and activities throughout a career.

Networking as an Undergraduate: Selecting a Blueprint

First-generation students, especially women, receive less social support than other students (Jenkins et al. 2013); they report a diminished sense of belonging in their college communities (Stebleton, Soria, and Huesman 2014), and fewer interactions with faculty (Soria and Stebleton 2012). Stephens, Fryberg, and Markus (2012) attribute some of their difficulty to the transition from a "culture of interdependence" to a "culture of independence." Cultures of interdependence affirm values for student learning such as "learning to work together with others" and "asking for help," versus values of independence such as "learning to express oneself" and "influencing others." First-generation students typically have values more consistent with interdependence (e.g., "I want to bring honor to my family") and do better academically in a learning environment with interdependent values. Stephens and colleagues termed this "cultural match." What I want to suggest is that this interdependent orientation equips first-generation students well for networking. Let me explain why I believe this is so.

Because of their backgrounds in low-resource communities, first-generation students understand what it is like to be aware of and concerned about the needs of others. First-generation students understand the need to work together toward common goals. What we do not understand is flagrant self-promotion, pretention, and name-dropping—all things I had automatically associated with "networking." This inaccurate, preconceived notion kept me from being effective at relating to others in my earliest years of college. I assumed that networking amounted to devising a way to use others to my own advantage. I had no conception that quality networking is much more like the caring and collaboration I had seen in my community.

Thus, the first and biggest networking lesson for me involved learning what networking was and was not. Networking is not a specific script that everyone must follow. Rather, it is up to each person to approach networking in a way consistent with their own values, preferences, and goals. In this sense, becoming a skilled networker is like building a home for yourself—it must be one you are comfortable in and that reflects your personality and style. Thus, the first stage to leveraging the power of networking across a career is selecting a blueprint. It is in the undergraduate phase that the "layout" of networking can be discovered.

Am I putting myself in uncomfortable situations?

Having now completed my doctorate, I can admit with some embarrassment that I did not know what a Ph.D. was when I arrived as a freshman in college. Fortunately, I was referred to the McNair Scholars Program (for first-generation, low-income college students), which gave me information and opportunities that I needed to better understand and navigate higher education. With the explicit intent of mentoring us toward doctoral degrees, the McNair program provided us deliberate guidance in professional conduct, presenting, and networking. While we were given opportunities to practice these new skills, I must confess that I was uncomfortable, intimidated, and afraid of failing. My discomfort and doubts came, in part, from the impostor syndrome I previously described (Gardner and Holley 2011). Networking can feel at first like "posing"—not being true to one's roots, like a "game." Thankfully, I discovered over time that this was not the case.

Tim Sanders, in *Love is the Killer App* (2002), has articulated the same idea and applied it to the area of business success. Sanders recommends the qualities of a "Lovecat," who shares her knowledge, network, and compassion with others to ultimately foster her own success. The Lovecat principle works, says Sanders, because individuals gain the trust and attention of others through genuine interactions. Practical suggestions for making these types of worthwhile connections abound, for example, in Sanders' chapter on compassion, which describes strategies such as "quick ops" (e.g., small commitments of help, hallway conversations) and creating meaningful salutations, among others. Hearing that these were networking strategies that others had to work as adults to *learn* made me feel ahead of the game. I was thrilled to know that the values instilled in me by my family and community were consistent with successful networking. Specific networking behaviors (e.g., socializing, engaging in professional activities) have been linked with both personal perceptions of career success and objective measures such as total compensation (Forret and Dougherty 2004). As a first-generation student, it was such a relief to me to learn that I could be myself and network at the same time.

Research attests that social and professional connections made as an undergraduate can carry over for many years. For example, undergraduate networking experiences such as internships are related to later success, including greater salaries and job satisfaction (Gault, Redington, and Schlager 2000). Further, intentionally networking with individuals that are different in terms of race, gender, and social class is predictive of positive outcomes (Rhodes and Butler 2010). While first-generation students may already feel comfortable connecting and networking with others from similar backgrounds, college is a time to apply these skills more broadly. Use college as a time to test networking strategies and find a style that works for you. Stewart and colleagues (2014) provide several ideas to use as starting points. These include setting weekly networking goals for meeting new people or reconnecting with existing contacts, practicing asking sincere questions with those you know well, and offering to do something of value for a new contact. Any discomfort from working to improve your Lovecat skills and spread your network will be worth it.

Am I treating every encounter equally?

First-generation academics have no idea, especially at this stage in their development, to whom they might be speaking. In presenting at a student research symposium sponsored by McNair, I had a graduate student pass by my research poster. She showed a moment's interest in my work, so I pounced at the opportunity to tell her all about my project.

Through our conversation, she realized my research was in line with ongoing work of faculty in her department. Before the afternoon was over, she had convinced these faculty members to meet me. The exchange went quite well, and less than six months later I found myself enrolled in a master's program at that institution. Not only was the match perfect for my interests, the mentorship and relationships I gained through my time at that institution continue to impact my professional development. While I am by no means perfect at recognizing the potential of every encounter, I sometimes stop to wonder how my path would have been different had I not engaged professionally with the other student, asked her about her own research, and discovered the work that led to my own graduate career.

A few years later, I was presenting another poster as a graduate student at the leading research conference in my field. I was shocked to realize (after he had walked away) that I had been conversing with one of the leading researchers in my area, someone that I had cited heavily. I was courteous in our interactions, but unlike the previous interaction I described, I did not take the time to ask questions about his work, to understand his interest in my topic, or to make a meaningful connection. This was a missed opportunity.

The primary difference between the two interactions, I now understand, is the use and nonuse of the Lovecat principle. On the first occasion, I engaged with the other individual around *our* research and shared ideas. On the second, I wanted to make a good impression with my findings so badly that I overlooked openings to express genuine appreciation for his curiosity and to connect around our common interests. Each and every professional (and personal) interaction is potentially relevant to future goals and progress.

Networking in Graduate School: Laying the Foundation

A qualitative study on the transition to graduate school found that first-generation McNair graduate students found that building a social network in academia involved a "significant learning curve" and that developing professional interaction skill took time and intent (Willison and Gibson 2011). For some first-generation students in the study, graduate school marked their first time away from home, and this demanded separating from their primary network and forming new networks, all while balancing the academic work load. While the study participants acknowledged these difficulties, they also described the progress they had made in this area. One participant, now a college professor, stated, "Creating those relationships with those people is what helps you to learn to navigate places. Those are the situations that have really benefited me, how I've gotten the job where I'm at and things like that" (Willison and Gibson 2011, 9). Graduate school is the time when first-generation academics begin laying the foundation with the networking blueprint selected—and a house is only as good as its foundation. Thus, the more work put into networking at this stage, the better positioned the student will be to obtain a desired job and be successful in it.

Am I maximizing my opportunities?

Graduate students have great opportunities to network but will also be tempted to let them pass. For example, a professor's research lab may sponsor students to attend a professional conference to present collaborative research; there will be receptions and networking events, not to mention all the interesting research of peers and the leading colleagues in the field. These are all great opportunities to meet new people and become known in professional circles.

Yet graduate students also have limited funds to travel, and they deserve far more vacation than they can take. It wouldn't hurt to skip those open receptions, right? Wrong. I made this mistake. I mostly wasted the first conference I attended. (I did see basketball star Shaquille O'Neal at one of the local dives, but that has not proved to be beneficial to my professional advancement.) I suggest sightseeing in the evening. Better yet, plan ahead and save so you can take extra time for a real, guilt-free vacation. I realized this myself four years after the Shaq conference, when I met a well–respected expert in my field at a poster reception. We had a wonderful conversation that transformed over time into a formal mentoring relationship. This mentor now goes above and beyond to connect me with seasoned researchers and promising junior investigators across the country. I sure am glad I didn't opt for the trolley tour instead.

National conferences might come around once or twice per year. However, I suspect there are monthly, or even weekly, opportunities to network on campus or in the area. As first-generation academics struggle to achieve equilibrium between the fun, carefree college life of the past and the successful career of the future, there will be plenty of opportunities to choose amusement in the present over investment in the future. While there is certainly room for balance between the two, choose strategically.

Remember, too, that networking includes peer-to-peer interactions.

The connections that I built with fellow graduate students, both off and on my campus, continue to represent some of the most meaningful, supportive, and openly collaborative relationships I have. Say yes to yoga with a new classmate when you are feeling exhausted. Take a break from the mounds of assigned reading for chocolate pie with your cohort at a local diner. I am glad I did.

Am I talking with my peers and mentors about my next step and ultimate career goals?

Because of regular conversations with one of my master's advisors, she knew that I needed to relocate upon completion of my degree to meet the needs of my husband's educational plan. While she wanted me to stay on and complete my doctorate at her institution, she knew that this was not feasible for our family. When interacting with a friend of a friend at a regional conference, my advisor realized she was talking to someone from my soon-to-be new home. She mentioned my name and research accomplishments (merit does play a role!), and because of this networking, I forged a link with the institution at which I continue to work today. If she had not known about my plans and dreams for the future, she would not have had the opportunity to make this contact for me. Be sure that mentors are in a position to listen and share on your behalf. Do the same for others.

Networking as a Young Professional: Building the House

There is little research following first-generation scholars from graduate school into their professional careers. However, studies in the general population find that early-career networking is associated with later career success, both objectively (i.e., compensation) and subjectively (i.e., job satisfaction) (Kuijpers, Schyns, and Scheerens 2006; Vos, Dewilde, and Clippeleer 2009). To put it bluntly, what first-generation scholars do in the first few years in the field can set their career trajectory.

Unsurprisingly, early-career academics report that collegial relationships are critical (Carroll et al. 2010). Future funding collaborations, job opportunities, coauthored manuscripts, and other opportunities come from networks developed during this period (Ansmann et al. 2014). I discover every day how new connections transform the landscape of possibilities for the future. While I can renovate or expand at a later date, I realize that the house I am building now is the house in which I will live the rest of my professional career. Building this house is tireless but stimulating work.

Am I branding myself in a specific network?

In graduate school, you are likely to have done research exclusively in your department faculty's areas of interest. There may not have been opportunity to begin developing a unique, individualized research agenda apart from your mentors. As first-generation academics launch their own careers, it is time to define the area of research in which you want to make an impact. Continue to cast off those feelings of impostor syndrome and employ strategies to affirm your position and value. As first-generation professionals seek to make their own "brand," intentional investment is needed to link into a specific network. In six years' time, a new faculty member will need experts in their specific field to write letters for promotion, demonstrating national recognition and contribution to the field.

To have an opportunity to employ Lovecat skills, first-generation scholars must put themselves in positions to meet other key players in the field. At this career stage, young faculty are invited to engage in many service opportunities. Resist. Be picky. Only agree to the ones that align with targeted, valuable networks. Seek out committees on which leading researchers in your field or on your campus serve. Meet the people who need to know you.

I found the following to be helpful in making intentional connections. First, do research. When planning to attend national grantee meetings, research conferences, or other professional gatherings, review the program. Take note of who will be in attendance and who will be presenting. Next, reach out to contacts of interest. At a minimum, plan to attend the sessions of those you would like to meet. Stay late to introduce yourself, and ask meaningful questions. If you are feeling more adventurous, email ahead of time and tell them how much you admire their work and how it has impacted your interests, and request an opportunity to meet over a cup of coffee or make contact at a reception already on the program. Think of a couple key questions to ask when you can meet, but do allow for the conversation to develop naturally; be yourself. Finally, follow up. Email your new contact to thank them for their time. State that you look forward to interacting more in the future.

Do I still have mentors?

In graduate school, mentorship is a given. Students have to listen to and follow closely the advice of faculty to navigate the hoops to graduation. For first-generation scholars, graduate school may still include extra support through targeted programs like McNair. Most often, however, the workplace environment that follows graduate school does not provide structure for mentoring. While I have been fortunate in having a seamless transition to mentorships as an early career professional, some of my peers have not been so lucky. Find the faculty development office at your institution, if there is one. Seek out the early-career committee of your leading scholarly society, if there is one. Ask if they can recommend a mentor, or better yet multiple mentors or a mentoring committee (Janasz and Sullivan 2004). As new faculty members without the benefit of family connections or experience with higher education, it is critical for first-generation scholars to link to more experienced faculty to build local networks (see Haynes, Adams, and Boss 2008 for more advice on securing a mentor). Receiving mentorship predicts career success—both directly, by expanding their mentees' networks, and indirectly, by having a positive impact of their protégé's networking abilities (Blickle, Witzki, and Schneider 2009).

At a grant-writing workshop, I recently received some advice that is consistent with my observations and the existing literature on the importance of mentorship. The presenter admitted that the key to getting National Institute of Health (NIH) funding was getting NIH funding. That is, once a research has received NIH funding, subsequent support is easier to obtain. What's the key to getting the first grant, you ask? He said (and I can attest), it's *who* is helping the research through the critical stages. When writing a grant application early in your career, select a primary mentor who has a funding history with the targeted agency. Their experience and name will matter. To be in a position to do this, first-generation academics need to begin networking early with potential mentors. Asking for grant support during a first interaction will likely not work.

Of course, a good mentoring relationship is two-sided. To receive the best possible mentorship, first-generation scholars must be the best possible mentees. De Janasz, Sullivan, and Whiting (2003) describe specific strategies for becoming a good mentee—one who can capitalize on mentorship received. Though written from a business career standpoint, their work provides a range of helpful suggestions, including adapting to ever-changing mentoring relationships as they ebb, flow, and, ultimately, end. The authors emphasize the importance of providing an acknowledgment of the contributions of mentors, giving feedback and appreciation to mentors, and recognizing the degree to which mentors can contribute given their current obligations. From my personal experience, I have found that mentors particularly appreciate well-organized meetings and communications. I seek to set a regular, recurring meeting before which I organize an agenda of topics I would like to cover. I communicate these topics and between-meeting requests for input and feedback in brief, bulleted emails. My goal is to always respect the time of the mentor. These strategies can contribute to what de Janasz and colleagues describe as becoming the "perfect protégé" (2003, 22).

Networking in Mid-Career and Beyond: Practicing Hospitality

As family demands encroach and academics become increasingly capable of independent research, it will likely be tempting to reduce or stop intentional networking efforts. Female first-generation academics are particularly vulnerable to such temptation, as they report greater family responsibility than their non-first-generation counterparts (Seay 2010). Faced with this type of stress, continued networking may not seem as critical.

Perhaps surprisingly, a recent study of networking among faculty reports that the belief that networks improve social capital (i.e., "perceived network capital") and "agency behaviors" (e.g., writing papers, submitting grant applications, asking for resources) are more strongly correlated among full professors than among assistant and associate professors (Niehaus and O'Meara 2015). That is, the relationship between scholars' perceived network capital on the one hand, and their actual productivity on the other, increases rather than decreases across academic career stages. Given this finding, it is critical that scholars in more advanced career stages ensure that the hard work of their early careers is not wasted. Maintenance of one's network is the minimum; cultivation is the goal. To achieve these outcomes, one must practice hospitality. Over the course of many years of hard work, you have built a beautiful home. It's time to maintain its integrity and to extend its warmth and shelter to others.

Am I maintaining my networks?

I suspect that few academics are investing in their careers with the hope that their work will be forgotten as soon as they stop publishing. Rather, I believe that most academics hope their work has a long-term impact on the field and the researchers that follow them. We want to leave a legacy. To accomplish that goal, one's network must continue expanding and evolving across a career. Networking with other professionals at various career stages will maximize the likelihood that our work will have a lasting impact. The visibility gained through networking will also increase opportunities for the interdisciplinary and multi-site collaborations that are increasingly valued as the most transformative type of research.

One potentially unforeseen benefit of maintaining networks at the mid-career stage is that it can equip the academic with a collegial support group that can help process and strategize about the challenges that come with balancing personal and professional goals (Auster 2001). Given the reality of burnout and "mid-late career overload" in academic professions (Sanders et al. 2010), professional networking at this stage can provide a critical kind of support that friends outside the academic realm may not be able to offer. In turn, needed encouragement can be extended to others.

Perhaps these considerations are enough to prompt first-generation scholars to pick up the phone, compose an email, or send a handwritten note to a colleague. Plan to rendezvous at an upcoming conference session, catch up over a nice meal, or reconnect after an event or shared activity. Set calendar reminders to be intentional in keeping in touch with the contacts developed. Baldwin and colleagues (2008) recommend collaborating on a new project in an emerging field to rejuvenate professional energies at this career stage. Regardless of the action selected, efforts in this area will be much like going to the gym. The hardest step may be the first one, but the long-term benefits will outweigh the short-term sacrifices.

Am I using my network to pay it forward?

As first-generation scholars advance in our careers, let us not forget how hard it is to make those initial connections and how far we have traveled. In my experience, seasoned academics sometimes neglect to link young colleagues into networks or provide mentorship in networking strategies. Further, I have met with different reactions when employing the networking strategies that I have described above for young professionals. By and large, the researchers that I have sought to meet have been kind and courteous, taking time to converse with me and answer my questions. A few have asked helpful questions about my goals and provided insight specific to my situation. Very few have been rude or dismissive. I write this to encourage early-career academics to push the limits of their comfort in networking and as a catalyst for established scholars to consider where they fall on the continuum of openness to mentoring junior colleagues outside their natural networks.

I acknowledge that the mid-career phase is the one for which I am least qualified to offer advice. I also acknowledge that mentoring comes at a high price of valuable time and energy for the mentor. The encouragement I can offer is that other professionals providing mentorship report that the benefits outweigh the costs (Canter et al. 2012; Huybrecht et al. 2011). As an early career scientist, I strive to appropriately include my gracious mentors on manuscripts and grants to draw on their expertise. I belief the benefit extends to all parties. Mentees can increase leadership roles on projects while simultaneously helping mentors maintain productivity. With a proper negotiation of roles, funding and scholarly contributions can increase for all involved.

Finally, I urge mentors to intentionally network for mentees. Teach them the importance of networking and how to network for themselves. Encourage them to brag (appropriately) about their accomplishments. I have heard it said that credit does not divide, it multiplies. When it is deserved, give it away freely. It will reflect favorably on you. I cannot imagine where I would be if my wonderful mentors had not done this for me. I will close with the wise words of Winnie-the-Pooh: "You can't stay in your corner of the Forest waiting for others to come to you. You have to go to them sometimes." Let us build our houses in a high-traffic neighborhood. Let us ask our neighbors for a cup of sugar. Let us invite others into our homes.

Works Cited

Ansmann, Lena, Tabor Flickinger, Serena Barello, Marleen Kunneman, Sarah Mantwill, Sally Quilligan, Claudia Zanini, and Karolien Aelbrecht. 2014. "Career Development for Early Career Academics: Benefits of Networking and the Role of Professional Societies." *Patient Education and Counseling* 97 (1): 132–34.

Auster, Ellen. 2001. "Professional Women's Midcareer Satisfaction: Toward an Explanatory Framework." *Sex Roles* 44 (11): 719–50.

Baker, Wayne. 1990. "Market Networks and Corporate Behavior." *American Journal of Sociology* 96 (3): 589–625.

Baldwin, Roger, Deborah DeZure, Allyn Shaw, and Kristin Moretto. 2008. "Mapping the Terrain of Mid-Career Faculty at a Research University: Implications for Faculty and Academic Leaders." *Change: The Magazine of Higher Learning* 40 (5): 46–55.

Blickle, Gerhard, Alexander H. Witzki, and Paula B. Schneider. 2009. "Mentoring Support and Power: A Three Year Predictive Field Study on Protégé Networking and Career Success." *Journal of Vocational Behavior* 74 (2): 181–89.

Bourdieu, Pierre. 1989. "Social Space and Symbolic Power." *Sociological Theory* 7 (1): 14–25.

Canter, Kimberly S., Emily D. Kessler, Cathleen Odar, Brandon S. Aylward, and Michael C. Roberts. 2012. "Perceived Benefits of Mentoring in Pediatric Psychology: A Qualitative Approach." *Journal of Pediatric Psychology* 37 (2): 158–65.

Carpenter, Jenna. 2014. "The Role of Networking and Social Media in Career Advancement." *The FASEB Journal* 28 (1): Supplement 9.2.

Carroll, Jennifer K., Akke Albada, Mansoureh Farahani, Maria Lithner, Melanie Neumann, Harbinder Sandhu, and Heather L. Shepherd. 2010. "Enhancing International Collaboration among Early Career Researchers." *Patient Education and Counseling* 80 (3): 417–20.

Clance, Pauline R., and Suzanne A. Imes. 1978. "The Imposter Phenomenon in High Achieving Women: Dynamics and Therapeutic Intervention." *Psychotherapy: Theory, Research & Practice* 15 (3): 241–47.

Drew, Joshua Adam. 2012. "Impostor Syndrome Lecture." http://academiccommons.columbia.edu/catalog/ac: 154891.

Ellis, Albert. 1999. "Early Theories and Practices of Rational Emotive Behavior Therapy and How They Have Been Augmented and Revised during the Last Three Decades." *Journal of Rational-Emotive and Cognitive-Behavior Therapy* 17 (2): 69–93.

Forret, Monica L., and Thomas W. Dougherty. 2004. "Networking Behaviors and Career Outcomes: Differences for Men and Women?" *Journal of Organizational Behavior* 25 (3): 419–37.

Gardner, Susan K., and Karri A. Holley. 2011. "'Those Invisible Barriers Are Real': The Progression of First-Generation Students through Doctoral Education." *Equity & Excellence in Education* 44 (1): 77–92.

Gault, Jack, John Redington, and Tammy Schlager. 2000. "Undergraduate Business Internships and Career Success: Are They Related?" *Journal of Marketing Education* 22 (1): 45–53.

Haynes, Laura, Sherrill L. Adams, and Jeremy M. Boss. 2008. "Mentoring and Networking: How to Make It Work." *Nature Immunology* 9 (1): 3–6.

Huybrecht, Sabine, Wim Loeckx, Yvo Quaeyhaegens, Danielle De Tobel, and Wilhelm Mistiaen. 2011. "Mentoring in Nursing Education: Perceived Characteristics of Mentors and the Consequences of Mentorship." *Nurse Education Today* 31 (3): 274–78.

Janasz, Suzanne C. de, and Sherry E. Sullivan. 2004. "Multiple Mentoring in Academe: Developing the Professorial Network." *Journal of Vocational Behavior* 64 (2): 263–83.

Janasz, Suzanne C. de, Sherry E. Sullivan, and Vicki Whiting. 2003. "Mentor Networks and Career Success: Lessons for Turbulent Times." *Academy of Management Perspectives* 17 (4): 78–91.

Jenkins, Sharon Rae, Aimee Belanger, Melissa Londono Connally, Adriel Boals, and Kelly M. Duron. 2013. "First-Generation Undergraduate Students' Social Support, Depression, and Life Satisfaction." *Journal of College Counseling* 16 (2): 129–42.

Kuijpers, Marinka A. C. T., Birgit Schyns, and Jaap Scheerens. 2006. "Career Competencies for Career Success." *Career Development Quarterly* 55 (2): 168–78.

Ng, Thomas W. H., Lillian T. Eby, Kelly L. Sorensen, and Daniel C. Feldman. 2005. "Predictors of Objective and Subjective Career Success: A Meta-analysis." *Personnel Psychology* 58 (2): 367–408.

Niehaus, Elizabeth, and KerryAnn O'Meara. 2015. "Invisible but Essential: The Role of Professional Networks in Promoting Faculty Agency in Career Advancement." *Innovative Higher Education* 40 (2): 159–71.

Parkman, A. 2016. "The Imposter Phenomenon in Higher Education: Incidence and Impact." *Journal of Higher Education Theory and Practice* 16 (1): 51–60.

Portes, Alejandro. 2000. "Social Capital: Its Origins and Applications in Modern Sociology." In *Knowledge and Social Capital: Foundations and Applications*, edited by Eric L. Lesser, 43–67. Boston: Butterworth-Heinemann.

Rath, Tom. 2007. *StrengthsFinder 2.0.* New York: Gallup Press.

Rhodes, Colbert, and John Sibley Butler. 2010. "Organizational Membership and Business Success: The Importance of Networking and Moving Beyond Homophily." *Challenge* 16 (1): Article 5.

Sanders, Kathryn A., Alfiee M. Breland-Noble, Cheryl A. King, and Barbara A. Cubic. 2010. "Pathways to Success for Psychologists in Academic Health Centers: From Early Career to Emeritus." *Journal of Clinical Psychology in Medical Settings* 17 (4): 315–25.

Sanders, Tim. 2002. *Love Is the Killer App: How to Win Business and Influence Friends*. New York: Three Rivers Press.

Seay, Sandra E. 2010. "A Comparison of Family Care Responsibilities of

First-Generation and Non-First-Generation Female Administrators in the Academy." *Educational Management Administration and Leadership* 38 (5): 563–77.

Seibert, Scott E., Maria L. Kraimer, and Robert C. Liden. 2001. "A Social Capital Theory of Career Success." *Academy of Management Journal* 44 (2): 219–37.

Soria, Krista M., and Michael J. Stebleton. 2012. "First-Generation Students' Academic Engagement and Retention." *Teaching in Higher Education* 17 (6): 673–85.

Stebleton, Michael J., Krista M. Soria, and Ronald L. Jr. Huesman. 2014. "First-Generation Students' Sense of Belonging, Mental Health, and Use of Counseling Services at Public Research Universities." *Journal of College Counseling* 17 (1): 6–20.

Stephens, Nicole M., Stephanie A. Fryberg, Hazel Rose Markus, Camille S. Johnson, and Rebecca Covarrubias. 2012. "Unseen Disadvantage: How American Universities' Focus on Independence Undermines the Academic Performance of First-Generation College Students." *Journal of Personality and Social Psychology* 102 (6): 1178–97.

Stewart, Julie, Thomas Clark, Brian Clark, and Regina Troxell. 2014. "Sharing the Importance of Developing Networking Ties in Teaching Career Communication Skills." *Journal of Organizational Behavior Education 7.*

Tolle, Eckhart. 2004. *The Power of Now: A Guide to Spiritual Enlightenment.* Oakland, CA: New World Library.

Vos, Ans De, Thomas Dewilde, and Inge De Clippeleer. 2009. "Proactive Career Behaviours and Career Success during the Early Career." *Journal of Occupational and Organizational Psychology* 82 (4): 761–77.

Willison, Scott, and Emily Gibson. 2011. "Graduate School Learning Curves: McNair Scholars' Postbaccalaureate Transitions." *Equity and Excellence in Education* 44 (2): 153–68.

Wolff, Hans-Georg, and Klaus Moser. 2009. "Effects of Networking on Career Success: A Longitudinal Study." *Journal of Applied Psychology* 94 (1): 196–206.

Young, Valerie. 2011. *The Secret Thoughts of Successful Women: Why Capable People Suffer from the Impostor Syndrome and How to Thrive in Spite of It.* New York: Crown Business.

INDEX